Ambroise Dydime Lépine

Preliminary Investigation and Trial of Ambroise D. Lepine

for the murder of Thomas Scott, being a full report of the proceedings in this case before the Magistrates' Court and the several courts of Queen's Bench in the province of Manitoba.

Ambroise Dydime Lépine

Preliminary Investigation and Trial of Ambroise D. Lepine
for the murder of Thomas Scott, being a full report of the proceedings in this case before the Magistrates' Court and the several courts of Queen's Bench in the province of Manitoba.

ISBN/EAN: 9783337323851

Printed in Europe, USA, Canada, Australia, Japan

Cover: Foto ©Suzi / pixelio.de

More available books at **www.hansebooks.com**

JOSEPH DOUPE, C. E. and P. L. S.,
INSURANCE AND LAND AGENT.

PRELIMINARY INVESTIGATION

AND TRIAL OF

AMBROISE D. LEPINE

FOR THE MURDER OF

THOMAS SCOTT,

Being a full report of the proceedings in this case before the Magistrates' Court and the several Courts of Queen's Bench in the Province of Manitoba.

SPECIALLY REPORTED AND COMPILED BY

MESSRS. ELLIOTT AND BROKOVSKI,

OF THE CANADIAN PRESS.

[COPYRIGHT SECURED.]

1874

DISPUTED LIMITS A SPECIALTY.
OFFICE, CORNER OF ASSINIBOINE & NOTRE DAME STREETS, WINNIPEG, MA.

THE PACIFIC LAUNDRY,

N. B. CHURCH, Proprietor,

Is now prepared to wash every article of Clothing, both Ladies' and Gents', and guarantee satisfaction to every patron. All kinds of LACE and EMBROIDERY and CLOTHES cleaned to order. We will not allow any other establishment to surpass us in the business. We call for clothes and deliver them. All articles lost or destroyed will be replaced, or the money paid for the same.

NEAR THE GRAND CENTRAL HOTEL, WINNIPEG.

MANITOBA CARRIAGE FACTORY,

WINNIPEG.

THOMAS LUSTED,

Corner of McDermott Avenue and Arthur Street.

General Jobbing, Horseshoeing, and all kinds of Blacksmithing and Repairing. THE LARGEST ESTABLISHMENT AND STOCK WEST OF ST. PAUL.

ONE AND ALL GIVE HIM A CALL.

JAMES STEWART,

Druggist and Pharmacist,

GARRY ST., WINNIPEG.

PHYSICIANS' PRESCRIPTIONS CAREFULLY PREPARED.

W. W. CLARKE,

Baker and Confectioner,

MAIN STREET,

WINNIPEG.

THOS. H. PARR,
Civil Engineer,
WINNIPEG, MANITOBA.

Plans and Specifications of Buildings and Engineering Works prepared.

OFFICE, NOTRE DAME STREET, WEST.

The "Canadian Illustrated News,"
THE NATIONAL PICTORIAL PAPER OF THE DOMINION.
WEEKLY—16 pages.

Illustrations of current Events, prominent Personages, Canadian Scenery, Public Buildings, the Fashions, etc. Literary, Artistic, Scientific, Domestic, and Miscellaneous subjects treated in the letter-press by competent writers.

Steadily advancing in Popular Favor,

and equal, in every respect, to the best European and American Publications.

Subscription Price, $4.00 per annum, in advance.

THE BURLAND-DESBARATS LITHOGRAPHIC CO.,
PUBLISHERS, MONTREAL.

The Canadian Patent Office Record
& MECHANICS' MAGAZINE,

ISSUED MONTHLY—60 to 80 PAGES.—Publishes, under the official direction of the Canada Patent Office, the abridged Specifications and reduced Drawings of all Inventions patented in Canada. In the "*Magazine*" columns, every branch of Engineering, Mechanics, and Manufactures are treated, especially Railways, Ship-building, Lumbering, Mining, Architecture, Machinery, Cabinet-making, and the manufacture of Cloth, Linen, Cotton, Paper, Tobacco, and other articles of Home Industry. Practical Chemistry, Mineralogy, and Natural Philosophy also receive attention. Original articles are contributed by distinguished Canadian scientists, engineers and manufacturers, and the whole is profusely illustrated.

The Subscription to the Magazine is only $2.00 per annum,
PAYABLE IN ADVANCE.

THE BURLAND-DESBARATS LITHOGRAPHIC CO.,
PUBLISHERS, MONTREAL.

SIGN OF THE BIG BOOK AND WATCH,
MAIN STREET, WINNIPEG.

H. S. DONALDSON & BRO.,
DEALERS IN
BOOKS, STATIONERY, FANCY GOODS, CLOCKS, WATCHES & JEWELRY.

A large stock of School Books, Wall Papers and Drawing Materials kept constantly on hand.

JOHN ANGUS,
Watchmaker and Jeweller,
GOLD & SILVER ELECTROPLATING.
ALL WORK WARRANTED.
Main Street, Winnipeg, Manitoba.

WASHINGTON & BRO.,
DEALERS IN
Books, Stationery, Fancy Goods and Toys,
WALL PAPER, Etc.,
GARRY ST., WINNIPEG.

C. D. NORTHGRAVES,
DEALER IN
Watches, Clocks, Jewelry,
FANCY GOODS & STATIONERY,
MAIN STREET, WINNIPEG, MANITOBA.

W. CHAMBERS,
PRACTICAL GUN MAKER,
GARRY STREET, Opposite Grace Church,
WINNIPEG, MA.
FINE BUCK-LOADING SHOT GUNS A SPECIALTY.
REPAIRING CAREFULLY AND NEATLY DONE.

J. M. McGREGOR,
Auctioneer for the Province,
BUYS AND SELLS REAL ESTATE,
LOCATES LANDS AND LAND WARRANTS, Etc.,
"FREE PRESS" OFFICE, WINNIPEG, MANITOBA.

WOLSELEY HOUSE,
POINT DOUGLAS, OPPOSITE THE UNITED STATES CONSULATE,
MAIN STREET, WINNIPEG.
NOW OPEN TO THE TRAVELING PUBLIC AND SUPERIOR TO ANY OTHER HOUSE IN THE CITY.

Parties wishing to secure apartments can do so by telegraphing to the manager from any station between Moorehead and Winnipeg.

W. G. FONSECA, Proprietor and Manager.

MAIN STREET, WINNIPEG, MANITOBA.
INVESTMENT AGENCY,
Real Estate, Insurance and General Agent.

The subscriber is prepared to make Investments in this Province on eligible Security, First Mortgages, &c., at rates of interest varying from 10 to 15 per cent. per annum. All information regarding Investments will be promptly supplied on application.

JOHN BREDEN, P. O. Box 106, WINNIPEG.

REFERENCE: Merchants Bank of Canada, Winnipeg.

W. J. MACAULAY & CO.,
MANUFACTURERS AND DEALERS IN
LUMBER, SHINGLES, LATH, PICKETS, &c., &c.
Macaulayville Mills, Minnesota.   Winnipeg Mills, Manitoba.

MACAULAY & JARVIS,
MANUFACTURERS AND DEALERS IN
DOORS, SASH, BLINDS AND MOULDINGS OF EVERY DESCRIPTION.
SASH AND DOOR FACTORY, WINNIPEG.

Terms Cash, or approved paper at 30 days from purchase, bearing interest after due at 15 per cent. per annum.

JOHN SCHULTZ,
Office on Main Street, Winnipeg, next door to McMicken's Bank,
DEALER IN FURS AND REAL ESTATE.

Agent for MANITOBA INVESTMENTS in Mortgages on Real Estate.

Improved Farms in the Settlement Belt, and City Lots in Winnipeg for Sale.

JOSEPH RYAN,
BARRISTER & ATTORNEY AT LAW,
PORTAGE LA PRAIRIE, MANITOBA.
SPECIAL ATTENTION GIVEN TO LAND AND REAL ESTATE MATTERS.

KEW, STOBARD & CO.,

28 FENCHURCH STREET, LONDON, ENGL'D,

AND MAIN STREET, WINNIPEG,

WHOLESALE DEALERS IN

DRY GOODS, BLANKETS, CLOTHING & INDIAN TRADING GOODS.

J. FREEMAN, Agent.

JAMES H. ASHDOWN & CO.,

IMPORTERS AND DEALERS IN

Shelf and Heavy Hardware,

WAGGONS, PLOWS & HARROWS,

AND ALL CLASSES OF AGRICULTURAL IMPLEMENTS,

STOVES AND JAPANNED WARE,

MANUFACTURERS OF ALL CLASSES TIN AND SHEET IRON WARE.

Contractors', Emigrants' & Farmers' Outfits Complete

AT THE LOWEST POSSIBLE RATES.

WINNIPEG, MAIN STREET NORTH.

SNYDER & ANDERSON,

MAIN STREET SOUTH, WINNIPEG, MA.,

DEALERS IN PORK, HAM, BACON, FLOUR, FEED, OATS,

Groceries of all kinds, California Fruits and Pickles, Glass and Crockery.

NOTIONS & CONFECTIONERY,

WHOLESALE & RETAIL.—LOW FOR CASH ONLY.

ARCHIBALD WRIGHT,

MANUFACTURER OF AND DEALER IN

Trunks, Harness, Saddles, Horse Collars, Blankets,

HALTERS, WHIPS, &c., &c.,

WRIGHT'S BLOCK, next to Court House, MAIN STREET, WINNIPEG.

☞ ALL REPAIRING DONE PROMPTLY AND NEATLY.

ALFRED W. BURROWS,

Winnipeg, Manitoba,

OFFERS FOR SALE

1,600 CITY LOTS

IN WINNIPEG,

Being the subdivisions of the tracts lately known as the Mulligan, Land, Ness, Tristan, Sarjent & Magnus Brown properties.

These estates are eligibly situated in the Western and Northern parts of the City, and are intersected by the only two main thoroughfares—Main Street and the Assiniboine Road—leading to the Settlements.

Several Thousand Dollars have already been expended by the proprietor upon these properties, in Sidewalks, Tree Planting, Free Lots for building and residence, and Parks (of which there are two), and having reserved a proportion of the lots from sale, purchasers may be assured of continued efforts to increase their value.

He also offers for sale

500 LOTS

in Gallie's subdivision of the Town of Morris, at the junction of the Southern R. R. (Manitoba) with the Red River, and a few choice quarter sections selected with a view to future commercial advantages.

Mr. Burrows will spend the winter in Ontario and may be addressed until March, 1875,

Care of G. & H. B. MORPHY, Solicitors, &c.,

EXPRESS BUILDINGS,

TORONTO.

☞ **Later at WINNIPEG.**

MANITOBA COLLEGE,
WINNIPEG.

BOARD OF MANAGEMENT:

A. G. B. BANNATYNE, Chairman.
Rev. THOMAS HART, M. A., Secretary.
D. MACARTHUR, Esq., Treasurer.

Rev. John Black.	John Sutherland, M.P.P.	Kenneth McKenzie, Esq.
Gilbert McMicken, Esq.	Rev. Sam'l Donaldson, B.A.	Hon. Donald Gunn.
Hon. William Fraser.	Hon. D. A. Smith, M.P.	John F. Bain, B.A., Esq.
Rev. Alex. Matheson.	Duncan Sinclair, Esq.,	Rev. Prof. Bryce.

STAFF:

REV. GEORGE BRYCE, M.A., Professor of Science and Literature.
REV. THOMAS HART, M.A., Professor of Classics and Modern Languages.
REV. JOHN BLACK,
REV. JAMES ROBERTSON, } Lecturers in Special Course.
MR. A. FERGUSON, Elementary Tutor.
PROF. GAUVIN, French Tutor.
G. B. ELLIOTT, Esq., Phonography.

This College, like Upper Canada College, Toronto, educates for second year in the University of Toronto. Commercial Department specially attended to. Students prepared for Surveying, Medicine, etc. Instruction is also given to Theological Students. Two Medals presented by the Governor General are open for competition.

Calendar, with Fees and Board rates, can be had from Prof. Bryce.

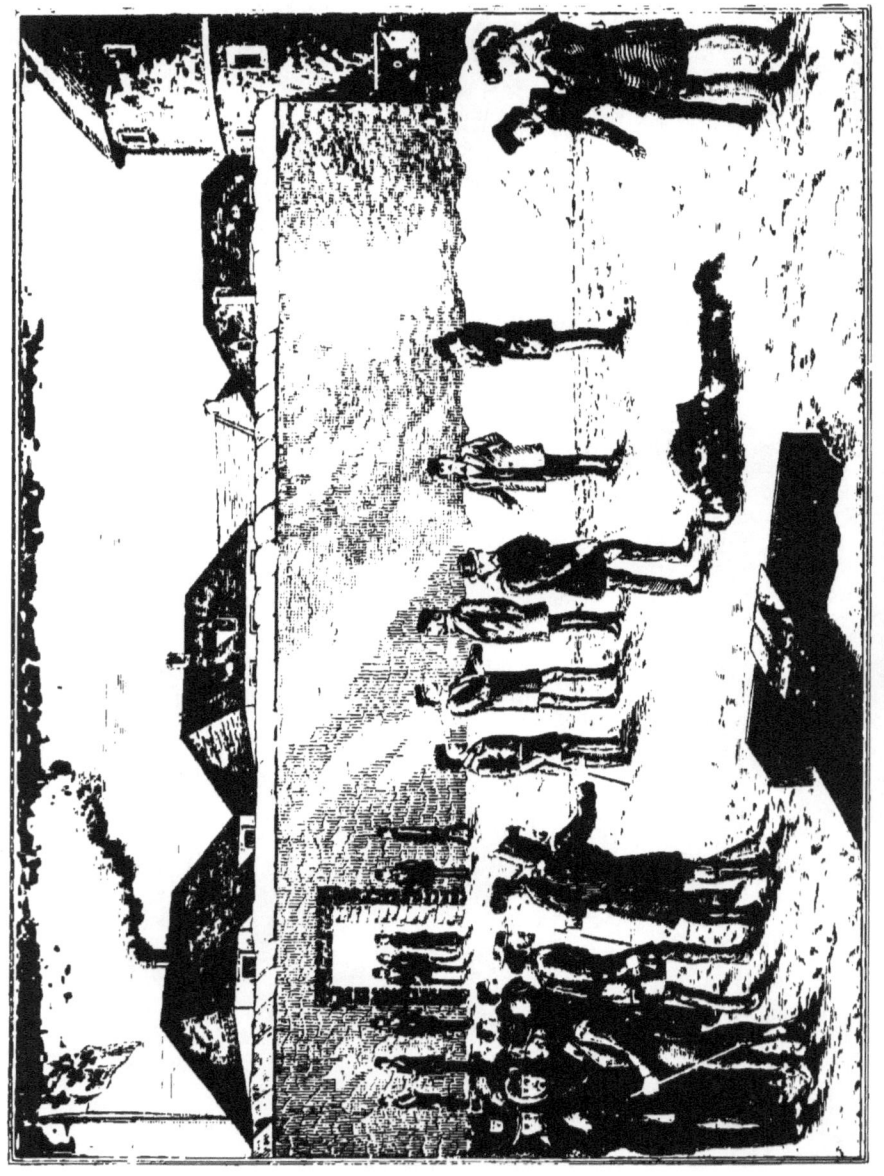

THE EXECUTION OF SCOTT.

AND TRIAL OF

AMBROISE D. LEPINE

FOR THE MURDER OF

THOMAS SCOTT,

Being a full report of the proceedings in this case before the Magistrates' Court and the several Courts of Queen's Bench in the Province of Manitoba.

Specially Reported and Compiled by

MESSRS. ELLIOTT AND BROKOVSKI,

OF THE CANADIAN PRESS.

[COPYRIGHT SECURED.]

1874

Entered according to Act of Parliament of Canada, in the year 1875, by ELLIOTT AND BROKOVSKI, in the Office of the Minister of Agriculture.

PRINTED BY THE BURLAND-DESBARATS LITHOGRAPHIC COMPANY,
MONTREAL, CANADA.

PREFATORY.

Owing to the many mistaken opinions which prevail with regard to the facts and particulars connected with the murder of Thomas Scott, and also to the great demand for an impartial record of the evidence elicited both at the preliminary investigation and the trial of Ambroise D. Lepine, for the murder of the said Thomas Scott, we have been encouraged to publish the proceedings in the case, commencing with the preliminary investigation and ending with the sentencing of Lepine by His Lordship Chief Justice Wood. No opinions are expressed, our purpose being simply to give a fair and impartial record of the proceedings, the demand for which as we have already intimated, has been so great as to encourage us in the publication of the evidence, together with cuts of some of the celebrities connected, directly and indirectly, with the case

THE COMPILERS.

WINNIPEG, 4th January, 1875.

HON. J. A. CHAPLEAU.   LOUIS RIEL.   HON. JOSEPH ROYAL.
AMBROISE D. LEPINE.

PRELIMINARY INVESTIGATION

AND TRIAL OF

AMBROISE D. LEPINE

FOR THE MURDER OF

THOMAS SCOTT,

Being a full report of the proceedings in this case before the Magistrates' Court and the several Courts of Queen's Bench in the Province of Manitoba.

ISSUE OF WARRANT AND ARREST OF LEPINE.

On the 15th of September, 1873, an information was laid before John H. O'Donnell, J. P., in the town of Winnipeg, by one W. N. Farmer against Ambroise Lepine, charging him with the murder of Thomas Scott. Farmer had been one of the prisoners at the time of the Rebellion of 1869-70, and was one of the party of Canadians who came from Portage La Prairie for the purpose of liberating the prisoners confined in Fort Garry by the order of Louis Riel and others. Upon his information, the Magistrate accordingly issued the following warrant:

CANADA,
PROVINCE OF MANITOBA,
County of Selkirk.

WARRANT TO APPREHEND.

To all or any of the Constables or other Peace Officers in the County of Selkirk.

WHEREAS Louis Riel and Ambroise Lepine and others have, this day, been charged upon oath before the undersigned, one of Her Majesty's Justices of the Peace, in and for the said County of Selkirk, for that they, the said Louis Riel, Ambroise Lepine and others unknown, did, on or about the fourth day of March, in the year of Our Lord 1870, feloniously kill and murder one Thomas Scott, at the said County of Selkirk :

THESE are, therefore, to command you in Her Majesty's name forthwith to apprehend the said Louis Riel, Ambroise Lepine and others, and to bring them before me or some other of Her Majesty's Justices of the Peace, in and for the said County of Selkirk, to answer unto the said charge, and to be further dealt with according to law.

Given under my hand and seal, this fifteenth day of September, in the year of Our Lord one thousand eight hundred and seventy-three, at the town of Winnipeg, in the County of Selkirk aforesaid.

[Signed,]   JOHN H. O'DONNELL, J. P.   [L.S.]

This warrant was placed in the hands of Constables Ingraham, Kerr and Dupont, who succeeded in making the arrest two days after (September 17th, 1873).

Lepine was confined in one of the rooms in Fort Garry, until the sitting of the Magistrates' Court.

From the date of Lepine's return to Manitoba from St. Paul, Minnesota, and up to that of his arrest, he was pursuing his ordinary avocation of a farmer, and had made no attempt at escape. The arrest created some excitement both amongst the French and English speaking nations of the Province, as no circumstances had transpired to lead to the belief that any arrests would be made at that time ; by the former, it was received with indignation, but the English speaking, or what is termed the Canadian party, felt that there was some prospect of the matter of the Scott murder being thoroughly investigated, and that the arrest of Lepine was the first step towards this.

PRELIMINARY EXAMINATION OF AMBROISE LEPINE.

On Tuesday, September 23rd, 1873, Ambroise Lepine was brought before Mr. Justice Betournay, sitting as Police Magistrate at Fort Garry, upon the charge that he did, on the 4th day of March, 1870, kill and murder Thomas Scott, at Fort Garry.

The examination was deferred for the production of evidence for the prosecution, and the prisoner was remanded until the following Friday.

ADJOURNED COURT.

The Court was opened pursuant to adjournment by Mr. Justice Betournay, and Gilbert McMicken, Esq., on the Bench.

Messrs. Cornish and Thibaudeau for the prosecution. Hon. Messrs. Royal, Dubuc and Girard for the defence.

Hon. M. Dubuc raised the question of jurisdiction, addressing the Court in French.

Hon. M. Royal repeated the argument in English, of which the following is the substance :

If the Imperial Statutes giving Canada legislative power (91st clause) were clear, there would be no room for raising a question of jurisdiction. The only clause upon which jurisdiction can be claimed is upon 34 Vic., cap. 14, sec. 2. Manitoba was not constituted like the other provinces prior to Confederation.

The circumstances of this country prior to transfer were entirely different, and the jurisdiction was exercised here by other provinces. Were the act cited clear, it would be a logical sequence to clause 146 of Imperial Act. We do not raise the question of constitutionality of the law. Your Honors are only to construe the law. The next question is, whether Canada, in assuming the jurisdiction, did so in accordance with Imperial Statute. It may be said, seeing that Ontario and Quebec did exercise jurisdiction in the North-West before transfer, that since Confederation the Dominion succeed to jurisdiction; but we claim that the Imperial Statutes giving jurisdiction to Ontario and Quebec in the North-West were never repealed, nor was that jurisdiction transferred to Canada. The first Act for giving Ontario and Quebec jurisdiction in the North-West was passed in 1803, which made offences amendable to the same, as in Ontario or Quebec. But in all cases the magistrates had to convey the criminal to Ontario or Quebec. This Act is based upon an old French law, existing in New France.

The second Imperial Statute bearing upon this matter was passed in 1821. The 6 h and 7th sections of this Act gave similar power in civil cases. The 8th clause gives the Governor of Quebec power to issue commissions to administer law in the North-West, same as Ontario. The 11th clause gives the King power to issue commissions for the trial of offences in the North-West.

The 12th provides that such commission may not try an offence sujecting offenders to capital punishment or transportation, or upon any civil matter exceeding £200. Jurisdiction created by these Acts was of a limited and exceptional character.

For the offence of murder the offender had to be sent to Ontario or Quebec for trial.

If, as before said, it could be shown that Confederation had fused former jurisdiction of Ontario, Quebec and Canada, the course would be clear; but it cannot, it was exceptional. In 1841, Imperial Statute vested the powers of Ontario and Quebec before cited in United Canada.

If the same could be said of the British North American Act, the jurisdiction would be beyond dispute. Act of 1867 repealed Act of 1841.

The next Imperial Act upon this matter is that of 1868. The fifth clause of this Act says that from a certain day to be named by Order in Council, Canada shall succeed to full powers in Rupert's Land.

The Order in Council necessary was not passed till June, 1870. The address upon which the accession of the North-West was based, states that it is for the *future* welfare and government. Sixth clause of the Manitoba Act provides that there shall be no retroactive action. The Rupert's Land Act was passed in 1868, but the Order in Council which put it into effect was not passed until 1870.

Not till 1871 was the Manitoba Act framed, which clearly states that there can be no retroaction; and we claim that this Court has no power to investigate matter of the kind now before it, that transpired prior to 1871.

Where, then, does the jurisdiction fall? Not upon the Local Government; not upon the Federal Government; but upon the Imperial Government. The Provisional Government was recognised at Ottawa by the reception of the delegates from the same.

Our position is, that from the time of the resignation of the Government of Assiniboia, in 1869, until Canada assumed the Courts by Act of Parliament in 1871, the jurisdiction in the North-West belonged to the Imperial Government.

The offence now for the consideration of the Bench partakes of a political feature; and seeing that we may reasonably expect efforts on part of witnesses to make the case so and so, we would abjure proceeding to it with caution.

Mr. Cornish, for the prosecution, said that it was not for this Court to determine upon jurisdiction; but the duty of the Bench was to determine whether the crime alleged has been committed, and whether there was sufficient grounds upon which to send the prisoner to his trial, at which time the arguments advanced to-day would be in place. A careful reading of the Statute quoted would clearly establish the claim of jurisdiction, bringing it down to the present ime.

But he did not propose to argue this point now.

This Court had simply to determine whether a *prime facie* case could be made out. He was sorry to hear his learned friend insinuate that there was a political significance; for he knew of none. The allusion to the Provisional

Government was also out of place. And if he understood what he (Mr. Royal) alluded to, it must have been a usurpation of Her Majesty's power.

Mr. Justice Betournay said that he could not determine the question of jurisdiction at this time; it would be determined in a higher Court, if there was evidence enough to send the prisoner there.

The Court then proceeded to examine the witnesses, the examination of whom occupied five days, during which an interval of adjournment took place.

On Thursday, October 9th, after the prisoner Lepine was brought into Court, he was asked by Mr. Justice Betournay if he had anything to say to the Court, in answer to which he read an address in French as follows:

"May it please the Court,—From the very first moment that I could be heard, I have respectfully repelled the accusation brought against me, and denied any magistrate appointed by the Government of Manitoba the right to issue warrants for deeds committed or actions done in the Settlement of the Red River between the 1st of July, 1869, and 15th of July, 1870. I have also in the meantime declined the competency of the Court to take cognizance of any accusation of this character. I beg to renew the same declaration.

"On the other hand, the accusation that has so suddenly been brought against me has taken, by the examination just now concluded, a character essentially political. That fact is clearly established by the evidence of all and every one of the witnesses; and these witnesses are not mine, but those of the prosecution. They have made those affirmations not at the instance of my counsel, but of the counsel for the prosecution. It is, therefore, the political man that is aimed at in this prosecution, and not the pretended murderer.

"In view of these facts, and in answer to the request of the Court, I beg to declare and to enter respectfully but energetically my protest against a proceeding by which the sworn faith is trampled upon, as well as the arrangements made at Ottawa in the spring of 1870, between the Dominion Government and the delegates of a Provisional Government recognised and supported by at least three-fourths of the population of the Colony of the Red River.

"I also do respectfully but energetically enter my protest against a proceeding by which myself, out of a thousand, is selected to bear exclusively the responsibility of acts done by a Government acting in the *plénitude* of powers with which the people of a country had publicly and voluntarily invested it.

"In conclusion, I repel with all my strength the heinous accusation directed against me, because it is false, mendacious, and got up, not by a spirit of justice, but by a spirit of injustice, and by political passions and feelings.

"Such is my declaration, that in my soul and conscience I deem it my duty to make to the Court, after I have heard and well weighed all the evidence that the counsel for prosecution has brought against me.

"[Signed]

"AMBROISE LEPINE.

"Fort Garry, Oct. 9th, 1873."

Mr. Dubuc addressed the Court on behalf of the prisoner in French, the substance of which was as follows:

First,—That it is not proved that Scott is dead. He has been seen wounded, but no medical man was present to say that these wounds caused his death.

Second,—That the death of Scott is not a murder, but a sad occurrence arising from political difficulties.

If it is not an ordinary murder, the part Lepine took was too remote to accuse him of murder, and he is only as guilty as any other man who took part with the Government of that day. If it is not a murder, it is then a political offence. The evidence shows that Scott was condemned by a council of war. There were two parties in conflict; one the Canadian party, headed by Colonel Dennis, who had no more right to take Lower Fort Garry than the native party had to take Fort Garry. Colonel Dennis professed to be acting for the Canadian Government, whilst his authority was only from the Hon. Mr. McDougall, who was officially blamed by the Canadian Government for having issued a proclamation under the Queen's name without the sanction of the Government, as will be proved by a letter from the Hon. Mr. Howe to Hon. Mr. McDougall. The proclamation of McDougall destroyed the authority of the Hudson's Bay Company, and therefore the Government of Riel was the Government of the people, and therefore *de facto* the only government, there being no other in the country. There being two parties in conflict, the death of Scott was the result of that conflict.

The third reason is, that we protest against the jurisdiction of this Court, and therefore decline to accept its decision.

Mr. Cornish, on behalf of the prosecution, said:—That so far as the evidence of the proof of Scott's death, it had been proved to the Court most conclusively that Scott met his death at the hands of a number of men with arms, and that amongst the men who were active in thus causing Scott's death, it was clearly proved that the accused was one of these. That the written defence of the prisoner did not say that Scott had not been killed, that he had not had anything to do with it, but that it was done at a time when political feelings were high, and done under the political necessities of the time. That the question of jurisdiction put in by the prisoner could not be entertained here, as it was not for this Court to determine, but that it was the duty of a Supreme Court to do this, and that evidence enough had been adduced to warrant the present Court to commit the prisoner for trial at a higher Court, where the question of jurisdiction could only be considered. That there was nothing in the whole course of the prosecution to show that political feeling had anything to do with the present prosecution, nor was it so; for the whole tenor of the evidence was a positive proof of the truth of the accusation without any political motive. The question now before the Court was only to be considered by it, and that the evidence of Duncan Nolan clearly proved that Lepine was the man who led out Scott to the place of his death, and who had command of those who were instrumental in the death of Scott; and that the evidence of Mr. Bruce was given clearly, and went to show that Lepine was well aware of what was or was not to take place, as he had told him (Bruce) that some of the prisoners taken by Riel would have to be shot. The evidence of Chambers proved that Lepine, as the so-called Adjutant-General, gave the signal for the firing party to fire upon Scott, and that from the beginning of the evidence to the end of it, the actions of Lepine in causing Scott's death had been traced out clearly. That he did not intend to argue the question of judisdiction, as it was not for an inferior Court to say as to the jurisdiction of a superior one, but that he would now move that the prisoner be committed for trial.

The Court reserved its decision until the morning of Tuesday next, October 14th, at 10 a.m.

TUESDAY, Oct. 14.

Court opened at 10.30 a.m. Mr. Justice Betournay on the bench.

More than usual interest was seemingly taken in this morning's proceedings, as instanced by the unusual number of spectators. The prisoner was brought into court about 11 o'clock; and on his appearance, Justice Betournay proceeded to give his decision.

JUSTICE BETOURNAY'S DECISION.

" This is a preliminary examination upon a charge of murder preferred against the accused, Ambroise Lepine,—First: On the part of the defence, it was urged that there was no proof of the death of Scott. Second : That if Scott was murdered, there is no proof that he was murdered by Lepine; and that besides, it was not an ordinary murder, but the action of a then existing government.

"Objection has also been taken to my having jurisdiction in the case.

"As to the first point, there is conclusive proof of the arrest and imprisonment of Thomas Scott, and his detention by a party of whom Lepine was apparently the leader. It has been sufficiently established by the evidence that Scott was shot on the 4th of March, 1870, by a party under the command of the accused, who, it appeared, had charge of Scott on the occasion.

"As to the second point, the presence of the prisoner on the occasion of Scott's death, and his participation in the crime of which he stands accused, render him guilty of it; and sitting as I do in this matter, I cannot recognise such a pretended government as that claimed by the defence. Now, as to the question of jurisdiction, I cannot sustain the views of the defence. It is my duty, under the law, to see if a sufficient case is made out to commit; it will rest with a higher tribunal to determine the question of jurisdiction.

"I find a made-out case. Therefore, my judgment is: That you, Ambroise Lepine, stand committed to the common goal of this Province until the next criminal Assizes for the Province of Manitoba of Oyer and Terminer and general gaol delivery, when bills of indictment will be preferred against you for the offence with which you stand charged."

Upon the conclusion of the examination and commitment for trial, Lepine was conveyed to the Provincial Penitentiary at Lower Fort Garry for safe keeping, there being no jail at that time in the town of Winnipeg.

NOVEMBER TERM.

PLEA AGAINST JURISDICTION OF THE COURT.

During the following month of November, an extra-term of the Court of Queen's Bench was held and which was opened on Wednesday, November 12th. Mr. Justice McKeagney on the Bench. At this term, on Saturday, November 15th, a True Bill was found by the Grand Jury against Lepine, upon the following Indictment:

CANADA,	COURT OF QUEEN'S BENCH,
PROVINCE OF MANITOBA.	(CROWN SIDE.)

NOVEMBER TERM, 1873.

The Jurors of Our Lady the Queen upon their oath present,—That Ambroise Lepine, on the fourth day of March, in the year of Our Lord one thousand eight hundred and seventy, at Upper Fort Garry, a place then known as being, lying, and situated in the District of Assiniboia, in the Red River Settlement, in Rupert's Land, and now better known as being, lying and situate at Winnipeg, in the County of Selkirk, in the Province of Manitoba, Dominion of Canada, feloniously, wilfully and of his malice aforethought, did kill and murder one Thomas Scott, against the form of the Statute in such case made and provided, and against the peace of our said Lady the Queen, her Crown and Dignity.

HENRY J. CLARKE, Q.C.,

Attorney-General.

The following are the names of the twelve Grand Jurors : N. T. Lonsdale (foreman), J. T. Grant (half-br ed), Alex. Murray (half-breed), W. Fraser, J. Higgins, W. Henderson, Geo. Setter, D. Cassitor (half-breed), W. A. Farmer, U. Delorme (half-breed), B. Lavalette (half-breed), B. Falcon (half-breed).

On the 15th, Lepine was arraigned upon the Indictment found against him by the above Jurors.

On being asked by the Clerk of the Court as to his plea, the counsel for the prisoner, Hon Mr. Royal, said that before the plea of the prisoner was given, he questioned the jurisdiction of this Court in the matter.

The Attorney-General argued that a plea must be entered, or failing that, the prisoner must enter a *demurrer* at once.

His Lordship decided that the matter should lay over until Monday, in order that a *demurrer* should be prepared against the jurisdiction of the Court.

This was objected to by the Attorney-General, but His Lordship decided that the case lay over until Monday.

Accordingly, on Monday, November 17th, the prisoner was again placed at the bar, when he put in a written protest against the jurisdiction of the Court.

Hon. Mr. Royal asked the Court that in this case a plea of jurisdiction of this Court would be put in on behalf of the prisoner, and submitted the question to the Court as to whether the prisoner could put in a plea of " Not guilty," subject to the plea of jurisdiction. That there had been precedent for this at last Court.

The Hon. Attorney-General, on behalf of the Crown, objected to the stand of prisoner's counsel, that this Court had no jurisdiction in the matter, and that the asking of a plea for the prisoner of " Not guilty " was an unusual course; but the prosecution was not one of vengeance, but one of justice ; and that, in order that the matter might be brought to an issue, he would consent to a plea of " Not guilty " being entered, after which he would join issue with his learned friend as to the jurisdiction of this Court.

The prisoner was then arraigned and pleaded " Not guilty."

Hon. Mr. Royal quoted legal authorities to show that the question of geographical territory, or limits, could not apply in the case now before the Court, and that cases involving capital punishment could not be tried by any Court within this Province, but according to Imperial Statute the case must be sent to Upper or Lower Canada for trial, and that in this view he was borne out by Chief Justice Gray in his work of " Legal Reviews."

The Attorney-General objected to this quotation, as it had not been given by Col. Gray as a Chief Justice, but as a private person merely writing a book.

Hon. Mr. Royal held, that even if written by him as Mr. or Col. Gray, this work was an authority to be quoted and relied upon.

The question arose, did the British North American Act transfer the jurisdiction from the Lower Provinces to this, and when did this take place? That by the Imperial Act of 1867 the jurisdiction of the Courts held by the Hudson's Bay Company was taken away from them, and the Act returning this privilege to them did not come into force until June 23rd, 1870, by the passage of an Order in Imperial Council proclaiming the Act passed in 1868 as in force in Rupert's Land. Whenever this question of jurisdiction was talked of in Canada, the same answer was given by all, that sec. 2, chap. 14 of the Dominion Statutes settled the matter; but he would say that the Dominion had no power to pass such a law with regard to jurisdiction in the North-West, as there had been no transfer of this Province between 1868 and 1870, and therefore the Dominion had not the power to pass any law establishing territorial jurisdiction over any crimes called felonies, and that any person committing these between these periods must be sent to the Lower Provinces for trial. That the power given to this Province in criminal matters was exceptional, and that according to the laws cited, he did not believe that this Court had the power to try the prisoner, but that he ought to be sent down either to the Province of Quebec or Ontario to be tried.

ARGUMENT ON THE PLEA TO THE JURISDICTION OF THE COURT OF QUEEN'S BENCH.

The Hon. Attorney-General Clarke, Q.C., in reply to the Hon. Mr. Royal, said :

My Lord,—The pretention of the learned counsel for the defence, although there is really nothing in it when the sophistry in which it was enveloped is brushed away, compels us to glance back over a period of about 200 years to the reign of King Charles the Second of England. To do this with any degree of precision must necessitate the occupation of so much of the valuable time of this Court, that I must not attempt it, and consequently will confine my argument to the narrow limits necessary to show your Lordship that over that vast extent of territory over which King Charles the Second gave exclusive rights and jurisdiction to " *The Governor and Company of Adventurers of England trading into Hudson's Bay,*" commonly called the " *Hudson's Bay Company,*" — that vast extent of territory over which several Imperial Acts of Parliament gave limited jurisdiction to the Governor of Lower Canada, and to the Governor of Upper Canada, and to the Governor General of United Canada—that over all that territory, a very small spot of which now constitutes Manitoba, your Lordship, as a Judge of the Court of Queen's Bench of this Province, has as certain and undoubted jurisdiction as it is possible for law to constitute and establish, or for time and usage to consecrate and render permanent and lasting.

My Lord, I must now most respectfully draw your attention to the fact that must be patent to every one, viz.: that the powers and jurisdiction secured to " *Hudson's Bay Company*" by the charter granted by Charles the Second, and which were again and again recognized by Acts of Parliament, were never taken away or contested by any recognized legal authority up to the time—15th of July, 1870 — when the whole of the North-West Territories were transferred to and became part and parcel of the Dominion of Canada, under and by virtue of the provisions of the " *British North American Act,* 1867." That being the case, how can there be any serious question raised as to the undoubted jurisdiction of this Court ? No such question can be sustained by logical reasoning, much less on any legal grounds ; and to me it is perfectly plain that the whole object of the prisoner's counsel is to throw obstacles in the way of the prisoner's trial, and if possible send it over to the next term of this Court, hoping that something may be done elsewhere in the meantime to save the prisoner, and others quite as guilty and far more cowardly than him, from the consequences of their cold-blooded and diabolical crime, committed on the fourth day of March, 1870, when in their brutal ferocity they slaughtered a defenceless man outside the walls of Fort Garry.

My Lord, I need hardly ask you if you have made yourself acquainted with the " Hudson's Bay Company's " charter ; I am certain that you have. That being the case, can you doubt your jurisdiction as a Judge of this Court ? Impossible ! if you are satisfied that the Hudson's Bay Company did, by a solemn Act, cede and transfer to Canada all their rights and powers to and in these North-West Territories, and that under and by virtue of an Imperial Act of Parliament, which precludes the possibility of any question being raised as to whether they could legally transfer their powers as a Government. Where, then, can the question arise as to the jurisdiction of this Court to try the prisoner Lepine and his fellow criminals, Riel and others, for the murder of Thomas Scott, at Fort Garry, in March, 1870? Where is there room for a doubt?

The counsel for the prisoner has treated us to-day to a printed re-hash of the arguments used by his partner on the question of jurisdiction before the magistrate at the preliminary examination of the prisoner, previous to his committment for trial before this Court, with only one part of that argument left out or dropped, that is, the pretention that the prisoner and Riel and a few others were a *de facto* Government, and that as such their victim was legally put to death. I think it is just as well that they have let that pretence drop, and yet it was just as sound in fact and in law as any or all of their other pretences; and I think, my Lord, we will be able in a very short time to show such to be the case. Let us see how the Imperial Act 43 George III., cap. 138, affects this case, or what effect it had *quod ad* the jurisdiction of the Hudson's Bay Company. By that statute it was enacted, That all offences committed within the Indian Territories, or parts of America not within the limits of Lower or Upper Canada, or of any civil government of the United States of America, *shall be and be deemed to be offences of the same nature, and shall be tried in the same manner, and subject to the same punishment as if the same had been committed within the Provinces of Lower or Upper Canada.* Now, my Lord, was murder a crime in Lower Canada and in Upper Canada at the time of the passing of that Act? Certainly it was. If so, what does the Act declare? Why, simply, but with very great certainty, that murder when committed in the Indian Territories shall be tried and punished in the same way that the same offence would be tried and punished in either of these Provinces. That is the provision of the Act of 1803, the 43 George III., cap. 138, which seems to have escaped the attention of the counsel for the prisoner, but which your Lordship will perceive completely established the criminal law of England, then in force in the two Canadas, in the Indian or North-West Territories. With the remaining provisions of that Act, giving power to the Governor of Lower Canada to appoint Justices in the Indian Territories, for the proper hearing and committing for trial in Lower Canada, and also giving to the Governor of that Province, if the case seemed to require it, power to order the trial to take place in Upper Canada, your Lordship is no doubt quite well acquainted, so that I need not dwell on the subject, but proceed to examine the next Imperial Act relating to this country, which is the Act passed in 1821, being the 1st and 2nd George IV., cap. 66, which *extended the Act of 1803 to all the Territories of the Hudson's Bay Company.* It also gave power to the Crown to issue commissions under the Great Seal, to empower justices to hold Courts of Record for the trial of criminal offences, and also of civil cases, " *notwithstanding anything contained in the Hudson's Bay Company's Charter.*" My Lord, why did the Imperial Parliament deem it necessary to so strongly mark the intention of the Act? Simply because the Hudson's Bay Company by its charter, up to that time, had positive and concurrent jurisdiction, and it became necessary to prevent any doubts which might arise as to jurisdiction in the Hudson's Bay Territories; and for fear that any doubts might still remain, the last section clearly sets forth *that all the rights, privileges, authorities and powers conferred on the Hudson's Bay Company, shall still remain in full force, virtue and effect, as if the Act had never been passed.* This, my Lord, will satisfy the greatest legal hair-splitter in Canada, that the Hudson's Bay Company's power to punish crime under the laws of England was never questioned. Now, let us see what is done by the Act of 1859, 22nd and 23rd Vict., cap. 36. It recites the principal provisions of both the former Acts, 43 George III., cap. 138, and 1st and 2nd George IV., cap. 66; its provisions empower the Crown, either by commission or Order in Council, to authorize such justices as might be appointed, to try in a summary manner all crimes, misdemeanors and offences whatsoever, and to punish by fine or imprisonment, or both. It also provides that in cases punishable by death, or in which, in the Justice's opinion, fine and imprisonment would be inadequate to the offence, they might try the offender in the ordinary way, or send him to Upper Canada to be tried under the Act 1st and 2nd George IV., cap. 66, or they could send him to British Columbia, to be tried by any court having jurisdiction of like offences committed there. This Act is *declared not to extend to the territories of the Hudson's Bay Company.* What then was the object of the statute? It is very clear *that it was to provide for the administration of justice in the Indian Territories, outside of the jurisdiction of the Courts established under the Company's charter, and leaving to the courts established by the Hudson's Bay Company within their own territories, the powers, authority and jurisdiction that belonged to them;* the same power that, up to the transfer of this country to Canada, was exercised by the general Court, the power to hear, try and determine capital felonies, a power that was exercised by that Court and its sentence carried into execution. Now, my Lord, I ask myself, is there any doubt as to the full power and jurisdiction of this court to try the prisoner at the bar? and I reply to the question with the Hudson's Bay Company's charter before me—with all the Imperial Acts relating to this country before me—with the statutes of the Dominion of Canada and of this Province before me: No! If there is any force in statutory enactments; if there is any meaning in the word justice; if there is any power in the Crown of Great Britain to punish crime, this Court has legal jurisdiction, power, and force to satisfy the ends of justice, and to punish any crime committed within these North-West Territories, wherever the Hudson's Bay Company's power extended. I do not think, my Lord, that it can be doubted that all the powers given by the Imperial statutes to the Governors of Lower Canada and Upper Canada, were transferred, on the union of the Provinces, to United Canada, by the Act of 1840, 3rd and 4th Victoria, cap. 35, sections 45, 46 and 47, so that, up to the time of Confederation, the Province of Canada was vested with all those powers, and the *British North America Act,* 30th and 31st Victoria, cap. 3, 1867, vests all those powers in the Governor-General of the Dominion of Canada, by sec. 12, so that any and all powers or jurisdiction given by any of the Imperial statutes to the separate Provinces of Upper Canada and Lower Canada, or to their Governors, or to the United Province of Canada, or its Governor, by the Act of 1840, were by the Imperial Act of 1867 vested in the Dominion of Canada and its Governor-General respectively. Now, my Lord, I must draw your attention to the very lengthy extracts read by the learned counsel for the prisoner, from a pamphlet written by Mr. Gray, better known as Colonel Gray, during his political career, and very erroneously cited by the learned counsel as the opinion of Chief Justice Gray. I must remind your Lordship that there is no such person as Chief Justice Gray; that the gentleman formerly known as Col. Gray, is now a puisné-justice in British Columbia, but at the time he wrote that pamphlet he was simply a member of Parliament, and that his opinion has no legal weight or significance before a Court of Justice. I have no doubt that the opinion of Col. Gray, now read by the prisoner's counsel, would scarcely be admitted as law by Mr. Justice Gray himself. Few, indeed, are the judges on the Bench who would like to accept or admit as sound law, all or even a small portion of what was written or spoken by them as politicians, or to advance the interests of their own party, or to throw obstacles in the way of their political opponents whilst they were in active political life. Surely the defence must be hard pressed for authority to sustain their pretensions, when they come into Court with printed arguments composed of extracts from political pamphlets. Not being at a loss for the authority of both Imperial and Canadian Statute law to support my arguments, I do not intend to even take the trouble to reply to the opinion of *Col. Gray,* as read by the learned counsel to the Court, and which has already done duty in the hands of himself and his law-partner before the committing magistrate. The counsel for the prisoner seems to have a most perverse disposition to misconstrue acts or sections of acts of Parliament, and in his reference to the Imperial Act 31st and 32nd Victoria, cap. 105, 1863, he certainly was mistaken, to say the least. Section 5 of that Act enacts :—" It shall be competent to Her Majesty by " any such Order or Orders in Council as aforesaid, on Address from the Houses " of Parliament of *Canada*, to declare that *Rupert's Land* shall, from a date to " be therein mentioned, be admitted into and become part of the Dominion of " *Canada* ; and thereupon it shall be lawful for the Parliament of *Canada*, from " the date aforesaid, to make, ordain and establish within the Land and Terri- " tory so admitted as aforesaid, such laws, institutions, and ordinances, and to " constitute such Courts and officers, as may be necessary for the peace, order " and good government of Her Majesty's subjects and others therein ; Provided " that, until otherwise enacted by the said Parliament of *Canada*, all the powers, " authorities, and jurisdiction of the several Courts of Justice now established " in *Rupert's Land*, and of the several officers thereof, and of all magistrates and " Justices now acting within the said limits, shall continue in full force and " effect therein." How can the learned counsel make the very grave mistake to suppose that this section of the Act is not a most convincing proof of the fallacy of his pretension ? Surely he must see that " all the powers, authorities, and jurisdiction " of the Quarterly Court "are continued in full force and effect " until otherwise enacted by the Parliament of Canada. Of this there is no room for doubt. Now, my Lord, what provision has the Parliament of Canada made under the authority given by the Imperial Act of 1867, 30 and 31 Vic., cap. III., called the " *British North America Act*," and in accordance with the provisions of the Imperial Act 31 and 32 Vic , cap. CV., also cited, whereby it is declared that the Courts then established in Rupert's Land and the North-West Terri- tories shall continue in full power and authority until otherwise provided for by the Parliament of Canada ? Let us see. By the Act 32 and 33 Vic., cap. III., passed in 1869 —" *An Act for the temporary government of Rupert's Land and the North-Western Territory when united with Canada* "—it is enacted, almost in the words of the Imperial Act, by the 5th section, " That all the laws in force in Rupert's Land and the North-West Territory at the time of their admission into the Union, shall, so far as they are consistent with ' THE BRITISH NORTH AMERICA ACT, 1867,' with the terms and conditions of such admission approved of by the Queen under the 146th section thereof, *remain in force until altered by the Par- liament of Canada, or by the Lieutenant-Governor under the authority of this Act.*" By the 6th section of the same Act, all public officers or functionaries holding offices in Rupert's Land and the North-Western Territories, at the time of their admission into the union, are continued in office until otherwise ordered by the Lieutenant-Governor. By the Act 33rd Vic., cap. III., passed in 1870—" *The Manitoba Act* "—the provisions of the Act 32 and 33 Vic., cap. III., are re-enacted and continued. Again by the Act 34 Vic., cap XVI., 1871, the same provision is made for continuing the laws in force in Rupert's Land and the North- Western Territories. Now, my Lord, I direct your attention to the Act 34 Victoria, cap XVI, 1871, " *An Act to extend to the Province of Manitoba certain of the Criminal Laws now in force in the other Provinces of the Dominion.*" And therein we find the jurisdiction of this Court fully and completely established beyond the possibility of any doubt. The 2nd section of the Act enacts as follows :— " *The Court known as the* GENERAL COURT " *now and heretofore existing in the Province of Manitoba, and any Court to be* " *hereafter constituted by the Legislature of the said Province, and having the powers* " *now exercised by the said General Court, shall have power to hear, try, and deter-* " *mine in the course of law*, ALL TREASONS, FELONIES AND INDICTABLE OFFENCES COM- " MITTED IN ANY PART OF THE SAID PROVINCE, OR IN THE TERRITORY WHICH HAS NOW " BECOME THE SAID PROVINCE." Is this not most positive and clear ? Can there be any doubt as to the jurisdiction given this Court by this Act ? For after all I will show your Lordship that this Court of Queen's Bench is only the GENERAL COURT under a new name. The 6th section of the Act provides for the repeal of all laws inconsistent with its provisions, and then makes this proviso; Provided " always, that no person shall, by reason of the passing of this Act, be liable to " any punishment or penalty for any act done before the passing thereof, for " which he would not have been liable to any punishment or penalty under the " laws in force in the said Province or Territory now constituting it, at the time " such act was done; nor shall any person, by reason of the passing of this Act, be " liable to any greater or other punishment *for any offence committed before the* " *passing thereof*, than he would have been liable to under the laws then in force " as aforesaid; and this Act and the Acts hereby extended to the said Province " shall apply only to the procedure in any such case, *and the penalty or punish-* " *ment shall be the same as if this Act had not been passed*." My Lord, a good deal of stress has been laid on this section of the Act by the prisoner's counsel. Why so, I can only account for by the fact that they have, up to the present time, been treating the Court to reading from Col. Gray's pamphlet, and have not, or cannot, read the statutes and take in them meaning for themselves. And still the provision of the statute is so simple and clear that there is no mistaking its object. Certainly no man should or could be condemned by the Court to any greater punishment than he was liable to under the laws as they stood at the time the offence was committed. What then? Was not murder always a capital felony in Rupert's Land? If not, the prisoner cannot be condemned to death for the murder of Thomas Scott, in March, 1870. If it was, and of that there can be no doubt, then the prisoner, if proved to be one of the murderers, must be convicted under the law as it stood then, and as it stands now, for I am proceeding under the laws of England as they were in force in Rupert's Land at the time the murder of Thomas Scott was committed at Fort Garry.

My Lord, I have now to direct your attention to the remaining series of statutes that complete the chain of authority which gives jurisdiction to this Court to try the prisoner. I have already shown you that the General Court of Rupert's Land had full power and jurisdiction in all cases, criminal or civil, up to the time of Confederation, from the time the charter was granted " *The Governor and Company of Adventurers of England trading into Hudson's Bay* " by Charles the Second. Under that charter the Company's powers, prerogative, and jurisdiction to administer justice were never doubted. The Imperial Acts of 1803, 1821 and 1859 did not take away any of the powers of the Courts of law that were established by the Company by virtue of its charter. All they did do, or attempted to do, was to give a certain amount of limited concurrent jurisdiction within the Company's territory to certain Imperial officers in Canada, and to establish some kind of a limited system of criminal and civil jurisdiction within the Indian Territories of America belonging to the Crown of England. After three-quarters of a century's experience, it was found that the Imperial legislation still remained a dead letter, so far as the enforcement of criminal law was concerned in the Indian Territories. It is true that the murderers of Mr. Reveny, De Reinhard and McLelland and others were tried under the Act 43 George the Third, cap CXXXVIII., at Quebec, in 1818, and that a trial took place at Three Rivers, in 1838, under the same Act and the Act of 1821, 1st and 2nd George Third, cap. LXVI., for a murder committed at the Rocky Mountains, and certain trials in Upper Canada for the murder of Governor Semple, in 1818, with which exceptions the Imperial Statutes were so much waste paper, so far as their utility was concerned, for seventy years. Not so the Courts established by virtue of the Company's charter. They acted regularly—in fact with wonderful regularity, considering the circumstances of the country—their judgments were carried into execution in all civil cases to any amount, and even in capital felonies. Well, my Lord, that Court—*the General Court*—was, we have seen, continued by Imperial and Canadian Statutes, and its jurisdiction extended to the whole of the Province of Manitoba, outside of the limits of the " *District of Assiniboia*," which bounded its jurisdiction under the Company. I now tell your Lordship, without fear of contradiction, *that this Court is the*

"*General Court*" *under the name of the Court of Queen's Bench*, having all its former powers given to it by Imperial, Canadian and Manitoba Statutes. By virtue of the powers vested by law in the Legislature of this Province, the "*General Court*" was defined by our statute, 34 Victoria, cap. II., 1871, "*An Act to Establish a Supreme Court in the Province of Manitoba,*" section 39, wherein it was enacted: "Till a judge of the Supreme Court shall be appointed by the Government of the Dominion of Canada, *the General Court existing in this Province shall exercise throughout the Province all the functions, and possess all the authority hereby conferred on the Supreme Court.*" Well, my Lord, no Judge was ever appointed by the Canadian Government under that Act. Canadian ministers had so little care for Manitoba and her interests, that we were left without a judge, and so, in self-defence, the Legislature in 1872, by Act 35 Victoria, cap. III , changed the name of this Court from "*Supreme Court*" to "*Court of Queen's Bench,*" and provided for the appointment of *three Judges*. We have got two of them after waiting a year, and are left during that time without any Courts for want of Judges. Well, my Lord, now you, as one of the Judges of the Court of Queen's Bench of Manitoba, are told that you have no jurisdiction to try the prisoner, and you are to decide the question. Are you prepared to render your decision? I should think so. Your Lordship would certainly not preside in this Court, and at the same time not have your mind made up as to what jurisdiction you have by virtue of your position as a Judge of the Court. The objections of Col. Gray have not been sprung upon you to-day for the first time. They have been hawked around the Province by the counsel for the prisoner during the past two months, and a great many people, not knowing Colonel Gray under the new designation erroneously given him, thought they were reading the solemn and well-considered opinion, if not decision, of a Chief Justice. Your Lordship could not be thus mistaken. You know Col. Gray and were in Parliament when he wrote that pamphlet to assist his party, which is now given, nominally by the prisoner's counsel, but in reality by the "*Revue Légale*" of the Province of Quebec, a semi-legal-political newspaper, which has been trying for a long time to convince its readers, not that Louis Riel and others are not murderers, but only that there is no law in Manitoba to punish them. One more authority, my Lord, and I will have done. What were the criminal laws in force in Rupert's Land on that portion of it known as the "*District of Assiniboia*" over which the *General Court* had jurisdiction up to the time of the extension of the criminal laws of Canada to this Province by the Act 34 Victoria, cap. XIV., 1871? If your Lordship be satisfied on that head, then I can ask for your decision on this trumped-up question of jurisdiction at once. Here it is, my Lord; we have no difficulty in finding it. On page 17, section 64, of the "*Laws of Assiniboia*," under the caption of "ADMINISTRATION OF JUSTICE," "*amended 7th January, 1864,*" we find the following—" To REMOVE ALL DOUBTS as to the true construction of " the 53rd article of the code of 11th April, 1862, the proceedings of the Court " shall be regulated by the Laws of England, *not only of this date of Her present* " *Majesty's accession*, so far as they may apply to the condition of the colony, but " also by all such laws of England of subsequent date as may be applicable to the same." *In other words, the proceedings of the General Court shall be regulated by the existing laws of England for the time being, in so far as the same are known to the Court and are applicable to the condition of the colony.* Now, my Lord, I have done, and have only to pray that you will render your decision at once, so that the prisoner's trial may be proceeded with, and that the world may know that murder in any British territory cannot be done and the guilty parties escape.

Hon. Mr. Royal, by permission of the Court, replied to the arguments of the Attorney-General. (The reply took similar grounds to those used by the hon. gentleman at the preliminary investigation. This speech not having been reported, it is impossible to produce it here.)

2

Upon the conclusion of the argument, His Lordship said he would defer his decision.

APPLICATION FOR BAIL.

On Saturday, Dec. 6th, an application for bail on behalf of Lepine was heard in Chambers before His Lordship Judge Betournay. The counsel for prisoner, Hon. J. Royal, put in a petition from Lepine (which was read in French), and argued the question. The Hon. Attorney-General, on behalf of the Crown, opposed the question of bail. Application ordered to lie over until Tuesday.

On Tuesday, December 9th, the application was again heard before His Lordship and lengthy arguments heard from the counsel for the defence (in French). The Attorney-General opposed the application; one of the grounds taken by him was that the petition asked for bail for one Ambroise Lepine, now a prisoner in Winnipeg, in the County of Selkirk, Province of Manitoba, when there was no such person confined there, consequently His Lordship could not be cognizant of the case. The petition had also been sworn to on the 19th of November, when the prisoner had been waiting the decision as to jurisdiction. The petition, as sworn to, was alone considered by the Attorney-General as containing important matter affecting the prisoner's trial, and he asked His Lordship that the document be impounded, as it was his intention to make use of it at the time of applicant's trial. Hon. Mr. Royal stated to His Lordship that the reason that the application for bail had not been presented within the delay asked from the date of petition until December 3rd, was that he, Mr. Royal, had other matters occupying his attention; and that the reason that the petition had been sworn to on November 19th was to save the expense of journey down to the Lower Fort.

Decision was reserved until following Saturday.

APPLICATION IN CHAMBERS.

DECISION OF MR. JUSTICE M'KEAGNEY.

His Lordship decision was as follows:—

The Queen vs. Ambrose Lepine.—Application at Chambers.

This is an application for the admission to bail of Ambroise Lepine, against whom, at the last term of the Court of Queen's Bench, an indictment for murder was found by the Grand Jury.

Mr. MacKenzie has appeared in support of the application, and Mr. Carey for the Crown.

The principle upon which a party committed to take his trial for an offence may be bailed, is founded chiefly upon the legal probability of his appearing to take his trial.

It appears that the deceased Thomas Scott, with complicity in whose murder the prisoner has been charged, came to his death in March, 1870, in a public manner, by the act of parties claiming to exercise supreme authority in this country; that whatever part the prisoner may have taken in that unhappy transaction, was publicly known at the time, and promulgated not only here, but throughout the Dominion of Canada.

It does not appear that he "fled for it," concealed himself, or in any way sought to evade justice.

Now, after a lapse of nearly four years, have proceedings been instituted against him, and it would appear the officers of justice have had no difficulty in finding the prisoner, who quietly submits himself to the law, and comes in with every appearance of being desirous of obtaining an adjudication of his case.

As the prisoner, then, has been living with his family in this place for nearly the last four years, made no effort to escape, and seemed ready when required to submit himself to justice, I think I may fairly presume that if let out on bail, he will, when called for, appear and take his trial for the offence charged against him, and this is all that the law—that public justice requires.

I regard it, however, as a most important fact in this application, and by which it is distinguished from the generality of cases of this kind, that the Crown has not only not opposed the application, but has assented to it.

In the Queen vs. Jeffers, and the Queen vs. Hoy and others, bail was refused, but I look upon these cases as being in many respects dissimilar to the present one.

In the first of the former cases, the accused confessed his guilt in open Court, which put it out of the judge's power to bail him.

In the second case, the application for bail was most strenuously opposed by the Crown (in this case the Crown assents to it), and from the surrounding circumstances, it was rendered more than doubtful that the parties, if bailed, would have surrendered themselves to justice.

In the present case no such doubt would seem to exist. On the contrary, the conduct of the prisoner, ever since the commission of the crime charged against him, goes to strengthen the probability that he has no desire to evade justice.

In conclusion, I desire to say that I chiefly ground my decision on the fact that, although the prisoner has sought no means of concealment, done nothing to evade justice, the prosecution has allowed nearly four years to elapse without moving in the matter; and also on the no less important fact that the Crown has not only not opposed this application, but has assented to the prisoner's being enlarged on bail.

I therefore think he ought to be bailed, himself to be bound in $4000, and two sureties each in the sum of $2000.

Bail to justify.

J. C. McKEAGNEY, J. C. Q B

December 22nd, 1873

Bail was accordingly taken for the prisoner's appearance at the next term of Court—himself in the sum of $4,000, Andrew G. B. Bannatyne, Esq., in the sum of $2 000, and André Beauchemin, Esq., M.P.P. in the sum of $2,000.

NOTE.—Mr. D. Carey, Prothonotary and Clerk of the Crown and Pleas for Manitoba, appeared for the Crown in place of Attorney-General Clark, who was absent in Canada.

A provincial statute provides that this officer shall act on behalf of the Crown in cas of the absence of the Attorney-General or other Crown Prosecutor.

FEBRUARY TERM, 1874.

This term of Court opened on Tuesday, Feb. 10th, 1873. Mr. Justice McKeagney on the Bench.

Ambroise D. Lepine was in attendance awaiting the decision of the Court as to its jurisdiction for the hearing of the charge against him, and which had been reserved from the November term until the sitting of this Court.

Attorney General Clarke asked for His Lordship's judgment on the pleas to the jurisdiction of the Court, as he was not in a position to decide what further steps to take in the case, until His Lordship's decision had been given.

His Lordship.—In that case I do not intend to give judgment till next term. I do not think myself competent or justified in deciding a question of such great importance without a full Bench; I will therefore await the appointment of a Chief Justice till next term, and if at that time there is no Chief Justice appointed, I will have the question re-argued before myself and my learned brother Betournay, and then decide the question.

Attorney-General.—Pardon me, my Lord; surely your Lordship will not refuse to give a decision on a question so simple as that of your own jurisdiction as a judge of the Court. Four months have now elapsed since the question was argued before you, and there has been absolutely no other business before you during all that time. I do not think I am asking too much at your Lordship's hands in praying for judgment, so that the Crown may proceed with the case.

His Lordship.—I don't think it would be right in me to take upon myself to decide the question. I will wait for the appointment of a Chief Justice before deciding the case or giving my opinion. I do not think it would be right to do otherwise. One judge is not enough to decide a matter of such grave importance to the prisoner.

Attorney-General.—My Lord, I must, in the interest of the administration of justice in this Province, call your attention to the statute by virtue of which your Lordship now sits on that Bench, and remind you that the law declares that any one judge of this Court has full power and jurisdiction to hear and determine all questions arising before the Court, and it is only in cases of appeal from the decision of one judge that the full Bench is appealed to. Now, surely your Lordship is not going to allow it to be understood that you will appeal from your own fears to the full Bench, and in reality shirk your duty and cast doubts on your own competency and the jurisdiction of the Court of Queen's Bench of the Province.

His Lordship.—Mr. Attorney-General, can't I do as I please in the matter?

Attorney-General.—No, my Lord, most certainly not. You cannot do just as you please. Judges can but hear questions arising before them and decide according to law and justice. Judges cannot shirk their duty, no matter how unpleasant and repugnant to their feelings the performance of such duties may be. If it were otherwise, I fear, from what experience I have had in this Court, that unpleasant duties would only too often be passed over and the ends of justice defeated. I respectfully pray your Lordship not to allow it to go to the world that you are not competent to decide your own jurisdiction. It will strike a fatal blow at the foundation of our administration of justice. It will be a fearful thing if the people of Canada are allowed to think that the judges of our Courts in this young Province are incompetent or afraid to administer justice—that life and property must depend on the decision of a Court that cannot or will not decide, after four months' deliberation, a question, a very simple question raised as to its jurisdiction.

His Lordship.—I will do as I please. I won't hear any more argument on the subject. I want my brother judge at least to hear the question argued before there is any decision given.

Attorney-General.—His Lordship Mr. Justice Betournay has already heard the question argued. There was nothing new in the argument before your Lordship last term. It was the very same argument (read from Mr. Grey's pamphlet) that was urged before your brother judge on the application for the commitment of the prisoner Lepine.

His Lordship.—Well, I will not give any decision now. I will wait till next term.

Attorney-General.—My Lord, once more I beg of you, do not drag our administration of justice in the dust. Do not, I pray you, make this Court the jeer and the scoff of every man of sense in the Dominion. If your Lordship wishes to play into the hands of any political party, let us understand it at once, and we will then know that your object is to gain time, so that efforts may be made in another quarter for a pardon—but do not let it go to the world that you do not know your own power or jurisdiction.

His Lordship (much excited).—I will not allow you, Mr. Attorney-General, to proceed any further. What do you mean to insinuate, I should like to know

Attorney-General.—I do not insinuate anything, my Lord. I think I speak plainly and try to be fully understood. I am determined, if the Court will not, or cannot perform its duty, that I will not shrink from reminding the Court of the fact, and at the same time endeavor to perform my duty fully and fearlessly.

Mr. Dubuc.—Will you consent, Mr. Attorney-General, to the prisoner's bail being enlarged?

Attorney-General.—I will not consent to anything, as the Court cannot decide on its own jurisdiction. I will leave this man suspended like Mahomet's coffin, till there is a decision given. The Court must take the whole responsibility.

His Lordship.—I think the bail may be enlarged. I see no objection.

The counsel for Lepine then moved that his recognizances be enlarged, which was granted.

JUNE TERM, 1874.

This term of the Court of Queen's Bench for the Province of Manitoba, which was opened on Tuesday, June 16th, was presided over by Chief Justice Wood, who had recently arrived in the Province in the capacity of Chief Justice of the Province. Justices McKeagney and Betournay were also in attendance on Monday, the 15th, when the Chief Justice announced that he was ready to hear the arguments of the learned counsel with reference to the jurisdiction of the Court in the Lepine case.

After the prisoner was placed at the bar,

Hons. J. Royal and J. Dubuc for the defence. Attorney-General Clarke for the Crown.

Hon. Mr. Royal addressed the Court, arguing that the Courts of the Province of Manitoba, as now constituted, were not competent to try any offences alleged to have been committed during the interval between the time of the transfer of the Province in 1869 and 70.

Attorney-General Clarke followed, taking the similar ground on his argument for jurisdiction as those in his address at the November term of 1873.

On the conclusion of the arguments by counsel, His Lordship the Chief Justice proceeded to render the following decision:

THE QUEEN vs. LEPINE.—The prisoner, in the November term, 1873, of this Court, was indicted for the murder of Thos. Scott on the 4th of March, 1870, at Upper Fort Garry, a place then being in the District of Assiniboia, in the Red River Settlement, in Rupert's Land, within the territories heretofore granted to the "Governor and Company of Adventurers of England trading into Hudson's Bay," and now within the territory forming the Province of Manitoba, one of the Provinces composing the Dominion of Canada.

On this indictment the prisoner was, on the 15th of November last, arraigned, and entered a plea to the jurisdiction of the Court, alleging that the territory now forming the Province of Manitoba, at the time the offence is alleged to have been committed, formed no part of the Dominion of Canada, and at that time the Dominion of Canada had no jurisdiction in this Province, or in the territory now forming the Province, and that the offence could only be heard and determined by the Imperial authorities, and the Imperial authorities never transmitted to or conferred upon the Dominion of Canada power to take cognizance of the offence; and that therefore neither the Dominion of Canada nor the Court of Queen's Bench in Manitoba had or has jurisdiction over the offence charged in the indictment.

To this plea the Crown demurred.

The case was argued in November term, 1873, before my brother McKeagney (my brother Betournay having sat on the preliminary examination in the Police

Court, and on the question of jurisdiction being raised, having over-ruled the plea), who reserved judgment until the next term (March, 1874), and who then further reserved judgment until the present June term, stating he would like to have the assistance of the Chief Justice, and to have the case argued *de novo.*

The case has now been ably argued both on behalf of the prisoner and the Crown, and as I have no doubt as to the judgment that should be given, I do not think any good end can be gained by delay, and I have, therefore, decided to follow the argument by immediate judgment:

The Province of Manitoba is a portion of Rupert's Land, and is embraced in the Royal grant and charter made by King Charles the Second, in 1670, to Prince Rupert and his associates, incorporated under the name of " The Governor and Company of Adventurers of England trading into Hudson's Bay."

By the terms of the charter, the Company was granted all the lands and territories upon the countries, coasts and confines of the seas, bays, lakes, rivers, creeks and sounds, in whatsoever latitude they should be, that might lie within the entrance of the straits commonly called Hudson's Straits ; and all this territory was to be called Rupert's Land, and reckoned one of His Majesty's plantations or colonies in America ; and the Company was to be the lord proprietor, under the Crown, of the same forever; and the Company was clothed with absolute legislative and judicial power over all these lands ; provided the laws were to be reasonable and not contrary to the laws of England ; and it was empowered to employ an armed force to protect its territory and to enforce its laws.

It is scarcely necessary to observe that under its full and ample powers, the Company could establish Courts, both civil and criminal, of unlimited jurisdiction, in which justice might be administered according to the laws of England.

The limits of Rupert's Land seem to be such territories as were drained by or formed the watershed of all the rivers, lakes and waters which flowed into Hudson's Straits, or into the Hudson's Bay, which were not then possessed by any subjects of His Majesty, or by the subjects of any other christian Prince or State. There was, at the time the charter was granted, and is yet, a vast extent of country in the North-West not within the limits of Rupert's Land, nor within the limits of what now comprises Quebec and Ontario, called " Indian Territories." It would seem, after the cession by the French crown to the British crown of territorial rights in North America by the Treaty of Paris in 1763, and the establishment first of the Province of Quebec and subsequently of the Provinces of Lower Canada and Upper Canada, that there were extensive regions not comprehended in Rupert's Land and beyond the boundaries of the two Canadas, in which crimes and offences were committed, and which were not within the limits of the jurisdiction of any courts, or any civil government, and beyond the cognizance of any jurisdiction whatever; and by reason thereof great crimes and offences had gone, and would continue to go, unpunished, and would greatly increase (Preamble to 43 Geo. 3, c. 138, 1803) ; whereupon the Parliament of Great Britain passed the Act 43 Geo. 3, c. 138, intituled :

" An Act for extending the jurisdiction of the Courts of Justice in the Provinces of Lower and Upper Canada to the trial and punishment of persons guilty of crimes and offences within certain parts of North America adjoining to the said Provinces.'

The first section of this Act provides :

" That from and after the passing of this Act, all offences committed within any of the Indian territories or parts of America not within the limits of either of the said Provinces of Lower or Upper Canada, or of any civil government of the United States of America, shall be and be deemed to be offences of the same nature, and shall be tried in the same manner, and subject to the same punishment as if the same had been committed within the Province of Lower or Upper Canada."

The second section provides:

"That it shall be lawful for the Governor or Lieutenant-Governor, or person administering the government, for the time being, of the Province of Lower Canada, by commission under his hand and seal, to authorize and empower any person or persons wheresoever resident or being at the time, to act as civil magistrates and justices of the peace for any of the Indian territories or parts of America not within the limits of either of the said Provinces, or of any civil government of the United States of America, either upon information taken or given within the said Provinces of Lower or Upper Canada, or out of the said Provinces in any part of the Indian territories or parts of America aforesaid, for the purpose only of hearing crimes and offences and committing any person or persons guilty of any crime or offence to safe custody, in order to his or their being conveyed to the said Province of Lower Canada to be dealt with according to law; and it shall be lawful for any person or persons whatever to apprehend and take before any person so commissioned as aforesaid, or to apprehend and convey, or cause to be safely conveyed with all convenient speed, to the Province of Lower Canada, any person or persons guilty of any crime or offence, there to be delivered into safe custody for the purpose of being dealt with according to law."

The third section in substance provides for the trial of offenders in Upper Canada, if the Governor of Lower Canada, from any circumstances of the crime or offence, or the local situation of witnesses for the Crown or the defence, should think the trial could more conveniently take place and justice be more conveniently administered in relation to such crime or defence in Upper Canada than in Lower Canada—clothing the courts with power of punishment and with authority to enforce the attendance of witnesses.

Section four directs that if the offender be not a British subject, or the offence be committed in any colony, settlement, or territory belonging to any European State, he shall be acquitted.

The remaining section, however, declares that if the offender be a subject of His Majesty, although the offence may have been committed in some colony, settlement, or territory belonging to some European State, he shall, nevertheless, be tried as in other cases.

I am thus particular in referring to all the provisions of this Act, inasmuch as subsequently, by direct enactment, it is made applicable to Rupert's Land, or what is commonly called the Hudson's Bay Territory. Although this Act is very general and comprehensive in the description of the territory to which it was intended to apply, it is supposed its language would not necessarily include Rupert's Land. On the trial of De Reinhard and Archibald McLellan for the murder of Owen Keveny at a place called Dalles, on the River Winnipic, near the north-west angle of the Lake of the Woods, and within Rupert's Land, before Chief Justice Sewell at Quebec, in 1818, the question of the geographical boundary of Upper Canada was much discussed; and although De Reinhard was convicted of murder, the verdict was never carried into execution; not, as it is apprehended, on the ground urged at the trial, that the courts in Upper Canada had sole jurisdiction over the offence because of its having been committed within the geographical limits of Upper Canada, as defined by the Act of 1791 and the King's proclamation issued in pursuance thereof, but on the ground that the offence was committed, not within the "Indian Territories" referred to in 43 Geo. 3rd, chap. 138, but within Rupert's Land, to which it was doubtful if on a strict construction the Act had any application.

Accordingly we find that shortly thereafter, in 1821, was passed the Imperial Act 1 and 2 Geo. 4th, chap. 66, intituled:

"An Act for regulating the fur trade, and establishing a criminal and civil jurisdiction within certain parts of North America."

As giving an historical glimpse of the unsettled state of affairs in the Indian territories and other parts of British America adjoining the Provinces of Lower and Upper Canada, and of the feuds and animosities existing between the North-West Company and the Hudson's Bay Company, and as throwing light upon the proper interpretation of 43 Geo. 3rd, chap. 138, I cite the preamble of this Act in full. It reads:—

"Whereas the competition in the fur trade between the Governor and Company of Adventurers of England trading into Hudson's Bay, and certain associations of persons trading under the name of the North-West Company of Montreal, has been found for some years past to be productive of great inconvenience and loss, not only to the said Company and associations, but to the said trade in general, and also of great injury to the native Indians and other persons subjects of His Majesty: And whereas the animosities and feuds arising from such competition have also, for some years past, kept the interior of America, to the northward and westward of the Provinces of Upper and Lower Canada, and of the territories of the United States of America, in a state of continued disturbance: And whereas many breaches of the peace, and violence extending to the loss of lives and considerable destruction of property, have continually occurred therein: And whereas, for remedy of such evils, it is expedient and necessary that some more effectual regulations should be established for the apprehending, securing and bringing to justice all persons committing such offences, and that His Majesty be empowered to regulate the said trade: And whereas doubts have been entertained whether the provisions of an Act passed in the forty-third year of the reign of His late Majesty King George the Third, intituled: 'An Act for extending the jurisdiction of the Courts of Justice in the Provinces of Lower and Upper Canada to the trial and punishment of persons guilty of crimes and offences within certain parts of North America adjoining to the said Provinces,' extended to the territories granted by charter to the said Governor and Company, and it is expedient that such doubts should be removed, and that the said Act should be extended."

The first section of the Act provided for giving a royal license to any corporation, company, or person or persons, for the sole and exclusive privilege of trading with the Indians in all such parts of North America as should be specified in such license, not being parts of the lands or territories granted to the Hudson's Bay Company, or of any of the Provinces of North America, or of the United States of America.

The second section limits the term of the licenses to twenty-one years.

By the third section the Hudson's Bay Company, and every corporation or company, or person or persons, to which or to whom any license should be granted, were required to keep accurate registers of all persons in his or their employ, and once a year make a return of a duplicate thereof to His Majesty's Secretary of State, and were further required to enter into such security as should be demanded by His Majesty for the due execution of all processes both criminal and civil, as well in the territories included in any such license, as within those granted by charter to the Hudson's Bay Company, and for the producing and delivering into safe custody, for purpose of trial, all persons in their employ, or acting under their authority, charged with or guilty of any criminal offence, and also for the due observance of all such rules, regulations and stipulations as should be contained in any license, either for the diminishing or preventing the sale of spirituous liquors to the Indians, or for promoting their moral and religious improvement, or for any other object which His Majesty might deem necessary for the remedy or prevention of other evils which had theretofore been found to exist.

Section four provides that such licenses should not interfere with the trade of the United States west of the Stony (Rocky) Mountains.

Section five reads as follows:—

"And be it declared and enacted that the said Act passed in the forty-third year of the reign of His late Majesty intituled, 'An Act for extending the jurisdiction of the courts of justice in the Provinces of Lower and Upper Canada to the trial and punishment of persons guilty of crimes or offences in certain parts of North America adjoining to the said Provinces,' and all the clauses and provisoes therein contained, shall be deemed and construed, and it is and are hereby respectively declared to extend to and over, and to be in full force in and through all the territories heretofore granted to the Company of Adventurers of England trading into Hudson's Bay; anything in any Act or Acts of Parliament, or this Act, or in any grant or charter to the Company to the contrary notwithstanding."

Section six provides that the courts of judicature established in Upper Canada should have cognizance of causes arising in the Indian territories and other parts of North America, and of actions relating to lands, to be decided according to the laws of England; and by section seven the authority of the courts, and all processes and proceedings issuing from them, were to have the same force and effect in those territories and other parts as in Upper Canada they would have in actions arising therein; and the eighth section makes provision for the Governor of Lower Canada, by commission under his hand and seal, authorizing all persons who should under the Act be appointed justices of the peace within the said Indian territories, or other parts of North America as aforesaid, or any one who should be specially named in such commission, to act as a commissioner within the same for the purpose of serving, executing, and enforcing subpœnas and all processes, decrees, judgments, orders, injunctions, and other processes or proceedings of the said courts, and on disobedience of any person, to apprehend and deliver offenders over to the said courts to be dealt with according to law.

The ninth section provides for the assignment of recognizances and the bringing of actions thereon; and the latter part of the clause, in these words: "Notwithstanding anything contained in any charter granted to the said Governor and Company of Adventurers of England trading to Hudson's Bay," shows that sections six, seven, eight, as well as section nine, apply to the Hudson's Bay Company.

Section ten provides for the appointment of justices of the peace by His Majesty, as well in Rupert's Land as in the Indian territories and other parts of America, and also for the taking of evidence under commissioners by the courts of Upper Canada, and if expedient so to do, to have the issue tried by the commissioners, who were to be justices of the peace appointed by the Crown under the Imperial Act now in recital.

The eleventh and twelfth sections have an important bearing on the case under consideration.

Section II.—And be it further enacted, that it shall be lawful for His Majesty, notwithstanding anything contained in this Act, or in any charter granted to the said Governor and Company of Adventurers of England trading to Hudson's Bay, from time to time, by any commission under the great seal, to authorize and empower any such persons so appointed Justices of the Peace as aforesaid, to sit and to hold Courts of Record for the trial of criminal offences and misdemeanors, and also of civil cases; and it shall be lawful for His Majesty to order, direct, and authorize the appointment of proper officers to act in aid of such courts and justices within the jurisdiction assigned to such courts and justices in any such commission; anything in this Act, or in any charter of the Governor and Company of Merchant Adventurers of England trading to Hudson's Bay, to the contrary notwithstanding.

Section XII.—Provided always, and be it further enacted that such courts shall be constituted as to the number of justices to preside therein, and also such places within the said territories of the said Company, or any Indian territories or other parts of North America as aforesaid, and the times and manner of holding the same, as His Majesty shall from time to time order and direct; but shall not try any offender upon any charge or indictment for any felony made the subject of capital punishment, or of any offence, or passing sentence affecting the life of any offender, or adjudge or cause any offender to suffer capital punishment or transportation, or take cognizance of or try any civil action or suit in which the cause of such suit or action shall exceed in value the amount or sum of two hundred pounds (£200); and in every case of any offence subjecting the person committing the same to capital punishment or transportation, the court or any judge of any such court, or any justice or justices of the peace before whom any such offence shall be brought, shall commit such offender to safe custody, and cause such offender to be sent in such custody for trial in the Court of the Province of Upper Canada.

Section thirteen gives the right of appeal to His Majesty in civil suits in like manner as in Upper Canada, and in any case to which the right or title to any land should be in question.

The fourteenth and last section preserves to the Hudson's Bay Company the right, privileges, authority, and jurisdiction which it might lawfully have claimed and enjoyed under its charter.

Another Imperial Act was passed in 1859, 22 and 23 Vic., C. 26.

The preamble recites 43 Geo. 3, c. 138, and 1 and 2 Geo. 4, c. 66, and declares that "no Courts of Record had been established or authorized as provided in the Act 1 and 2 Geo. 4th, chap. 66, and that it was expedient to make further provision for the administration of justice in criminal cases in the said Indian territories and such other parts as aforesaid of America." And then in the first section it gives Her Majesty authority by commission to clothe the justices of the peace to be appointed under 1 and 2 Geo. 4th, chap. 66, within the limitations contained in such commission as to territorial jurisdiction and other matters, to take cognizance of, hear, try, and determine, in a summary manner, all crimes, misdemeanors, and offences whatsoever, and, on conviction, to award punishment; but in case the offence was punishable with death, or for other reasons the justice or justices should think it advisable to do so, he and they was and were directed to commit the offender to safe custody and have him delivered for trial to Upper Canada, as provided by the Act of King George the Fourth, or, if thought expedient, to British Columbia, there to be tried by any court having cognizance of like offences committed there, and like powers were given such court as were by the Acts recited given to any court in Canada in the like cases.

By the last section it is especially declared that nothing in that Act contained should extend to the territories heretofore granted to the Hudson's Bay Company; so that Rupert's Land, and consequently the Red River Settlement, and Winnipeg, which formed a portion of Rupert's Land, are entirely excluded from the operation of any of the provisions of the Act 22 and 23 Vic., chap. 26, and neither British Columbia nor any of its courts ever had anything to do with or any jurisdiction over or cognizance of the crime charged in this indictment, or any crimes or offences committed within any part of Rupert's Land, as has been popularly supposed, and as was apparently assumed on the argument of this demurrer.

It would appear from the declarations in the Acts to which I have referred, that though authority was given the Crown to set up Courts of Record in the Indian territories and other parts of America, and in Rupert's Land, none such were established by the Crown as late as 1859, and I think it quite safe to say none were constituted by the Crown down to the time of the transfer of all these territories to Canada in 1870, by the Order in Council of the 23rd of June, which took effect on the 15th of July of that year, in pursuance of the Imperial Act called "Rupert's Land Act, 1868," 31 and 32 Vic., chap. 105.

Although the Crown did not establish any courts, yet it appears the Hudson's Bay Company, by virtue of the powers conferred on it by its charter, as far back as 1839 constituted its factors and others in its employ justices of the peace in Rupert's Land and in other parts of the North-West Territories where it had trading posts, who exercised both civil and criminal jurisdiction in small claims and in minor offences, in a summary manner, in the respective districts in which they were stationed; and also about the same time established a Court of Record called the "General Court of Assiniboia," the seat of which was at Winnipeg, with a geographical jurisdiction which does not seem to have been strictly defined, and having cognizance and jurisdiction of all civil claims and demands, of whatever nature or amount the same might be, and of all crimes, misdemeanors, and offences whatsoever, with all the powers necessary to enforce its judgments, orders, decrees, and sentences in both civil and criminal matters, even to the extent of inflicting capital punishment. The Company appointed Mr. Adam Thom the first judge of this court, with other officers, in or about the year 1839. The sole authority and basis of this court and its officers rested upon the powers conferred on the Company by the charter granted it in the reign of King Charles the Second, but on no legislative enactment whatever. Mr. Thom presided over this court till about the year 1851. After his retirement, Mr. Johnson of Montreal, now a judge in the Province of Quebec, was appointed judge, who, having for some years discharged the duties of his office, retired, and was succeeded by Mr. Black, who was the judge in 1869-70 when the difficulties occurred at Winnipeg out of which arises the offence charged in this indictment. It would therefore appear that this court, with its judges and officers, in 1870 had been in existence for thirty years, trying civil cases to any amount whatever and exercising criminal jurisdiction even to the extent of inflicting capital punishment (for in one instance at least a person was tried for murder, convicted, and executed), without its basis or jurisdiction ever having been formally and authoritatively questioned by the Imperial Government. On the contrary, by the last clause of "Rupert's Land Act, 1868," the validity of this Court and the legality of its jurisdiction over capital offences, which were then well known to the Government and Parliament of England (see proceedings of Committee on Hudson's Bay Company, House of Commons, 1857), and of its officers, and of the magistrates and justices then being in Rupert's Land, seem to be fully recognized and admitted. It says:

"It shall be competent to Her Majesty, by any such order as aforesaid (Orders in Council for admission of Rupert's Land), on address from the Houses of the Parliament of Canada, to declare that Rupert's Land shall, from a date to be therein mentioned, be admitted into and become part of the Dominion of Canada; and thereupon it shall be lawful for the Parliament of Canada, from the date aforesaid, to make, ordain, and establish within the land and territory so admitted as aforesaid, all such laws, institutions and ordinances, and to constitute such courts and officers as may be necessary for the peace, order, and good government of Her Majesty's subjects and others therein; provided that until otherwise enacted by the Parliament of Canada, all the powers, authorities, and jurisdiction of the several courts of justice now established in Rupert's Land, and the several officers thereof, and of all magistrates and justices now acting within the said limits, shall continue in full force and effect therein."

Attention is called to the words of the proviso in this section. To what "courts and officers thereof" do they refer? The Crown had established no "courts" or "officers thereof" in Rupert's Land. It may have appointed some justices of the peace, but even that is doubtful. The only court then existing in Rupert's Land was "the General Court," established by the Hudson's Bay Company under its royal charter, and the only "officers thereof" were those appointed by that Company, and I think I may safely say, if not all, nearly all "the magistrates and justices then acting or being within the said limits," in like manner derived their authority from and were appointed by the Hudson's Bay Company, which by its charter had power and authority—

"From time to time to assemble itself for or about any of the causes, affairs or businesses of the said trade, in any place or places for the same convenient within the dominions or elsewhere, and there to hold court for the said Company and the affairs thereof, and to make, ordain and constitute such and so many reasonable laws, constitutions, orders and ordinances, as should seem necessary and convenient for the good government of the said Company; and of all governors of colonies, forts, and plantations, factors, masters, marines, or other officers employed, or to be employed, in any of the territories and lands aforesaid; and for the better continuance of the said trade or trafic and plantations, and the same laws, constitutions, orders and ordinances so made, to put in use and execute accordingly; and at its pleasure to revoke and alter the same, or any of them, as the occasion should require; and should and might impose, ordain, limit, and provide such pains, penalties and punishments upon all offenders contrary to such laws, constitutions, orders, and ordinances, or any of them, as to the said governor and Company for the time being, or the greater part of them, then and there being present, the said governor or his deputy being always one, should seem necessary, requisite or convenient for the observation of the same laws, constitutions, orders and ordinances; and the same fines and amerciaments should by its officers and servants in that behalf levy, take and have to the use of the said Company, without the impediment of the Crown, and without any account thereof to be made to the Crown; and all and singular the laws, constitutions, orders and ordinances so as aforesaid to be made His Majesty did will should be duly observed and kept, under the pains and penalties therein to be contained; so always as the said laws, constitutions, orders and ordinances, fines and amerciaments were reasonable, and not contrary or repugnant, but as near as might be agreeable to the laws, statutes or customs of the realm.   *   *   *   *   *   *   *   *   *

"And all the lands, islands, territories, plantations, forts, fortifications, factories or colonies, where the said Company's factories or trade might or should be, within any of the forts or places afore limited, should be immediately and from thenceforth under the power and command of the said Company (saving the faith and allegiance due to be performed to His Majesty, his heirs and successors); and the said Company were given liberty, full power and authority to appoint and establish governors and all other officers to govern them, and the governor and his council of the several and respective places where the said Company should have plantations, forts, factories, colonies, or places of trade within any of the countries, lands or territories thereby granted, might and should have power to judge all persons belonging to the said Company, or that should live under it, in all causes, whether civil or criminal, according to the laws of the kingdom of England, and to execute justice accordingly; and in case any crime or misdemeanor should be committed in any of the Company's plantations, forts, factories, or places of trade within the limits aforesaid, where judicature cannot be executed for want of a governor and council there, then in such case it should and might be lawful for the chief factor of that place and his council to transmit the party together with the offence to such other plantation, factory or fort where there should be a governor and council, or into the Kingdom of England, as should be thought most convenient, there to receive such punishment as the nature of his offence should deserve."

And these rights, powers, authorities and jurisdictions were in no way revoked, abridged, superseded, or limited by any Act of the Parliament of England; on the contrary, in the Act I and II Geo. 4, cap. 66, and in the concluding and last section thereof, it is enacted and declared:—

"*That nothing in this Act contained shall be taken or construed to affect any right, privilege, authority or jurisdiction which the Governor and Company of Adventurers* trading to Hudson's Bay are by law entitled to claim and exercise under their charter; but all such rights, privileges, authorities and jurisdictions shall remain in as full force, virtue and effect as if this Act had never been made; anything in this Act to the contrary notwithstanding." And in the concluding and last section of 22 and 23 Vic., c. 26 (1859), it is enacted and declared that " *Nothing herein contained shall extend to the territories heretofore granted to the Company of Adventurers trading to Hudson's Bay.*"

Therefore, notwithstanding that by the Imperial Act of 1803, which gave criminal jurisdiction to the Courts of Lower and Upper Canada within the Indian territories and other parts of North America, and made provision for the apprehension and transmission of offenders to those Provinces for trial and punishment, and nothwithstanding that by the Imperial Act of 1821, the Act of 1803 was extended and made applicable to Rupert's Land, and further provision was made for the administration of justice, both criminal and civil—the Crown taking power to appoint justices of the peace to act as such, as well in the Hudson's Bay Territory as in the Indian territories and other parts of North America, and to constitute such justices a Court of Record to try civil cases where the recovery should not exceed two hundred pounds, and to hear and determine criminal offences where the punishment inflicted was not death or transportation ; nevertheless the Courts of Lower and Upper Canada had only a concurrent, not an exclusive jurisdiction ; for the Act 1 and 2 Geo. IV., c. 66, conferring jurisdiction in Rupert's Land (the Hudson's Bay Territory) on the Canadian Courts, and giving power to the Crown to appoint justices and establish a Court of Record therein, explicitly enacts and declares, " That the rights, privileges, authorities and jurisdictions of judicature granted to the Hudson's Bay Company by its royal charter, should not be in any way affected by anything in that Act contained, but should remain in as full force, virtue and effect as they would if that Act had not been passed."

Again, I do not think it can be successfully contended that " The Supreme Court " established by the Manitoba Act (34 Vic., chapter 2) was not clothed with jurisdiction over all criminal as well as civil matters arising or existing in the Province of Manitoba, or in the territory which had then become that Province at the time it was passed, independent of 34 Vic., chap. 14, sec. 2, altogether ; for by section 92, sub-section 14, of the British North America Act, 1867, " the administration of justice in the Provinces, including the constitution, maintenance and organization of Provincial Courts, both of civil and criminal jurisdiction, including procedure in civil matters in those Courts,' belongs exclusively to the Legislature of the several Provinces. In this Act the legal existence and extensive jurisdiction of the General Court established, as I have mentioned, by the Hudson's Bay Company, are fully recognized   Section 39 says :

" Till a judge of the Supreme Court of the Province shall be appointed by the Government of the Dominion of Canada, the General Court sitting in this Province shall exercise throughout the Province all the functions and possess all the authority hereby conferred on the Supreme Court ; and all the provisions of this Act respecting the Supreme Court shall apply in like manner and to the same extent, for all purposes whatever, to the said General Court, and to the judge and officers thereof, and to all suitors therein, and to the attendance of jurors, grand and petit, thereat, and to all proceedings in the said Court, in as full and ample a manner as if such provisions had been made in express reference to the said General Court."

Section 40 says :

" From and after the appointment, as aforesaid, of a Chief Justice of the Supreme Court, all cases pending in the General Court in the last section mentioned shall be transferred to the said Supreme Court in the same state and condition as they may there be, and shall be treated in all respects as if they had been commenced and carried on in the Supreme Court."

Section 41 says:

"Judgments of the General Court in the last two preceding sections mentioned shall be enforced, set aside, or otherwise dealt with in all respects as if they were judgments of the Supreme Court."

This Act, as I have said, fully recognizes and admits the legal existence of the General Court, with a jurisdiction, both civil and criminal, as extended as that of the Supreme Court which it established, and it substituted or continued the General Court with its extended jurisdiction over all matters, civil and criminal, arising or existing within the Province, and within the territory which had become the Province, until by the appointment of a Chief Justice of the Supreme Court by the Government of Canada, the latter Court should be organized and brought into operation.

This Act of the Manitoba Legislature was passed on the 12th of May, 1871. Prior to the passing of this Act, on the 14th of April, 1871, the Parliament of Canada, under the authority of "The British North America Act, 1867," and "Rupert's Land Act, 1868," had passed the Act 34 Vic., chap 14, to extend to the Province of Manitoba certain of the criminal laws then and now in force in the other Provinces of the Dominion; and by the second section thereof it is declared and enacted that—

"The Court known as the General Court (the Court established by the Hudson's Bay Company) heretofore existing in the Province of Manitoba, and any courts to be hereafter constituted by the legislature of the said Province, and having the powers now exercised by the said General Court, shall have power to hear, try, and determine in due course of law all treasons, felonies, and indictable offences committed in any part of the said Province, or in the territory which has now become the said Province."

Simply re-iterating what was already declared to be the fundamental law of the Province by sec. 92, sub-section 14 of the British North America Act, 1867.

It would therefore appear to follow that when the offence charged in the indictment was committed (the 4th of March, 1870), the General Court established by the Hudson's Bay Company had jurisdiction over the crime; and that by the last clause of "Rupert's Land Act, 1868," such jurisdiction was continued down to the 15th of July, 1870, the time of the transfer of the territories to Canada and the formation of the Province of Manitoba (33 Vic, chap. 3, Statutes of Canada), and thence on (34 Vic., chap. 2, sections 39, 40, and 41, Statutes of Manitoba) until the Supreme Court of Manitoba, now called the Court of Queen's Bench, was organized and brought into operation by the appointment of a chief justice thereof—an event which took place in the autumn of 1872, by the appointment to that office of the Hon. Alexander Morris—and from that time and by that Act, and by the direct and express declarations of the several Acts to which I have referred, as well Imperial as Canadian and Provincial, unquestionable jurisdiction over and power and authority to hear, try, and determine in due course of law, as well the offence charged in the indictment, as also "all treasons, felonies, and indictable offences committed in any part of the said Province or in the territory which has now become the said Province," were given to, conferred upon, and vested in the Court of Queen's Bench, in which this indictment was found, and in which I am now sitting.

It has been argued that the General Court of Assiniboia had not, at the time of the committing of the offence charged in the indictment, power and authority to hear, try, and determine capital felonies. For the reasons I have given I think it had. However that may be, it can in nowise affect the conclusion at which I have arrived, based as it is on the express power given to the Court by the Canadian Act (34 Vic., chap 14, sec. 2), which Act is authorized by the Imperial Statute called Rupert's Land Act (31 and 32 Vic., chap. 105, sec. 5). and although passed on the 14th of April, 1871, and now on the statute book for upwards of three years, has not been disallowed or questioned by the Imperial authorities as being *ultra vires* or otherwise objectionable.

On the argument it was suggested that the second section of this Act was *ultra vires, ex-post facto* and *retroactive*, and therefore unconstitutional. It is expressly authorized by the Imperial Rupert's Land Act, 1868, and cannot be said to be *ultra vires*. I am unable to see in what respect it is either *ex-post facto* or *retroactive*. It does not make nor create any new offence. It does not make that an offence which, when it was done, was no offence. Every British colony wherever it may be planted, and all the members of it, unless the contrary is manifested by express Act of Parliament, carry along with them, and are protected by and subject to the common law of England. By the common law, whosoever, being of sound mind, with malice aforethought, taketh the life of a human being in the Queen's peace, is guilty of murder, and death is the penalty. That is the offence charged in the indictment. The statute does not make that a crime which, before it was passed, was no crime. It does not introduce any new rules or new principles of evidence or procedure by which that which, according to the common law, is murder, shall be heard, tried and determined. It simply points out the Court which, in accordance with due course of law, shall hear, try and determine the offence charged—the guilt or innocence of the prisoner. Seemingly from an apprehension that some objection of this sort might be raised, the Statute itself settles the question forever. Sect. 6, 34 Vic., cap. 14, says:

"All provisions of law heretofore in force in the country now constituting the Province of Manitoba, inconsistent with or repugnant to any of the Statutes enumerated in the first section of this Act, are hereby repealed ; *provided always that no person shall, by reason of the passing of this Act, be liable to any punishment or penalty for any act done before the passing thereof, for which he would not have been liable to any punishment or penalty under the laws in force in the said Province or territory now const tu'ing it a' the time such act was done ; or shall any person, by reason of the passing of this Act, be liable to any greater or other punishment for any offence committed before the passing thereof, than he would have been liable to under the laws then in force as aforesaid ; and this Act and the Acts hereby extended to the said Province shall apply only to the procedure in any such case, and the penalty or punishment shall be the same as if this Act had not been passed.*"

I, therefore, fail to see any ground whatever for questioning that this Court has jurisdiction of the offence charged in the indictment.

There is another aspect of the case which leads to the same conclusion, and which it may not be inappropriate to glance at, to settle the public mind on a much vexed question.

The Imperial Act 43 Geo. 3, c. 138, provides that the Governor of Lower Canada might, under his hand and seal, issue commissions appointing any person or persons, wheresoever resident or being at the time, to act as civil magistrates or justices of the peace for any of the Indian territories or parts of America not within the limits of either Lower or Upper Canada, or of any civil government of the United States of America, either upon informations taken or given in either of the Provinces of Lower or Upper Canada, or out of those Provinces, in any part of the Indian territories or other parts of America, for the purpose only of hearing crimes and offences, and committing any person or persons guilty of any crime or offence to safe custody, in order to his or their being conveyed to Lower Canada to be dealt with according to law ; and it was made lawful for any persons whatever to apprehend and take before any persons so commissioned by the Governor of Lower Canada, or to apprehend and convey, or cause to be conveyed with all convenient despatch, to Lower Canada any person or persons guilty of any crime or offence, there to be delivered into safe custody for the purpose of being dealt with according to law.

It was declared by the Act that all offences committed within the territories and places referred to, should be deemed to be offences of the same nature, and should be tried in the same manner and subject to the same punishment as if the same had been committed in the Provinces of Upper or Lower Canada respectively.

Every offender was to be prosecuted and tried in the Courts of the Province of Lower Canada, or, if the Governor of Lower Canada should, from any of the circumstances of the crime or offence or the local situation of any of the witnesses for the prosecution or defence, think that justice can be more conveniently administered, in relation to such crime or offence, in the Province of Upper Canada, and should, by any instrument under the great seal of the Province of Lower Canada, declare the same, then every such offender might and should be prosecuted in the Court of the Province of Upper Canada.

Here, in the year 1803, we have the Governor of Lower Canada empowered, as an Imperial officer, by commission under his hand and seal, to appoint magistrates and justices of peace wherever they might be or reside, for the purpose of handing over offenders in the Indian territories and other parts of North America for trial by the Courts of Lower Canada, or if the Governor should think it more convenient, and should so declare under the great seal of the Province of Lower Canada, by the Court of Upper Canada. Indeed, any person, whether so appointed or not, was authorized to apprehend and to transmit all persons charged with any crime or offence to the authorities of Lower Canada, to be dealt with in the manner indicated according to law.

Now, it will be observed that the appointment of magistrates and justices for the purposes mentioned was an executive act and rested solely with the Governor of Lower Canada, as an Imperial officer, in his relations as such to the Government of Lower and Upper Canada (there then being only a Lieutenant-Governor of Upper Canada), and in direct communication with, and receiving his instructions directly from the Imperial authorities, and was to be performed by an instrument under his hand and seal, not under the great seal of the Province; but when he came to deal with the question of directing any offender to be tried by the Court in Upper Canada, it being an act of administration within the Province, that was to be performed under the great seal of the Province. Considering that the government of a country embraces the Executive and his duties, the Legislature and its duties, the Courts of justice and their duties, with such ministers and officers and their duties as may be necessary, it is manifest that in the present case both duties, the one Imperial and executive, the other Provincial and administrative, equally related to the government of the Canadas.

It will be further observed, from what has already been said, that this Act did not apply to Rupert's Land (the Hudson's Bay Territory), a portion of which, on the 15th of July, 1870, became and now is the Province of Manitoba.

By the Imperial Acts 1 and 2 Geo. 4, c. 66 (1821), among other things, 43 Geo. 3, c. 138, with all its clauses and provisions, was in express terms made applicable to Rupert's Land, or the lands and territories by the charter of Charles the Second granted to the Hudson's Bay Company—still leaving with the Governor of Lower Canada the power of appointing magistrates, etc., as before.

From that time the Governor of Lower Canada had the Imperial executive authority in Rupert's Land, and the Provincial administrative authority in the Province of Lower Canada, in relation to the government of Upper Canada as I have mentioned; and the courts in Lower Canada and the court of Upper Canada had jurisdiction, concurrent not exclusive, as has already been shown, of all "offences committed" in Rupert's Land; and the Governor continued to possess such authority, and the courts such jurisdiction, unaffected by any legislative enactment, till the tenth day of February, 1841, when the Imperial Act for uniting the Provinces of Upper and Lower Canada, and for the Government of Canada, passed in 1840 (3 and 4 V., c. 35) came into operation, and the Provinces of Upper and Lower Canada became the Province of Canada.

But this Act declared and enacted that—

"All powers, authorities, and functions, which by the said Act, passed in the thirty-first year of the reign of His Majesty King George the Third, or by any other Act of Parliament, or by Act of the Legislature of the Provinces of Upper and Lower Canada, respectively, are vested in, or are authorized, or required to be exercised by the respective Governors or Lieutenant-Governors of the said Provinces, with the advice, or with the advice and consent of the Executive Council of such Provinces, respectively, or in conjunction with such Executive Council, or with any number of members thereof, or by the said Governors or Lieutenant-Governors individually and alone, shall, in so far as the same are not repugnant to or inconsistent with the provisions of this Act, be vested in and may be exercised by the Governor of the Province of Canada, with the advice, or with the advice and consent of, or in conjunction, as the case may require, with such Executive Council, or any members thereof as may be appointed by Her Majesty for the affairs of the Province of Canada, or by the said Governor of the Province of Canada individually and alone, in cases where the advice, consent, or concurrence of the Executive Council is not required. (Sec. 45).

"All the courts of civil and criminal jurisdiction within the Provinces of Upper and Lower Canada at the time of the union of the said Provinces, and all legal commissions, powers, and authorities, and all officers, judicial, administrative, or ministerial, within the said Provinces respectively, except in so far as the same may be abolished, altered, or varied by, or may be inconsistent with the provisions of this Act, or shall be abolished, altered, or varied by any Act or Acts of the Legislature of the Province of Canada, shall continue to subsist within those parts of the Province of Canada which now constitute the said two Provinces respectively, in the same form and with the same effect as if this Act had not been made, and if the said two Provinces had not been re-united as aforesaid." (Sec. 46.)

From the Union of the Provinces to Confederation (1st July, 1867), the Governor-General of the Province of Canada was vested with and possessed, and it became and was his duty to exercise, all the Imperial executive authority in Rupert's Land and the Province of Canada, in relation to the government of the Province of Canada, and the courts in Lower and Upper Canada continued to possess and enjoy, and were capable of exercising all the jurisdiction over all offences committed in Rupert's Land, that were respectively vested in and possessed by the Governor of Lower Canada, and that were possessed, enjoyed, and capable of being exercised by the courts of Lower and Upper Canada before the Union, unaffected in any manner whatever by the Imperial Act 22 and 23 V., c. 26 (1859), or by any other Act, Imperial or Provincial.

The question now is, what became of this Imperial executive and administrative power and authority, and of this jurisdiction of the courts of the Province of Canada on Confederation? It has been argued that it ceased altogether or reverted back to the crown in England, and therefore could be exercised only by the Imperial authorities and the criminal courts of England; and this argument is based entirely on the phrase, "In relation to the Government of Canada," in the 12th sec, and the phrase, "in relation to the Government of Ontario and Quebec respectively,' in the 65th section of the British North America Act, 1867. These sections are substantially the same in phraseology, and are substantial copies of section 46 of the Union Act of 1840, which has been quoted in full—the only difference being in the words, 'in relation to the Government of Canada," in the former, and "in relation to the Government of Ontario and Quebec respectively" in the latter. It is admitted that had these phrases been omitted, or in other words, had these sections been precisely in the words of section forty-six of the Union Act of 1840, the power and authority of the Governor-General of Canada, and of the courts of Quebec and Ontario in respect of offences committed in Rupert's Land, would have remained and continued just the same after as before Confederation: but it is argued that the Imperial Parliament, having in view the further acquisition by Canada of Rupert's Land and the North-West Territories, introduced these phrases with the intention of taking from the Executive of Canada these powers and authorities, and from the courts of Ontario and Quebec this jurisdiction. If this were the intention of Parliament, it seems to me it might easily have found words, phrases and language more fittingly expressive of its meaning. Is not this giving a strained construction to the Statute, unsupported by any substantial reason, and contrary to the express declarations of other parts of the Act? Is it not manifest, on a moment's reflection, why the phrases in question were used? These two sections (12 and 65) were dealing with the Imperial executive and Canadian administrative and ministerial powers and authorities of the Governor-General of Canada in respect of all matters and duties delegated to, and imposed upon him, in "relation to the Government of Canada," that is, all matters and duties which were general, not local, and which related to all the provinces alike, but to none in particular, *on the one hand*, and to the Provincial executive, administrative and ministerial powers and authorities, which, from their limited and circumscribed nature, and their local application, were to be exercised only in reference to such matters and duties as were required to be done in relation to the government of the provinces respectively, *on the other hand*; and, to draw a line between the executive duties of the Governor-General, an Imperial officer and in direct correspondence with the Crown through its Imperial ministers, and those of the Lieutenant-Governors of the Provinces, holding their appointments from, and being responsible to, and in correspondence only with the Governor-General, the phrases referred to were properly used; and it was necessary that these or similar words should be employed to mark the respective executive, administrative and ministerial powers and authorities of each. Neither of these sections has any relation to the courts of Upper and Lower Canada, Ontario and Quebec. I therefore fail to see how any argument can be derived from them that the Act of Confederation swept away the jurisdiction of those courts over offences committed in Rupert's Land and in the North-West territories. The only question that can be raised is, "Had the Governor-General, after Confederation the executive power of appointing magistrates, &c., in Rupert's Land and other parts, to take informations, &c., and transmit offenders for trial and punishment to the courts of Ontario and Quebec?" It is quite clear that neither the Lieutenant-Governor of Ontario nor of Quebec had any such power; and I think it equally clear, for the reasons given and for many others which might be mentioned, the Governor-General had such power until the transfer of Rupert's Land and the North-West territories, and the establishment of the Province of Manitoba—events which took place on the 15th day of July, 1870—and therefore, during, at the time, and after the crime charged in the indictment was committed. And from the 129th and 130th sections of the Confederation Act, apparently overlooked by counsel on the argument, the 129th being almost if not quite an exact copy of section 47 of the Union Act of 1840, which says:—

"129. Except as otherwise provided by this Act, all laws in force in Canada, Nova Scotia, or New Brunswick at the Union, and all courts of civil and criminal jurisdiction, and all legal commissions, powers, and authorities, and all officers, judicial, administrative, and ministerial, existing therein at the Union, shall continue in Ontario, Quebec, Nova Scotia, and New Brunswick respectively, as if the Union had not been made; subject nevertheless (except with respect to such as are enacted by or exist under Acts of the Parliament of Great Britain or of the Parliament of the United Kingdom of Great Britain and

Ireland) to be repealed, abolished, or altered by the Parliament of Canada, or by the Legislatures of the respective Provinces, according to the authority of the Parliament or of that Legislature under this Act.

"130. Until the Parliament of Canada otherwise provides, all officers of the several Provinces having duties to discharge in relation to matters other than those coming within the classes or subjects by this Act assigned exclusively to the Legislatures of the Provinces, shall be officers of Canada and shall continue to discharge the duties of their respective offices, under the same liabilities, responsibilities, and penalties as if the Union had not been made."

And section 5 of "Rupert's Land Act, 1868," which says:

"It shall be competent to Her Majesty, by any such Order or Orders in Council as aforesaid, on address from the Houses of Parliament of Canada, to declare that Rupert's Land shall, from a date to be therein mentioned, be admitted into and become part of the Dominion of Canada; and thereupon it shall be lawful for the Parliament of Canada from the date aforesaid to make, ordain, and establish within the land and territory so admitted as aforesaid, all such laws, institution, and ordinances, and to constitute such courts and officers as may be necessary for the peace, order and good government of Her Majesty's subjects and others therein: Provided, until otherwise enacted by the said Parliament of Canada, all the powers, authorities and jurisdiction of the several courts of justice now established in Rupert's Land, and of the several officers thereof, and of all magistrates and justices now acting within the said limits, shall continue in full force and effect therein."

I think it unquestionable that the jurisdiction of the courts of Ontario and Quebec continued over offences committed in Rupert's Land and the Nord-West territories, and therefore over the crime charged in the indictment; and that all the magistrates, etc., acting or being within those limits, had power and authority, and it was their duty, to apprehend and bring to trial, either in the court of Assiniboia or in the courts of Ontario or Quebec, all persons who had committed crimes or offences within their respective jurisdictions, and therefore those persons who were charged with the murder of Thomas Scott—certainly until the transfer of Rupert's Land and a portion of it was formed into the Province of Manitoba, and it may be, until the passing of the Canadian Act of 1871 (34 V., c. 14), whereby it is declared that—

"The court known as the General Court, now and heretofore existing in the Province of Manitoba, and any court to be hereafter constituted by the Legislature of the said Province, and having the powers now exercised by the said General Court, shall have power to hear, try, and determine in due course of law all treasons, felonies, and indictable offences committed in any part of the said Province, or in the territory which has now become the said Province."

At the Confederation of the Provinces—certainly at the passing of this Act—the concurrent jurisdiction of the Canadian courts over crimes and offences committed in the territory which afterwards became the Province of Manitoba, ceased and was at an end, and the Courts then existing or subsequently established in Manitoba, had and have exclusive cognizance of, and jurisdiction over, all crimes and offences in Manitoba, originating in the territory now forming that Province, whether committed before or after the establishment of the Province. There has, then, been no interruption of jurisdiction, or want of authority in Courts existing in North America, to hear, try and determine all crimes and offences committed within the territory now forming the Province of Manitoba, but all such crimes and offences might have been *before* the Province was established, in Courts *then* existing, and by officers *then* clothed with full authority in that behalf, and *may now*, in the Court of Queen's Bench duly organized in Manitoba, be heard, tried and determined in due course of law, and punishment awarded accordingly.

The demurrer to the plea of jurisdiction is allowed. The prisoner is permitted to enter a plea of "Not guilty."

Judges McKeagney and Betournay both signified their hearty concurrence in His Lordship's decision.

The Attorney-General then asked the counsel when the prisoner would be ready to stand his trial.

Mr. Royal said not for six or seven days.

The Attorney-General objected to so long a time, and finally the time was fixed for Thursday next, at ten o'clock.

The prisoner's bail was enlarged on the responsibility of the Court until that time.

The business of this term of Court prevented Lepine's case being tried; it was accordingly fixed for the next term of the Court of Queen's Bench which would sit in October following.

During the Session of the Provincial House of Assembly, in July, 1874, a Bill was passed providing that in the case the business of a term of Court should not have been finished inside the time named in the former Statute, the Court should be empowered to sit until the business had been finished. This fully prevented any chance of the trial of Lepine's being delayed for the future.

COURT OF QUEEN'S BENCH.

OCTOBER TERM,
1874.

Chief Justice WOOD presiding.

THE QUEEN vs. AMBROISE LEPINE—MURDER.

TUESDAY.

Mr. Cornish appeared for the Crown; and Messrs. Chapleau and Royal for the defence.

The Court then proceeded to empannel the jury, and after a good deal of standing aside and challenging, the following were selected:

John Omand, Norbert Marion, John Forbes, Jas. Parks, Peter Harkness, Baptiste Dubois, Samuel West, Joseph Poitras, Cornelius Pruden, André Robillard, Maurice Bird, Norbert Nolin.

The following were challenged for the Crown:

Duncan McDougall, Moïse Goulet, Amable Marion, Paschal Piette; and about sixteen were challenged by the prisoner's counsel.

During the address of the Crown counsel, the Grand Jury entered the Court room and presented the following True Bills:

The Queen vs. J. Sanders and Chas. Bond, larceny.

The Queen vs. Rocan and Morneau, receiving stolen goods.

The Queen vs. Chas. Baird, assault.

The Clerk read the indictment against Ambroise Lepine, as follows:

PROVINCE OF MANITOBA.

COURT OF QUEEN'S BENCH,
Crown Side.

NOVEMBER TERM, 1873.

The jurors for the Court of Queen's Bench on oath present, that Ambroise Lépine, on the 4th day of March, in the year of Our Lord one thousand eight hundred and seventy, at Upper Fort Garry, then known as being, lying and situated in the District of Assiniboia, in the Red River Settlement, in Rupert's Land, and now better known as being, lying and situated at Winnipeg, in the County of Selkirk, in the Province of Manitoba, Dominion of Canada, feloniously, wilfully, and of his malice aforethought did kill and murder one Thomas Scott, against the form of the Statute in such case made and provided, and against the peace of our said Lady the Queen, Her Crown and Dignity.

MR. CORNISH'S SPEECH.

Gentlemen of the Jury:—You are now called upon to try one of the most important cases that have been under consideration in this Dominion for some time. You are aware that some few years since, this country was attached to the Dominion of Canada, and that, for some reason or other, certain individuals bound themselves together, and took upon themselves the right to imprison some of the people and murder one of them, and that one of those implicated in these high-handed proceedings is the prisoner at the bar. It is known to you that one of these prisoners, by the name of Thomas Scott, was the one who was killed and murdered by those who professed to have authority at that time, and of whom the prisoner was one of the principals. It appears that the prisoner at the bar resided in this country. I shall show you that early in the year 1870, the prisoner ordered the arrest, and foully and illegally caused the death of one of Her Majesty's subjects. This, gentlemen, will be the first fact upon which you are called upon to decide, and it will be for you to determine whether the life taken by these men, of whom the prisoner was one, was a foul murder or a justifiable act. It is for you to say whether the crime of killing Thomas Scott was a murder or not. It is for you to decide whether the prisoner at the bar is guilty of the crime for which he has been called upon to answer by this Court and by the people of this country. It is for you, gentlemen, to say whether the constitution of the country, on which we all depend, can be subverted and destroyed by acts of lawless men; whether the bulwarks of our constitutional liberty are to be rudely leveled in the dust, and whether the prisoner at the bar, who is accused of the crime, is to be punished or not. It appears that previous to the 4th of March, 1870, a number of persons took upon themselves the right to imprison and abuse a great number of Her Majesty's loyal and peaceful subjects. This was an illegal act. There was no authority or law to justify the imprisonment of those peaceful subjects for the length of time during which they were imprisoned. But, gentlemen, these lawless people who were guilty of this outrage were not satisfied with what they had done; they had to commit further wrong by putting to death one of the prisoners named Thomas Scott. This, gentlemen, was a foul murder. The men who did it had no authority for doing it. They had no right to commit that deed. The prisoner at the bar is accused of being one of those who ordered the execution of the unfortunate man Scott, and who took an active part in that murder. I need not tell you, gentlemen, that first you must come to the conclusion that the murder had been committed, and secondly, whether the prisoner at the bar is implicated in that murder. I will endeavor to show, by the evidence I will lay before you, that this unfortunate man Scott, after submitting to many hardships from these lawless men, on the morning of the 4th of March, 1870, was taken out of his prison and killed by a number of those men, among whom was Mr. Lepine, the prisoner at the bar. If that be so, and I am sure I have no desire to press conviction unless the evidence demands it, you will, gentlemen, see that the case is clear. Who, let me ask, was this Thomas Scott? A young man who, because of his loyalty to his Queen and country, was taken and killed, murdered foully so, because he dared to be loyal to his crown and country, by men of whom the prisoner was one. Gentlemen, we shall show you that upon that melancholy occasion, every effort was made by one whose name will be in the hearts of all, and memories of the good for all time, to save the life of poor Scott; but the unfortunate man was ordained to die by the hands of assassins and murderers. I speak, gentlemen, of the noble efforts made by the Rev. G. Young. It is true that for a long time justice was postponed, and that many of those equally guilty with the prisoner were at large and defied and laughed at justice; but the unerring dart has reached nearly all of them, and perhaps even before long, those too will find themselves in the hands of those whose duty it is to punish the transgressor and the murderer. It will be shown to you, gentlemen, that Scott was murdered, and that Mr. Lepine, the prisoner, was fully implicated in that deed. It is for you, gentlemen, to decide the question upon the evidence which will be laid before you. It will be your duty to render a verdict of acquittal if the evidence, in your estimation, is insufficient to prove guilt; and a verdict of guilty, if the evidence is sufficient. There is one feature in the closing part of this tragedy, gentlemen, that is not only suspicious-looking, but cowardly in the extreme. I allude to the spiriting away of the body of Thomas Scott, after the unfortunate man had been executed. Why was this done? If the execution was justifiable and according to law, why was this dark mysterious act committed? Surely, this act cannot be defended. Is it not a strong evidence of guilt of wrong, of a crime being committed that would not bear the light of day? No one to this day knows where the murdered clay of poor Scott lies buried, or if it was buried at all. I need not also tell you, gentlemen, that it is your duty, if you have any doubts, after weighing the evidence carefully and calmly, to give the prisoner the benefit of such doubts; but, gentlemen, let them be doubts, and do not allow prejudice or feeling to sway you from your duty in this matter. After the evidence has been laid before you, I will again be permitted, in accordance with the practice of the Court, to address you and sum up the evidence as it occurs to me. I trust that my learned friends who are conducting the defence will have no cause to complain. I shall now leave the matter in your hands, and lay before you the evidence upon which you are to adjudicate.

Joseph Nolin was the first witness called, but he did not appear, he not being present.

WM. Farmer sworn.—I reside at Headingly; I am the party at whose evidence the prisoner was arrested; on the 17th of February, 1870, I was made a prisoner about half a mile north of the Prairie Saloon; there was some forty-three of us; the late Thomas Scott was one of those arrested with me by a party of half-breeds headed by the prisoner Lepine and O'Donohue; they came from Fort Garry, i.e. the Hudson's Bay Fort; I was going home to the Portage; some of us were going to High Bluff, some to Headingly and some to the Portage; the half-breeds were armed with repeating rifles, revolvers and knives; we had been armed, but our arms were packed away in a sleigh at Kildonan; we dispersed on a note from the Fort, information being given to our party that we might proceed home without being molested; the cause of our coming down was to release some prisoners, of whom forty-five were in Fort Garry at the time; they were taken at Schultz's place; when we went down from Kildonan we met some five hundred, chiefly from St. Andrews North and South, St. Paul and St. Peters; our force amounted to about six hundred armed men; I was in command of the Portage force; we arrived at Kildonan about 10 o'clock in the morning, 15th February; the prisoners were released that night; next morning a communication was sent to Fort Garry by Northway and McKenny to Riel; I was not in the Council and know not what was in the note; there was a reply to the communication, stating that the prisoners had been released, and that our object having been accomplished, we could go home unmolested; it said nothing about the reward for apprehension of Dr. Schultz, or the restoration of Schultz's property; when we received this note, we were on our road home; some four or five, mistrusting that something might happen to them, went ahead of the others and reached their homes in safety; before we left Kildonan, an occurrence took place that induced several to go to their homes; a person by the name of Sutherland was shot; while in camp in Kildonan, a person came there, named Parisien, who was considered a spy; we arrested him and put him under guard; he escaped and went towards the river, but was pursued; John

Sutherland was coming across the river to Kildonan on horseback; Parisien as he escaped had seized a double-barreled gun loaded; he fired at Sutherland twice, one shot taking effect in his wrist and the other in the back; Sutherland fell from his horse and died about an hour afterwards. The persons pursuing Parisien fired at him and wounded him, but he was not killed; he escaped to the woods on the other side of the river; he was taken prisoner and brought back to the church; when he was retaken he was frozen in the hands; I saw him when I got out of prison, in the month of March following; he had not recovered from the effects of the freezing, but I think he had from the gun shot; the unfortunate occurrence of the death of Sutherland had the effect of inducing a great many to disperse and go home.

His Lordship.—Why did you go half a mile from town?

Witness.—We were advised to do so; we passed through about 10 in the morning.

His Lordship.—Did you know at that time whether the French force had any military designation?

Witness.—Lepine was styled Adjutant-General.

His Lordship.—Had he charge of the force when you were a prisoner?

Witness.—Riel and Lepine both came into our guard-room.

His Lordship.—Was the prisoner dressed differently to the rest?

Witness.—I could not swear what conversation; was between Riel and Lepine, and a half-breed named Poche; Lepine and O'Donohue commanded us to surrender; our arms were stacked in a sleigh; some had arms, but Major Boulton cautioned all of the party not to fire, and no one did fire; I did not see any resistance offered; the party from the Fort consisted of about forty mounted and a number on foot straggling along from the Fort; among the party that was taken was the deceased Scott; did not see him offer any resistance; the prisoner and O'Donohue rode in advance and spoke to Poche; he was known as an English half-breed and spoke the two languages; I do not know whether he conversed with the prisoner or O'Donohue in French or not; I did not hear them; when we saw them coming we stopped our sleighs; the prisoner did not cry out "Stop;" Poche, after speaking, came back and said that they came out to see that it was the Portage party going home; they surrounded us, and I was told there was a discussion in the French language between the parties as to whether we should be permitted to go home or be taken into the Fort, and O'Donohue decided that we should be taken into the Fort, and we were taken in without any resistance, as far as I could see, from any one of our party; I did not hear, in language that I understood, the prisoner give any command or direction respecting taking us prisoners, or taking us into the Fort; O'Donohue seemed to be in command; I heard O'Donohue say "Take them into the Fort."

Mr. Cornish.—When you heard O'Donohue say "Take them into the Fort," was he at that time in conversation with Lepine?

Witness.—I cannot remember.

Mr. Cornish.—I suppose you remember going to the Fort?

Witness.—I do; O'Donohue and Lepine went in company to the Fort; all rode together; we were marched into the court-yard, and some of us searched under the directions of Riel, Lepine and O'Donohue; Riel made his appearance at that time; they took some revolvers and knives, but nothing from me at that time; we were marched up to the Hudson's Bay Office and placed in the upper part of it; Scott was locked up at the same time; we were again searched there and placed in different rooms; I was placed in the same room as Scott; this was all done against my will; remained there a month; saw Scott daily during that time; frequently saw the prisoner Lepine; last saw Scott on the morning of the 4th of March, 1870; he came to the door of the room I was in, which was open; he said "Good-bye, boys"; I reckoned he was going away; this is the last time I saw him; I could not say whether he was with any person when I saw him; during my imprisonment I frequently saw the prisoner; he appeared to be in charge of the guard over us, and was spoken of as the Adjutant-General; he always spoke in French, and I do not understand French.

Cross-examined by Mr. Chapleau.—The prisoner was arrested on my information.

Q. Did you not take any part in finding a Bill against him? A. I was summoned as a Grand Juryman; I asked to be excused from the Attorney-General—the late one—and he said that if enough jurymen could be found, he would excuse me; when I first asked to be excused there were only eight; I did not make application before the Court; I was not called or examined as a witness; this morning, when the witnesses were ordered to leave the room, I remained in Court.

Q. Why did you not obey the order?

His Lordship said that he did not give any order; he merely told them to leave the Court until their evidence was given.

After some discussion it was decided that a witness could remain in Court after having given his evidence.

Witness.—In the month of February, 1870, in Major Webb's party, Colonel Dennis was immediately in charge, but not the whole time

Q. You have spoken of a certain Provisional Government, as you call it, as being in possession of the Fort; what time was that Provisional Government in existence?

A. I suppose from the 1st of December; it was two and a half months in existence then.

Q. Was it a Republic according to your information?

A. I cannot say; Riel signed proclamations and issued them through the country; I suppose he was the leader of the Government; I was aware that deceased had already been a prisoner before that day, from his own information; I think it was about Christmas time that he escaped.

Q. You have spoken of some property of Schultz and its capture; was it taken from him, and what was it?

A. I know nothing of it, only that I heard it had been seized; I understood it to mean personal property, goods in store; the party of which I was one, after we had decided to come to the Fort, determined only to release prisoners; never applied to any authority in the city here for the release of these parties; no one in the city had any power, except the Provisional Government, to liberate the prisoners; as I take it, no one appeared to have physical power enough at command to do it.

Q. By whom were you asked to come to Fort Garry to release those prisoners?

A. We were not asked; I was not the party that raised the force at the Portage; it was themselves; Scott, the deceased, was not with me when I went to the Portage; to the best of my knowledge, he came after the question was first spoken of; he escaped from the prison and enrolled himself with the party immediately after his escape.

Q. You said when you left Kildonan that the reinforcements that you had received from North and South St. Andrews raised the force to about five hundred armed men; in whose command were you then?

A. The Portage party under Major Bolton; the rest I could not say whose command they were under; the other parties each had their leader; Dr. Schultz seemed to be the most prominent man from down the river; Scott had no position at all in that force; he was a full private; about an hour after the meeting of Northway and McKenny, the shooting of Sutherland took place; the prisoners were liberated on the morning of the 15th; on the morning of the 16th, the message was sent; when the reply arrived the five hundred had dispersed; Dr. Schultz was represented by a General Council, and he himself agreed to the message; we met Northway and McKenny on our road home, and read it to them and some others; I took a copy of it in a memorandum book, but have lost it; that reply was signed, I think, by Louis Riel, to the best of my knowledge as President

DR. J. C. SCHULTZ.   THOMAS SCOTT.   HON. A. G. B. BANNATYNE.
SCOTT'S BROTHER.

after we came into the Fort and saw Riel, I did not ask him to make good that promise, nor did I hear anyone ask it; I did not see Governor McTavish or ask his permission to act as I did; I was not aware that Parisien had opposed the Government of Riel; I understood he was a soldier of Riel's; it is not commonly known that he had escaped from Riel as a prisoner; he came with a horse that was known not to be his property; he was put in the school-house at Kildonan; the guard were provided with arms, but did not carry them; if he had a gun I think they would not have left it with him; his horse was taken away and brought to me; when Parisien escaped, he was pursued by some of the Portage men armed; he appeared to me to be very much frightened; he was recaptured about four hundred yards from the school-house and brought back to the camp with his hands tied behind him, I think; when he came to the river he struggled with the guards, but when he found it was of no avail, he came quietly; I could not say whether they were dragging him by his feet or his hands; when he arrived he was taken to the school-house and two doctors attended him, Beddsome and Schultz.

His Lordship.—Was he still tied when you went back to the school-house?—A. No, my Lord; about half an hour after his escape he was brought to the school-house; during that time his hands were frozen.

To Mr. Chapleau.—This was on the morning of the 16th, about 10 o'clock; we left Kildonan school-house at 4 o'clock in the afternoon; at Redwood, coming back, we met Mr. Northway and another party with him; Redwood is about one mile and a half from here; the information we received was that as far as the French half-breeds were concerned, we were in perfect safety, but not as to the Americans in town; James McLean told us this; there were about thirty or forty Americans in town; I did not think of sending for any more information, but chose to pass round; when we met Poche we stopped to speak to him, and as soon as Poche had spoken to us, we put our arms in the sleighs and we supposed all was over; I heard O'Donohue say, "Take them to the Fort;" I heard considerable discussion in French going on, as far as I could see, between O'Donohue and Lepine, and it was stated to me that Lepine wished us to go on, but O'Donohue wanted us to go to the Fort, and after this I walked with them to the Fort; I had no conversation with the prisoner, and suffered no hardships from his hands, neither did Scott to my knowledge; by what I saw, Riel appeared to be the dictator in the Fort.

Geo. Newcombe sworn.—I reside at Emerson; in the fall of 1869, I resided at Poplar Point; about 15th or 16th of February, 1869, I was at Redwood; one night, Mr. Farmer was there as well, from Kildonan; I had come from Poplar Point to Kildonan; quite a number of people accompanied me; I was considered one of the Portage party; I went from Redwood home with the party; we started on the road towards St. James; a party came out from the Fort on horseback; the only one I recognized was O'Donohue; I did not recognize the prisoner; we were surrounded and told to march into the Fort; we did so and went between a row of armed men; there seemed to be some three or four in command of these armed men; one was a man named Louis Riel, another O'Donohue; cannot say I saw the prisoner giving orders, but recognize him as being there; we were searched after we were confined; the man Scott was with us; I was confined thirty-two days; the only time I saw prisoner in command was when I got out; before I was released, I was taken into a room where prisoner was sitting at a table or desk, and he had a book before him with an oath written in the book, and an oath was administered to me not to take up arms against the Provisional Government; I took this oath and signed my name in a book, and went back then, and got my overcoat and blanket and started; this was at least a fortnight after Scott's death; nearly the whole time Scott was in the same place as myself; saw him on the morning of the 4th of March; met him on the stairway; as I was going down he was coming up; he was shackled; he had rings on each ankle and carried a chain in his hands about as high as his middle; I think this was the last time I saw him; he went into his cell where he was left by himself at that time; he had been put in the night before about 8 or 9 o'clock; he told me the reason was he was going to be shot; on that same evening prior to his telling me this, O'Donohue, as I knew by his voice, came to the door of the room in which Scott and others were confined, and called out for Scott to come out; as Scott got up he made the remark to me that he was afraid he was going to get into trouble, and went out; I should say he was away about half an hour, when he returned with the guard; the door was left open by the guard, and he came in and took his blanket, the guard standing at the door waiting for him; I asked him what was the matter; he said, " I am going to be shot;" I asked him what for, he said he did not know, it was in French; I think he used the word trial, and then he went out; I saw no more of him that night; next morning I met him on the stairs; I think he had no shackles on when he came for his blanket; on the 4th of March, as we were standing in one room, I heard a voice from one of us saying: " There goes Scott to be shot;" I heard a report; this report was about a quarter of an hour afterwards; a man named Delorme was in charge of the guard; I used to hear Riel and O'Donohue, sometimes one and sometimes the other, occasionally scolding the men of the guard; I never heard the prisoner at any time; I have given all the reasons I know that have led me to suppose that he had any power there at all.

Cross-examined by Mr. Chapleau.—I saw Rev. Mr. Young going into Scott's cell after he had told me "I am going to be shot;" I think it was after 7 when I heard the voice; not to my personal knowledge did I ever hear the prisoner at the bar giving orders or scolding as the others did.

Court adjourned.

WEDNESDAY, Oct. 14.

Court resumed its sittings this morning, the Chief Justice presiding. Routine business having been disposed of, the Lepine trial proceded:—

Alexander Macpherson sworn.—I reside at Stone Fort; in 1870 resided in Winnipeg; was one of the party arrested in the month of February, at the back of the Prairie Saloon, by the French half-breeds; Thos. Scott was arrested with me; we were taken to the Fort, some forty or fifty in number; we were going to the Portage when captured; we were not armed to resist force, but had arms in our sleighs; when we got to the Fort, there were some four or five hundred men in the Fort—some armed; I cannot say all were; before we went we were told that they wanted us there but ten minutes; we expected to go home after Riel had spoken to us; when we were all surrounded inside, the only man that spoke to me was Thos. Scott; he said, " It is very cold, let us go down town and have a glass;" we started to go, but when we came near the gate we were pressed back again by the crowd in the Fort; Riel called John Taylor, of Headingly, to come into a room; Taylor was one of our party; all the rest were called in too; we went in, and nineteen of us were shut in a room; Thos. Scott was one of the nineteen; a short time after, O'Donohue came in and two or three men with him; they searched our pockets and took all we had from us; I did not know the parties that were with O'Donohue, then or now; remained there five weeks; Scott remained about two weeks; I only saw him once between that and the 4th of March; the first I saw I was looking out of the window, and Riel was ordering two French half-breeds to go into where we were; I saw this by his gestures; they seemed to hesitate, and after taking a few steps towards the house or room, stopped, when Riel turned over upon seeing them hesitate, and ordered them to proceed; do not know where these two men went; Scott's place of confinement was at the other end of the house; we had heard that Scott had been sentenced, and I thought that these were men ordered to go to Scott and take him out to be executed; I heard he was to be shot; did not hear Riel speak; do not speak the French language; Riel spoke to his associates in French usually; these men and Riel went away; then saw the Rev. Mr. Young and Thomas Scott coming out of the building where he was confined; there was another person going behind them; it was the prisoner Lepine; there were two or three men walking behind Lepine; Scott had a white cap on, and a handkerchief on his head; he was also tied, or handcuffed; cannot say whether it was his feet or hands, but know he had irons on; saw this from the window as they were going down stairs, outside the building into the court-yard; when they passed the corner of the house they went out of my view; they went in the direction of the gate, then opening on the main highway or Garry street, running east of the fort; I saw about six others following after; they had guns; they were also lost to my view by the building; these six followed right after the prisoner; the next thing I heard was a report of fire-arms; there was more than one gun fired; the sound seemed like a quick succession of shots; this occurred within less than ten minutes after they left my sight; the firing appeared to be in the direction they had gone outside the walls; the next thing I saw was about six or eight men coming in the walls with a box or coffin; they came from the direction the other men had gone out; they went from my view, hidden by the house that is within the fort; I do not remember seeing any party coming in with guns again.

Cross-examined by Mr. Royal.—I was in Schultz's building, but was not caught with that party; I was engaged with Colonel Dennis in the fall of 1869; I can't tell the month; it was in the fall; when the prisoners were taken at Schultz's house I got clear; Schultz had a store on Garry street, in town; it contained all kinds of goods; I went to the post-office to get some letters, and I did not go back again (laughter).

Chief Justice.—Why did you not go back?

Witness.—Because I was informed it was a farce on both sides; Schultz's store had a guard of armed men over it; there were forty or fifty of us armed men; we had ammunition; I was a constable, and also the other men guarding the stores; it was at the Stone Fort, before this affair, that we were sent for as constables to protect the peace; this was in the fall of the year; I was not sworn in by any magistrate; there were some thirty or forty collected at the instigation of Colonel Dennis; this was done in consequence of Riel taking Fort Garry; I never enquired under whose orders I was acting; we left guards over these stores about two days and two nights; on the third day I went to the post-office to get letters; our party was irregularly armed, but every one could get arms; to the best of my recollection, our only object was to protect the Government stores; I heard of no other object; after I went to the post-office, I stopped outside, and in an hour or so the party was all taken prisoners by Riel's party; I saw them being taken to the Fort; there had been, for a day or two, armed men from the Fort down about Schultz's premises; they were some two or three hundred day and night; I do not know whether they demanded the surrender of the place; this was after Riel had taken the Fort; I was told not to go in and expose myself, as there would not be a shot fired inside or outside; there were men all round the town surrounding it, and I could get out of it; if they had seen me I should have been captured; I went to the Stone Fort and stopped there a few days, and after that Colonel Dennis went away, and when he left, we left too; I went up to the Portage, was there some time, and a number of young men made up their mind to get the prisoners out of Fort Garry; Scott was taken prisoner with the party from Schultz's; I only know this from hearsay; he told me he had been confined in the Fort, but had escaped; I could not tell whether Farmer took any active part in the formation of the Portage party; I voluntarily joined; the party consisted of about eighty, and it seemed to act spontaneously, its only object being the liberation of the prisoners in Fort Garry; Thomas Scott was with us; he was not a principal actor; there were none;

some of us had guns, some pistols, and some guns without locks; none of us had any Bowie knives; we halted at Headingly for a day or two; we did not drill, but had officers; our horses having given out, some turned back at Headingly; I had no gun, only a good-sized stick; there were sixty or seventy of us on our way to Kildonan; it was on account of our small number that we did not try to rescue the prisoners from the Fort, but went to Kildonan; we passed through the town without being molested; it was during the night, most of us on foot; it was about the middle of the night; about one half of us in sleighs; as far as I recollect, none on horseback; we stopped at Boyd's first for a short time, and then went to the school-house at Kildonan; they began to gather from all parts of the country; while we were there, I saw a man coming on horseback, in the forenoon; I was inside of the school-house and ran out with others, and saw a man running towards another one on horseback; he raised his gun and shot him; the horse reared round, and he again shot him in the back and ran away, Sutherland falling from the horse; I saw Parisien run into the woods, a good many pursuing him; he was caught and taken back to the school-house again; I saw Parisien in the school-house; there appeared to be blood on his face; this was three-quarters of an hour afterwards; I did not see whether he was frozen; he was sitting in the school-house; as the prisoners were released, we decided upon going back; I could not tell you how many of us were at Kildonan, or who was in command; our commanding officer, Major Bolton, was most of the time about the Manse; I think I saw Dr. Schultz; I don't remember seeing Colonel Dennis there, or Dr. Lynch; I knew O'Donohue, and he was one of the parties that took us prisoners at Fort Garry; we were greatly excited, as we were told to go behind the town and promised that we should not be molested on our road home; it was said Riel made that promise; the majority of us were on foot; we sent a man to them to see what they wanted; a French half-breed named Poche, and they said "Peace, peace;" he talked with those that were in advance who appeared to be the leaders, as I thought with one who was the leader; the party from the Fort then came around us with Poche and surrounded us, and O'Donohue demanded which of us was the leader; no one in particular answered; then O'Donohue said, "Where is Major Bolton?" I do not recollect that any one answered; I do not recollect seeing the prisoner there; there were others who seemed to be in authority, but every one appeared to obey O'Donohue; there was so much talk and excitement that I could hardly tell what was going on; all I knew was that we were surrounded; we were then taken into the Fort; I cannot remember the prisoner at the bar as one of the two men who led; these two men were not armed; I think the two men who followed Scott down stairs were the same as Riel scolded; I occasionally saw Riel and O'Donohue scolding the guard, some three or four times; Riel appeared to be in command; I have often seen the prisoner at the bar going about the Fort, but could not say I heard him give commands or orders; I was in the upper storey looking down when I always saw him; I knew him by his stoutness; I could not tell how many times I saw him; it is now a long time since; I know another Lepine beside this; never heard of another brother, but only two of them; I think the distance of the house I was confined in and the house south is about the length of this Court-house hall; I do not remember any fence between; from this window I saw Scott and Rev. Mr. Young and two other parties going out; to the best of my knowledge, he was walking arm in arm with Mr. Young; I did not see him until he got out in the yard; the only thing that I heard was "Good-bye, boys;" I did not know who said it; the parties going out, I could not see their faces from my position; I could not see Scott's face, or any of their faces; that is the reason I could not say whether Scott was shackled, as I could not see in front; it is possible he might have gone out of the gate; I never saw them go out; I lost sight of them; I could see neither gate from my window; they may not, for ought I know, have gone out at all; I saw the box I mentioned coming by McTavish's house; I should think seven or eight men were carrying it; it is more like a dream the whole of it, so long ago; I think they carried it on their shoulders; from my position I suppose the party I saw going out were an armed party; this was after Scott went out; all I heard was the volley; my ears caught it, and I knew not what they were doing outside.

To Mr. Cornish.—It was between 10 and 12 I saw this party walking towards the gate; I think the third person following was the prisoner; I had frequently seen the prisoner walking to and from the yard; I was told it was Lepine; he was always called the Adjutant-General, and I took him to be him; to the best of my knowledge, he was the third person that followed Mr. Young; I did not see Scott's face or Mr. Young's face, but I knew it was them; by the same knowledge, I knew the prisoner.

Rev. Mr. Young sworn.—I reside in Winnipeg and am a Minister of the Methodist Church; in 1869 and 1870 I resided in the same place; I was in the habit of visiting Fort Garry, generally once a week in the months of January, February and March, to see the prisoners; there were two parties of prisoners; the first were taken from Dr. Schultz's building and the other party from off the prairie—the first party in December and the other party in February; I knew Thomas Scott; he was taken in both cases; these prisoners were in charge of Riel and certain officers under him, as I understood; I obtained permission from Riel first; for the first few weeks I invariably obtained permission whenever I went; subsequently I was not required to do this; I saw a number of others who were said to be in authority, acting as such; it was said that under Riel there was an Adjutant-General and several Captains; the prisoner Lepine held the office of Adjutant-General; I very often saw Lepine during my visits; he seemed to be in possession of power; Riel was first styled Secretary and subsequently President; Mr. Bruce was first styled President; I do not remember having any conversation with Lepine prior to this date; I remember the 3rd of March; nothing occurred till the evening to my knowledge; on that evening I returned home from the country, arriving home about 9 o'clock; soon after a messenger came from the Fort, named Turner, informing me I was required at the Fort; I asked him by whom, he told me by Riel; he had sent for me, as one of the prisoners had been sentenced to be shot, and the prisoner had asked me to be sent for; I went with him, and on entering the Fort I went at once to find Riel; I went to his room, and was told he was in St. Boniface and would not be back till next morning; then I went to see Scott; I found him in the corner of a room in the building that had been used as a prison; he was alone and not in irons; the door was guarded by a number of armed men; when I visited him the Saturday before, he was in irons; this was on Thursday evening; I asked him if it was in accordance with his wish I had been sent for; he told me it was; that he had been called before a council of war that afternoon, and condemned to die; he objected to the trial, as it was conducted in a language he did not understand, but was told it made no difference; he was a bad man and had to die, and was sentenced to be shot the next day at 12 o'clock. He told me he thought they were quite bad enough to do it, but he doubted if they dare do it; I instructed him the proper course for the both of us to do was to act upon the presumption that it would be done; the first matters attended to was to give me the address of his mother and brothers, and place in my hands his effects, all of which were forwarded to them after his death; having done that there was no further talk on the matter, all further discourse was relating to his spiritual welfare; I remained with him a considerable portion of the night, and I left him for a time, as he wished to write a letter to his mother; he had been furnished with pen and ink and paper for that purpose; early in the morning I thought to bring some things to bear in his behalf; first of all I thought to see Mr. Ross, who was then called the Chief Justice under that Administration; he was not at home; I then proceeded to see Mr. Bannatyne and other for the same purpose; they all seemed to be exceedingly surprised, and gave me an assurance that it would not take place; that it was only done to frighten the people ; I deemed it best to converse with Mr. Smith and told him of it ; he had not heard of it before, and did not believe it possible to be done, and engaged to use all his influence to prevent it ; a Roman Catholic priest named L'Estane came in a while talking to him; I asked him if he had heard of the sentence; he said he had ; I asked him if he would intercede with Mr. Riel for him ; Mr. Smith suggested that I should go and see Mr. Riel myself, thinking I should succeed without further trouble ; in case of failure to send him word and he would proceed at once ; I went and met Mr. Riel in his own room, and asked him if it was true that Scott had been sentenced to be shot, and if it was their intention to carry it into effect; he said he was sentenced by a council of war, all the members had concurred with one exception, and it would be carried out ; I asked if Scott had been guilty of any great crime to deserve such a sentence, and expostulated with him, but to no effect ; failing in that I urged that the execution be postponed at least twenty-four hours ; I wished more time; he had had but a few hours' notice, and could scarcely realize he was so near death as that ; upon the question of postponement, he spoke of calling the Adjutant-General and discussing with him ; in a few moments the Adjutant-General, the prisoner here, entered the room ; Riel stated my request, and I also spoke of it in their presence ; Lepine, the Adjutant-General, very energetically shook his head and rose up and left the room ; Riel told me it was utterly useless to press the matter any further, so I returned to the prison and sent a message to Mr. Smith to notify him of my failure ; Mr. Campbell was my messenger ; I remained with Scott then until he was shot, engaged in religious exercises until we were interrupted by the parties entering the room to lead him out to be shot; Goulet and a man named Nault and others, four or possibly five in all, were the parties who led him out ; when they entered the room, Scott was very much excited, exclaiming, " This is horrible.' " This is cold-blooded murder ;" I advised him not to make such remarks, hoping still that the sentence might not be carried out ; one proceeded at once to tie his hands behind his back, the other put a cloth about his head, that was used to blindfold him, a piece of white cotton ; they put it over his forehead ; until he went out he was not shackled ; I requested them to retire a few minutes, and they yielded to my request ; I then engaged in prayer with him ; when they came in, he requested permission to say " Good-bye" to the boys as he called them, and they granted that request also ; in passing out he went to each door where the prisoners were, and bade them " good-bye ;" Riel excitedly complained as regarded the delay (vociferating wildly) in the matter ; I explained to him that I had been the cause of the delay ; he spoke in French ; we passed down the stairs, down which I assisted him, as I was afraid he would fall, his arms being tied, and we were directed to the place ; I did not pay any attention to who directed us, my mind was too much occupied ; he passed through the gate ; the sleigh track at the time was near the walk ; we were halted at some little distance from the gate on the sleigh track ; as I supposed that this would be the place of execution, I had prayers with him there ; after prayers he asked me to draw the blindfold over his eyes, and if he should remain on his knees or stand up ; I told him it would be better to remain on his knees, and I withdrew away from him after drawing the blindfold as he had asked me; just then I met face to face two persons whom I urged to interfere ; one was Goulet and the other O'Donohue ; I knew they both spoke English ; Goulet said his time had come and must die ; O'Donohue said it had gone very far, but did nothing to prevent it ; during the time of this conversation they removed Mr. Scott from that point a short distance east, and in this place he was shot; the firing party consisted of six persons ; when they were about to fire upon him I turned away, not witnessing the act ; immediately after firing, heard his voice and returned ; he had fallen forward, the body lying partly on its side ; there was some indication of life, a slight twitching of the shoulder ; some one said, " Put him out of his misery," when one of the party took a revolver out of the pocket of another of the party, and put it to his head and fired it; I then, supposing the man to be dead, entered the Fort; before and after the firing of the pistol, I observed that Scott's coat had been pierced; I took it that the bullets had passed through his chest and out of his shoulder; passing within the gate I met Riel; I asked for the body that I might get it interred; at first he consented, but very soon recalled that consent; I met Goulet, and he said I had better get a sleigh; I said I should be glad to do so if I should be allowed; at that time the body was in the rough box or coffin; Nault said he objected; I then came to town and tried to use some parties' influence to get the body delivered up to them; I was told that if I would get the Bishop of Rupert's Land to guarantee that it would be burried quietly and without any demonstration, we should have it; accordingly, next morning the Bishop and myself waited on Riel for that purpose; he told us he was very sorry to disappoint us, but the Adjutant-General, who was responsible for this case, had instructed it to be interred in the walls of the Fort, as he had a right to dispose of the body; after the Bishop had left I importuned Mr. Riel to give me the body, as I wished to write to Scott's mother that day and inform her of the interment of her son's body, as it would be some little comfort for her to know that her son's body received Christian interment; the answer was as before, he could not interfere with the case; he seemed to be very much displeased with the remark that he had a mother left to mourn over him.

In reply to His Lordship.—I have no personal knowledge who were Riel's council; Nolin I knew as secretary for Mr. Lepine; I have obtained passes from him from time to time.

In reply to Mr. Cornish.—I should think the firing party distant about twenty or thirty feet; it did not so impress me at the time as being as far as across the hall; I do not recollect who commanded the firing party; I noticed a great deal of blood after the firing, on the snow, and heard his voice shout instantly after the firing, but did not recognize any words; there were two sounds, one like words and the other like a moan; this was previous to the discharge of the pistol shot; after this the box was closed; I have no doubt at all of his death.

EVENING SITTING.

D. U. Campbell sworn.—Have resided in Winnipeg off and on for five years; on the 17th December, 1869, a number of us were taken prisoners by a party of men that had assembled at the Fort; some time previous I was a prisoner there ten weeks with about forty-five others; Scott was not there all the time, about four weeks as far as I can recollect; he made his escape from the prison; got out of prison myself about the 13th of February; the prisoners were let out upon two separate days; I was liberated upon taking an oath of neutrality; about twenty others were released at the same time; the others were let out two or three days after; the oath was taken before Riel, O'Donohue and some others; did not go down to Kildonan; knew a party had come there from the Portage the next day but one after I was liberated; on the 17th February, the second party of prisoners were taken; (the witness corroborated the evidence of other witnesses with regard to the arrest of the Portage party;) visited Fort Garry a few days after, and daily after Thomas Scott was one of the prisoners; my object was to take provisions to the prisoners; was not interrupted except one day; I was not allowed to go out of the Fort; the sentry said that I should have to see the President; did not wish to see Riel; asked to see some one else; I was then directed to see the Adjutant-General; his name was not mentioned, but I knew who was meant, it was the prisoner Lepine; was going to his office, he met me at the door, spoke to him, "I wish to go out of the Fort, will you instruct the sentry to let me pass out"; he then beckoned to the sentry and said something to him that I could not understand; I spoke to Lepine in English and he appeared to understand me; had never conversed with him before that nor after; saw Scott on the 4th of March; went up with Mr. Schultz to the Fort and enquired for the Captain of the Guard; do not know his name; was told he was at the Council and that I should have to remain for some time; a short time after I had been there, the Rev. Mr. Young came in and went into Scott's room; he came out and requested me to go and see Commissioner Smith to intercede; I did so, came back and went into the guard-room; Mr. Young was there with Scott; a short time after two men came in—one having a cord and the other a piece of white cotton; they went into the room in which Scott was and tied his hands behind his back, and placed the cotton over his eyes; after, he (Scott) had permission to bid farewell to his fellow-prisoners; he did so and was then taken down stairs and taken towards the small gate of the Fort; Mr. Young was walking by his side; the men who went up to the room were with them; cannot tell whether they walked before or behind; I was looking through a window in the guard-room that looked in that direction; a number of men belonging to the Fort were standing armed with guns at the small gate, towards which Scott went; I think about twenty; saw others unarmed, about six or eight; saw the prisoner there, also O'Donohue and Riel; they were between the centre building of the Fort, Dr. Cowan's house and the small gate that was there then but is not now; Dr. Cowan's house was used as the officers' quarters; the Council was held there; Riel, O'Donohue and Lepine were together and conversing; they were in this position when Scott was going to the gate; he passed them; could not see Scott go out of the gate; the others passed towards the gate in the same direction; a party of men, five or six, went out towards the gate also; I supposed these to be the firing party; as near as I can recollect, the firing party went out before Riel, O'Donohue and Lepine; at the same time I saw a box being carried out; it was a rough box, such as is used to encase a coffin; this was taken in the same direction; a few minutes after heard a volley; I then saw a box and supposed it to be the same box they had carried out; this was after Riel, O'Donohue and Lepine had come in; it was borne by half a dozen men in their hands; it was taken towards the centre building and around the corner of McTavish's building, not in the same direction taken by Riel, O'Donohue and Lepine; after the discharge of the volley, did not hear any other shot; it was about ten minutes after the volley that I saw the box brought in; saw Riel, O'Donohue and Lepine together on March 10th, in Dr. Cowan's building; I went there to get a pass to go through the country; obtained the pass, went into Riel's office with three others; he was alone; he did not grant us the pass at once, but asked us to step in another room; we did so, he closed the door after us; we remained there a couple of hours, during which time O'Donohue and Lepine passed through several times, Riel twice; O'Donohue was, I understood, Treasurer of Riel's Government.

Court adjourned at 10.40 p.m.

THURSDAY, October 15.

Court met at 9.30 a.m., Chief Justice presiding.

Examination of D. U. Campbell, resumed.—I did not know the object of these three men being together; I had some further conversation with Riel; prisoner was then in his office; after about two hours' waiting, during which they walked to and fro from their offices, I intimated to Riel, through one of the guards, that I wished an interview with him; Riel at first had not appeared to be willing to grant the passes; after walking up and down he went to his secretary and told him to write out the papers for us; we received the papers from the secretary, whose name I did not know; on his signing them we then left; during the months of February and March, *i. e.* the ten weeks I was a prisoner, I saw the prisoner frequently, occasionally exercising authority ; on the 9th December, together with Riel and O'Donohue, he appeared to be directing the men on the occasion of hoisting their flag ; it was a flag with a white ground, fleur de lis and shamrock; there was great enthusiasm on hoisting the flag, and speeches made in French by Riel ; the prisoner did not speak, although taking part in the proceedings ; Riel appeared to be the leader of the ceremony ; there was a military demonstration, a flag-staff was there before, and on this the flag was raised ; as the flag was being hoisted up, Riel was addressing his soldiers, and as the flag reached the top of the staff, there was a volley fired, after which Riel continued to speak for some length of time, and then all was quiet; this was the only flag I saw there ; neither officers nor men wore any distinctive uniform ; there were none on horseback that day ; no platform erected ; Riel jumped up on some boxes a little higher than the ground, and spoke ; I cannot say by whose command the men dispersed ; on another occasion, during some little trouble, Riel came into the prison and ordered one of the prisoners to be put in irons ; the name of the prisoner was William Hallett, since deceased ; he lived about three miles from town, up the Assiniboine River; he was an English half-breed ; Lepine was present on the occasion ; Hallett was out warming himself at the stove in the guard-room ; there was no fire in the prisoners' rooms during the time I was a prisoner ; there was in the guard-room ; Riel came and said to the guard : " Why do you allow these dogs to come out into the guard-room?" upon which Hallett said: " I am the cause of all the trouble ;" Riel then ordered him to be put in irons ; Hallett went into his comrades, who said he should not be put in irons unless they were with him ; the soldiers were then drawn up round the prison by order of Riel and Lepine ; Riel and Lepine then came into the guard-room ; Lepine came to the door of the room where Hallett was, with a revolver in his hand, and ordered him out ; one of the prisoners, Franklin, stopped in between and took hold of Lepine; the Captain of the guard then took hold of Lepine and drew him back ; the guard was standing looking on with their muskets with their bayonets on, ready to use them ; one of the prisoners, Smith, went out and one of the guard made at him and his bayonet passed into the partition alongside of him ; the Captain of the guard closed the door and kept the prisoners and the guard apart ; Lepine was in the guard-room; Captain of the guard came into the room and advised them to let Hallett go out, and gave his word that no harm should come to him, on which Hallett consented to go ; he was then taken into another room and put in irons by the authority of Lepine and Riel ; there was n fire and no prisoners in the room he was put into; the window was open, and it was 30 deg. below zero at the time ; he was confined there about three weeks without any fire—in irons all the time; he was a man between sixty or seventy ; the weather continued cold all the time ; he had a capot on, and a buffalo robe and a blanket ; I might say that each found their own bedding ; he died about a year ago ; he had bad health from the time he came out ; he remained in the prison by himself until he was liberated with the other prisoners; he was very ill up to about six or eight months of his decease; during that six or eight months he was able to go out, but not well; I cannot explain his sickness; his mind was affected, and he committed suicide; I know of no other occasion of the prisoner exercising his authority.

Cross examined by Mr. Royal.—I was not at Kildonan when the party met the party from the Portage; I was a clerk at Dr. Schultz's store ; I saw the Portage party met by the party from the Fort from the place now called the Queen's Hotel, adjoining the Club House; I judged the Portage party to be about fifty, from the Fort about twenty horsemen, and between them and the Fort about sixty or eighty straggling; I had been about nine months in the country before this time; I used to visit the prisoners to take them food; I never expected to be paid by the Provisional Government for that food; Messrs.

Ashdown, Archibald, Mellon, Chisholm and a number of others made up the money to procure food; Dr. Schultz was not in the country then; I asked permission of the Captain of the guard to take food to the prisoners; I do not know his name, nor how many Captains they were; he spoke French; I applied to him in English; on the day I was not allowed to go in, I asked to see the prisoner; I went to him; he saw me coming; I met him at the corner of the building; I asked him to let me pass; the sentry could hear me; the prisoner made a motion, but I do not recollect what he said; I saw Mr. Young in the goal on the 4th of March, in a room with Scott; no one else in the room at first; it was about half-past ten in the morning; I was on the floor level with the cells; there were ten or twelve guards with me; prisoner was not amongst them; I spoke to Mr. Young of Scott's death; he came out and spoke to me, and said he had been to see the persons at the Council, Riel, O'Donohue and Lepine, to obtain a delay in the execution of Scott; I understood Mr. Young that he had seen Riel, O'Donohue and Lepine, all three; he said his request was denied, and asked me to see Commissioner Smith that he might intercede; I left Mr. Young and went to see Mr. Smith; while talking to Mr. Young, Scott was in his room by himself; Mr. Smith was generally known as Commissioner Smith at that time; Mr. Young did not ask me to see Governor McTavish; I saw Mr. Smith and told him that Mr. Young had requested him to use his influence for the delay of Scott's execution; Mr. Smith appeared to be somewhat surprised; there was no guard at his door; he said he would go and intercede in Scott's behalf; he was living in Governor McTavish's house; there were guards on promenade round the wall, but could not say if there was any at Governor McTavish's door; I did not see any; after leaving Mr. Smith I returned to the prison; Mr. Young was there with Mr. Scott; I did not see Lepine then; when Mr. Young and Mr. Scott left, I did not go with them; I lost sight of them by the building intervening; Mr. Young walked by the side of Mr. Scott, and had hold of his arm, I think; Scott had a coat on, a woollen one, an undercoat; I cannot say as to the order of the march; the men did not carry guns; there were some two or three men of large size present; I cannot say whether Lepine was present, or one of them; before the three men came in, I saw Riel, O'Donohue and Lepine between Dr. Cowan's building and John McTavish's with some others; they appeared, from their motions, to be giving orders; judged this by what I saw; they were passing to and fro; after Mr. Young and Scott had passed by McTavish's house, and I had lost sight of them, I saw O'Donohue, Riel and Lepine as described; the window I was looking out of was on the south side; there was a double window; it was about 20 or 25 deg. below zero; I do not consider this very cold for here; there were six men that stood by themselves, and they moved immediately after Mr. Scott; the crowd followed—a great number armed; I could not say how many; Riel, O'Donohue and Lepine were among the crowd; do not know if the windows were frozen; was conversing with a man named William McLean; he was looking on with me; next heard a volley; Lepine made no speech on the hoisting of the flag, only Riel; James Stewart was the man listening at the window and translated to us what he could pick up; I never saw Riel, Lepine or O'Donohue carrying arms; all those that had arms were the soldiers; I have seen the Hudson's Bay Comyany's flag, and seen it hoisted; Hallett went with Colonel Dennis to Pembina; I think he went as interpreter, as I understood; I believe Colonel Dennis engaged him on account of his being a loyal half-breed; have heard that he had a contract with the Boundary Commission; did not hear of any disagreement; heard of his losing money which he had to reimburse; saw in papers of the unfortunate occurrence of his suicide; I said Hallett's mind was affected; Dr. O'Donnell attended him first; I mean he was weaker in his mind than formerly; I did not know that he had to walk the distance with Colonel Dennis on snow-shoes; the window in Hallett's room was broken; to give an idea of the size, the hole was large enough to pass through.

Mr. Cornish then put a question to the witness as regarded the soldiers and the officers, but His Lordship ruled it of no importance.

Bishop of Rupert's Land sworn.—Resided in the country in 1869 and 1870; I was aware of prisoners being confined — two bodies, one taken at Dr. Schultz's house, in the end of 1869, and another in 1870 off the prairie; both parties were taken by the party in Fort Garry, who had risen in the country; they had taken up arms and occupied the Fort, and exercised a control over the country in general; latterly they were understood to be under the command of Mr. Riel; previous to this a Mr Bruce was, I believe, their leader; they held the Fort; I was at the Fort almost every week; Governor McTavish was the Governor of the country; I went there to visit him; to my knowledge the holding of the Fort was without Governor McTavish's consent; Governor McTavish died about May or June, upon reaching England; he was dangerously ill the whole period of the troubles, and before they began; I remember the Council of Assiniboia; when the first reports of the rising came, there was a meeting, and it was the opinion of the Council that it would not be practicable to resort any force; there were one or two efforts made to get the insurgents to disperse, but they failed; the general feeling was that any attempt at force made would raise the entire French population, and it would be impossible to raise a sufficient force in counteraction; the force was known to be in arms; there were two or three meetings of the Council; there was no forcible effort to make them disperse, as deplorable consequences might follow; it was thought that some days might be spent in bringing the English population together, and moreover it would not be desirable to bring the two bodies into collision after all; for these reasons nothing forcibly was done; there were negociations in which Mr. Dease took a part, and I believe the Governor and others did what they could; the intention was to get the party who had risen to disperse peaceably; I think I was the only member that suggested the use of force to put down the movement; the unanimous feeling of the other councillors was as I have stated; a proclamation was issued by the Governor, and I believe it was printed. (The blue-book being produced, His Lordship requested Mr. Carey to read the proclamation to the Court, dated 16th November, 1869, and signed Governor McTavish, Governor of Assiniboia.) This was distributed among the people; the people in the Fort paid no attention to this proclamation; I think at the date of the proclamation the Council no longer sat, as the Governor did not call any meeting; I suppose the Government had no longer any control over the country; we had one or two unsatisfactory meetings, and I wrote a letter to the Governor that I thought it would be better that the Executive would act themselves with the advice of any that the Governor might like to call, and I said I should be glad to act at any time he wished; the Governor never told me the reason the Council met no more; I visited the Fort to get the prisoners released who were taken in Dr. Schultz's house; I went with the Rev. Mr. Young, Rev. Mr. Black, and I rather think with Archdeacon McLean; we saw Riel and O'Donohue; I do not remember seeing the prisoner; I think it was on the evening of the 5th of March that Rev. Mr. Young called upon me to tell me that Thomas Scott had been shot that afternoon, and said Riel told him that if I asked, the body would be given up for burial; next morning I went with Mr. Young to Fort Garry and saw Riel; we told him we had come in regard to his statement that the body would be given up; he said he was sorry I had been brought there; the matter was in the hands of the Adjutant-General, and he would not hear of giving up the body; I understood him to refer to Lepine; there were a number of men digging in front, and we were informed that the body was to be buried there; I am not quite sure if the Adjutant-General was there; I knew him before under that designation; we failed in getting the body and made no further effort, as I felt it was useless; Mr. Young reasoned afterwards; there was a meeting of the Council of Assiniboia after the troops came in, myself, Archbishop of St. Boniface, William Frazer, John Sutherland, Robert McBeth and others; I think there was a sufficient quorum; the meeting was simply to draw up some resolutions to give Governor Archibald a congratulatory address; upon the arrival of Colonel Wolseley, Mr. Donald A. Smith assumed the command as Administrator of the Hudson's Bay Company, and I, as a member of the Council of Assiniboia, swore in two or three hundred special constables; I am not aware that Mr. Donald A. Smith took the oath of office.

Cross-examined by Mr. Royal.—The troubles arose unexpectedly; Riel called upon me a day or two before the execution of Scott, and said the French wanted land set apart exclusively; discussed on two points, desirability of a Province and of reserves; I think the desire for reserves was the cause of all the trouble; the French did not wish to be mixed, but to be all together; I heard of no understanding that the French had to settle on the upper part and the English the lower part of the river; there are cases of English and French half-breeds marrying, but of limited extent; there were two or three meetings convened of the Council of Assiniboia, after I heard of the troubles; I do not recollect the dates; at one meeting, in October, I think, Riel and Bruce met us by arrangement; they were sent for by Governor McTavish; the Council of Assiniboia was more for giving advice to the Governor than anything else. (A long and tedious cross-examination here ensued as to the meeting of the Council of Assiniboia and its action during the time of the troubles, up to the Proclamation of Governor McTavish of 16th November, 1869, and subsequently, the evident object being to ascertain the manner in which Riel was viewed by Government officials at the time.) The constables were sworn in after the arrival of the troops.

William Chambers sworn.—Lived in Winnipeg in 1869-70; knew Riel by sight; knew of prisoners being confined in Fort Garry; knew the late Thomas Scott; knew he was prisoner somewhere inside the Fort; last time saw Scott, it was ouside the Fort; saw him led out of the gate on east side of Fort; after Scott was brought out, he was knelt down in the sleigh track; Rev. Mr. Young knelt with him and prayed; Scott was then removed about twenty or thirty yards; body of armed men then came out of the Fort; they were drawn up in line about twenty or thirty paces from Scott; a man named Lepine appeared to be in command; should take the prisoner at the bar to be the man whom I then knew as Lepine; he stood a little in front of the firing party; took a handkerchief out of his pocket, held it up in his hand, and dropped it from one hand to the other; as he did so the party fired in the direction of Scott; he fell over, and cried out, "O my God! I am shot;" the crowd then gathered up around Scott; one of the firing party took a revolver and fired at Scott's head; saw a white cloth tied on his head; there was blood on the cloth; saw the coffin—a rough box—alongside; went into the Fort for a while; then went up town; that is the last I saw of it.

To the Chief Justice.—Did not know Lepine by any other title than Adjutant-General; recognized him that day when I saw him; should say the prisoner is the man; he stood about three or four feet from the firing party.

FRIDAY, October 16.

The first witness called was

William Chambers, who was cross-examined by Mr. Chapleau.— On the 4th of March, six armed men, I think, came out of the Fort; saw them coming out; don't remember seeing Riel coming out with the soldiers; my attention was attracted to the armed men only; don't remember seeing any one passing between the six armed men and Scott; can't say I saw the prisoner; knew O'Donohue at the time; if O'Donohue, Riel and the prisoner had passed, I might not have seen them, not paying particular attention; there were about hundred and fifty or two hundred spectators from the town, I should think; I noticed no one endeavoring to stop the proceeding; I don't remember seeing

Riel near me on that occasion; I did not pay any particular attention; I saw the man take the pistol out of the pocket—as I thought from his back; when Scott fell over, the party all mixed together, and the man stooped over that shot Scott; I could not tell if he had the revolver himself or not; some one in the crowd might have given him the revolver.

To Mr. Cornish.—I knew Lepine to be Adjutant-General; when I saw him, as I stated last night, I identified him then, and recognized him; I should say the prisoner was the man, but could not swear to him as a positive fact.

Alexander Murray sworn.—I reside near Winnipeg; in the years 1869 and 1870, I resided at Portage la Prairie; I remember the 17th of February, 1870; I was taken prisoner that day, at the back of the town, and was one of the Portage party then taken prisoners; saw prisoner there; I recognize him as Lepine; he and Mr. O'Donohue were on horseback in front of the others of the party; Poché advanced from our party to meet them; could not say whether Poché came back to the party at that time or not; two or three parties came to take my revolvers, but I would not deliver them up; I asked who was in command; they told me the Adjutant-General; (my arms were a gun and seven-shooting revolver;) I told them to stand back or I would knock them down; to bring their commander, and I would deliver them up in his presence; I then took them off; at that time the Adjutant-General was there; I told him I delivered these things up, but expected them back when the Government took hold of the country; he bowed his head and rode on; we went to the Fort and were re-searched; a pocket-book containing £6 was taken from me, I don't know by whose order; I saw O'Donohue, Riel and Lepine standing at the door, a little distance off; I do not know what became of the pocket-book; never recovered my money from these parties; my fellow-prisoners were searched; came from the Portage with Scott; was taken prisoner with him; saw him handcuffed; I remember the morning he was shot; saw what was said to be a coffin, a rough box of boards; I was down-stairs with a guard when I saw this; the guard took me back to my prison and I was locked in; in the building we were in there was a hall; from the guard-room five doors opened into five rooms; I was in the same room as the witness John Bain, at the north-west corner; at first Scott was kept in a room in the range with ours; a short time before the 4th March, Scott was placed in another room on the opposite side of ours; while in this room he lay in irons and handcuffed; I saw Scott on that morning; cannot say positively when Scott was removed; double guards were placed over us, and the cracks and openings looking into the guard-room were closed with rags or paper; a short time before he was taken out, Rev Mr Young and Scott stood at our door; the door was opened, I think, by one of the guards; Mr. Young said, "Good-by, boys;" Thomas Scott bowed his head; his hands were tied behind his back, and he had a white handkerchief over his forehead; the door was closed as they moved down-stairs; I never saw Scott afterwards; when Scott and Mr Young stood at the door, I did not recognize any other persons; I felt so sorry to see poor Scott taken out to be shot, and such a crowd in the room; I next heard report of guns that appeared to come from the road by the east gate; I then looked through the window, and saw Mr. Young in trouble; he was going towards Governor McTavish's residence; he appeared to be wiping tears from his eyes; the next thing I observed was the return of one of the firing party; I recognized the man then, and saw him last spring and also to-day; I cannot tell his name. (His Lordship instructed the witness to ascertain this man's name and inform the Court.) After that, the guards were drinking and fooling round, and got intoxicated that evening; I saw the prisoner that day, but I cannot say how long after Scott was said to be shot; I saw him up-stairs in the guard-room; he was apparently sober and talking to some of the guard; I knew Lepine well, while I was in the prison, I frequently saw him; I saw Riel, Lepine and O'Donohue on the night previous to Scott being shot; they were in the guard-room; Riel came and asked me if I was a

Canadian; I told him not but I belonged to that party; I went back to my room; he followed me up and apparently looking into my room; I closed the door and said, "Boys, keep quiet, for Riel, O'Donohue and Lepine are in the guard-room;" I knelt on my knees and looked through the key-hole; I heard a knock on the door where Scott was confined; the door was opened slightly by one of the guard; Scott said, "I want to get out;" the door was opened a second time; Riel stepped up to Scott, and Scott said he wished to be treated civil; Riel said he did not deserve to be treated civil, and called him a dog; Scott asked for his book, I think a pocket-book; Riel said he hadn't it; the door was then shut; I understood it to be a call of nature; this was about nine o'clock at night; during the opening and closing of the door, O'Donohue and Lepine were there; there were very few guards in the hall that night; Lepine was called the Adjutant-General; the guards told us, when we wanted some tea made, that they had strict orders from Riel and the Adjutant-General; I saw him one day giving strict orders not to allow us to get out in the guard-room; I got out under the influence of McKenny, Alfred Scott, and O'Lone; I was required to take the oath of their Government; the oath was taken in a building opposite the building he was confined in; it was used as the officers' quarters; I was taken there by these parties McKenny, O'Lone and Alfred Scott, and went into a room; there was a table; the man they call Goulet sat there; he asked me to take the oath; he read it to me in French; the parties with me translated it to me; I was sworn on the Bible or Testament, by Goulet; he had no clerk there; the nature of the oath was—I was to be quiet and not oppose the Provisional Government; I signed nothing as I recollect; I was then taken into the room where the Adjutant-General Lepine was; O'Lone and Scott were apparently half drunk, and were laughing and talking to Lepine; McKenny was sober: they conducted themselves very pleasantly; I did not laugh, I was in a great hurry to get my clothes changed; I did not understand what was said; they apparently said this fellow has got out and laughed over it; I went to town then, and then returned to see my fellow-prisoners with a bottle of wine and some whiskey; I tried to get in, but the guard would not let me; told me to go to the Adjutant-General to obtain leave; I went to him, showed him the flask, said it was for a sick man; he called one of the guard who was passing by, and asked him to explain what I wanted; the man did so; I got his permission, and went up-stairs to my fellow-prisoners; I have seen the prisoner Lepine since several times; I went to his house to get my things restored, in the spring of 1871 following the occurrence; I saw Lepine, I asked him through an interpreter for my things, viz., gun, revolver and pocket-book; he said he hadn't them, but that I had better keep quiet, the Fenians would be in shortly—O'Donohue was coming in with them; I referred to losing my things; he said he could not give them to me; this was all that occurred; (it was in the fall of 1871 that the Fenians came); I went from Lepine to Governor Archibald, and reported this to Governor Archibald.

Cross-examined by Mr. Royal.—I came to this country seven or eight years ago this fall; it was a year or so before the surveyors came, and before the Dawson Route was commenced; I was living at the Portage at the time of the troubles, on my farm; I joined the party at High Bluff first, supposed to be under the command of Colonel Dennis; a man named Hamilton was in immediate command, a young man who came up with the surveyors; about twenty in the High Bluff party; we drilled there about two weeks; it was nice weather: we got word to come down and join Schultz's party in Winnipeg; we had twenty rounds of ammunition apiece given us by the men who told me; Captain Webb gave Hamilton the order, and he told me; a despatch came up of the capture of Schultz's party, so I did not comply with the order; we remained there until further news; no more drilling, but kept guard; Colonel Dennis came up fleeing for his life to the Portage, as we supposed, from Winnipeg; sent his man to High Bluff for horses and a guide, which he got; a man named Paquin went as guide; he went across by the Pembina mountains, as I understood, to St. Joseph; he did not see our party, to my knowledge; we kept guard on the road by the house, so as to challenge any strangers to explain their business, and to prevent spies; we did not apprehend any attack; soon after that we disbanded; the next movement was when some persons who had escaped came to the Portage, and said that the prisoners were starving, and in filth and dirt; it was the report that Governor McTavish could have squashed the rebellion, if he had not given up the Fort, and arms, and ammunition, and provisions in it; that the French would have had no power to get up the rebellion; it was said he opposed no resistance, while he could have called in to protect the Fort a number of constables, amply sufficient to repel all attempts against it; this was the popular opinion; seeing that the legal authority had no wish, or was indisposed to protect our fellow-citizens, we naturally joined together to relieve them, and I felt it my duty to do so; there were Bolton, Farmer, Newcombe and Captain Webb with the Portage party; there was not much commanding by any one; we were about seventy-five or perhaps up to a hundred; we came from Headingly to Boyd's place, at Redwood; we were directed to march to Kildonan school-house; we did so; first one I met was Mr. Fletcher; I think by his influence we got possession of the school-house; I was keeping prisoners, John McKinny one, and I was told a man named Parisien was another; these prisoners were taken by us, were brought in after we reached the school-house; Major Bolton brought McKinny; I don't know who brought Parisien; McKinny was released; the other man got wounded; I heard they were spies; I kept them there one night and the better part of the day; after Parisien got wounded, McKinny was released; after Sutherland and Parisien got wounded, I was afraid for McKinny's life, from the infuriated people, and applied to have him put in a safe place; I believe he was sent up to Winnipeg to his home; after Parisien running away, he was brought back wounded; some of the officers were staying at Mr. Black's; we swore on the Bible at the Portage to do our best to release the prisoners and then go home; we were discontented with our leaders at Kildonan on account of our want of provisions, being left to shift for ourselves the best way we could; Major Bolton and Dr. Schultz, Mr. Powers, Farmer, and others appeared to be the leading spirits at Kildonan—also Prince of the Indian Settlement; there were a mixture of half-breeds and Indians, cannot say how many; there were some, not wild, but civilized Indians from the settlement below the Lower Fort; our object in going from the Portage to Kildonan was to get more force; we remained at Kildonan about twenty-four hours; I do not know what took place among the leaders; we came to disperse, because we had word the prisoners were released; Riel had given permission to return peacefully to our homes; our party was partly armed; if arms were distributed there, I did not know, as I was engaged inside; I saw one cannon—I should think about eight or nine-pounded; our party appeared to have plenty of ammunition; our arms were common domestic guns, with the exception of a few repeating Henry rifles; I was walking; my gun was in a sleigh ahead of us; I had on me my revolver; the party that met us was led by O'Donohue and the Adjutant-General; I was ahead of the sleighs walking; O'Donohue and the Adjutant-General were about hundred yards ahead of the others, I should think; I saw parties talking, *i. e.* Adjutant-General Lepine talking to Poché; Poché shook hands with Lepine; Lepine had no gun in his hand, to my knowledge; O'Donohue came round ahead of our party; Lepine stopped; I saw O'Donohue stop; did not see him talking to any one; he stopped when I drew up my gun to shoot him, and he came to a full stop; a voice from behind told me not to shoot; my gun was loaded; it was a double-barrelled gun; he was in a short distance of me, fully within reach; I did not see any arms on O'Donohue; after I had lowered my gun, he kept circling around; I heard Poché and Lepine talking, but could not understand them; they conversed two or three minutes; this was about the middle of February;

when I saw the imitation of a coffin, it appeared to come in the east gate, carried in the hands of two men; it was known by us then that Scott was to be shot; the hall in which the guards used to remain was a pretty good-sized one, with a large stove in it; when I was taken back to my room, I did not see the prisoner in the hall; when I went back from the Court-yard, soon afterwards, the guard was doubled; I was informed that Mr. Young was with Scott; the door of my room was closed until Mr. Young came; we could see through the cracks until they were stopped up; it is not in my knowledge that Scott kicked one of the guards; I heard a scuffle, as I thought Scott trying to get out; Riel was present when this scuffle took place, and O'Donohue and Lepine; I was looking through the key-hole; it appeared as if the door was opened; heard a noise—a commotion—saw Scott come at the door; I heard that Scott had difficulties with the guards more than once, but never saw it; door was opened by one of the guards; Mr. Young said, "Good-bye, boys," and Scott bowed his head; knew Mr. Young before; was close to Mr. Young, could not be mistaken; did not see Lepine there; saw a number of the guards; do not recollect the faces of the men behind Mr. Young and Scott; saw a number of guns and arms there; did not see if the men *immediately* behind Mr. Young and Scott were armed; there were often persons went into the guard-room to talk with the guards, apparently friends; the night that Scott got into trouble, I was in a room adjoining his; I should say it was about the hour of nine; it was after dark; I don't think there were quite so many guards that night; the distance between the door of the room and Scott's door was probably as far as from the witness box to the railing, probably some feet less; no light in my room; light in the guard-room; don't know if lamp light or candle light; Mr. McKenny sent Scott to intercede for me, and I think it was in consequence of my kindness to McKenny; I was asked to sign my name to a book; they looked into Lepine's room to see him, and asked me in to wait, so as we could come down together.

Girard sworn.—I have not that letter; I have made search for that letter, and have not it in my possession; (a letter to Mr. Ducharme; from the Governor.) Upon this, witness proving having searched through his office for this letter unsuccessfully, he retired from the witness box.

Joseph Nolen sworn.—I am a native of this country; reside at Point de Chêne; I know the prisoner at the bar; know him from a little boy; the years 1869 and 1870 I remember, also the troubles in the country at that time; the trouble was between the people of the country and the people of McDougall, who were to come here; I think the Company was in possession of the Fort about that time, in fall of 1869 and spring of 1870; saw some other people in the Fort during the winter; cannot say up to what time the Company had possession of the Fort; I do not know what they were doing there; I do not know who was in authority; I did not notice; I saw some armed persons guarding the entrances to the Fort; I think some person was in command of them, but cannot say for sure, who; there was a general report that Riel commanded the whole thing, and that O'Donohue and Lepine were officers; I did not see Lepine giving any command; heard the others stating that they took commands from him; Lepine was called in the Fort, Adjutant-General; during that winter there were prisoners confined in the Fort; I heard there was a great many, but did not see them myself; I only saw two or three in the Fort on one occasion, and on another, a number as they were taken on the prairie; when I visited the Fort, I had no conversation with Lepine, or with Riel in the presence of Lepine; don't know Lepine's duty there; had conversations with Riel on different subjects; I saw Lepine most every time I went to the Fort; I remember the day that Scott was shot; I was present at the Fort that day; did not go inside the Fort; as I was coming to enter the Fort, I met some parties taking Scott out, and that is why I did not enter; I remained standing outside of the wall—next to the door; stopped at the door-sill; Scott remained standing at the door, and I remained outside, with my hands behind, against the wall of the Fort; some time after I saw Mr. Lepine coming out and put down the white cloth that Scott had around his head; he went away with Scott along the wall; I only saw Lepine take Scott away; don't know what distance he went; saw Rev. Mr. Young speaking to Scott; Scott knelt down when Mr. Young spoke to him; Mr. Young spoke to him for a while, and after Mr. Young took him by the neck and was helping him, and bid him "Good-bye,"—so it appeared to me; from that spot he was taken to another place; I am not certain if Lepine took him or not; when he had reached there, he knelt down; then heard the noise of the clicking of the guns, as if cocking, and immediately afterwards heard the discharge of the guns and the cries of Scott; I looked to the spot and found that Scott had fallen down, and was turned on one side; as I was looking on a man came with a pistol; does not recollect if the man that had the pistol fired it or not; saw no smoke and heard no report; was very much excited at the time; immediately afterwards a box was brought there; do not know who was carrying it; Riel cried out that every body had to go into the Fort; the doors had to be closed, and witness went away. (In reply to His Lordship.) Scott fell on his left side; I had seen the guns in the hands of five or six, previous to the cocking of the guns; they were standing together when they fired; knew four or five: Auguste Parisien, Franço's Thibault, Marcel Comtois, Pierre Champagne, and another named Guilmette; this is all I know; I did not see them fire; these men whose guns I heard "click" might have been about twenty or thirty yards from Scott, but I could not tell; when Scott left the cell, could not say which direction he went; when he knelt down it was along the wall.

To Mr. Cornish—Along the wall towards the town; I knew Scott before; when first saw Scott, at the gate; cannot remember the position of handkerchief; his face was uncovered; saw the pistol pointed at Scott; think it was towards his head; saw Riel; do not remember seeing O'Donohue; do not know what became of Scott's body; never had any conversation with Lepine or Riel about the body; was told by Joe, his brother, and he had heard it from another person, that the body was thrown into the river; has heard it say by a great many other persons, but cannot remember who

Cross-examined by Mr. Royal.—Saw employees of the Hudson's Bay Company going round about the Fort frequently during its occupation; do not know if the occupation of the Fort prevented the Company from getting goods from the Fort; to the best of my knowledge, it was nine or ten o'clock when I came up to the Fort; the first person at that time that I saw was Mr. Bannatyne; remained in Bannatyne's quite a while, from there went straight up to the Fort; went up on foot and alone; saw some people going in the direction of the Fort; when I came to the Fort knew what was to be done; Mr. Bannatyne had told me; when I reached the small gate of the Fort there was a large crowd assembled; recollect noticing two or three persons that I knew—G. Richot, André Nault, and Daniel McDougall—of the latter I am not sure, think I saw him; they were mixed up with the crowd, going to and fro; was standing at the right side of the door as you go in, leaning on the outside of the wall close to the gate, with hands behind my back; when Lepine took hold of Scott's arm, Scott was standing at the door, within two feet of witness; I may be mistaken; to the best of my knowledge, Lepine took hold of Scott with his right hand and pulled down the cloth with his left; Scott was in a line where witness was standing, and Lepine a little in front; saw Lepine leading away Scott; did not see Mr. Young until they came to the first place where Scott knelt; when he saw Mr. Young, he was approaching Scott, and Scott was standing; the parties who carried guns were about thirty feet from me; when I first noticed them, they were outside the wall and I was nearly facing them (The exact position of the witness and the firing party was here explained to the Jury, by means of a plan of the Fort.) From the position I occupied, I saw the faces of the firing party it was not Lepine who had the pistol ; do rot know who gave the man the pistol; all I know I saw him with it.

OCTOBER 17th.

His Lordship upon taking his seat upon the bench, remarked that it had been suggested to him that the Jury would perhaps like to adjourn at four o'clock until Monday morning, for the purpose of obtaining a little exercise, and left it for them to decide upon during the recess.

Joseph Nolen continued his deposition. — I advanced to about three steps from Scott's body when it fell ; only thing I saw were some marks on the upper part of his coat near the shoulder ; saw no blood ; I think it was on the left shoulder ; the box was inside the small gate of the Fort ; had seen it previous to going out ; this box was brought out to where the body was through the small gate ; saw some one carrying the box, two or three, but do not know who they were ; believe that the corpse was put into the box and taken inside of the Fort ; cannot swear to seeing the body put into the box ; I cannot say whether I went into the Fort before the box was taken inside ; did not see the box after it went inside the gate ; heard from Modeste Lajemonière that the body was taken into the bastion ; saw this man in the Fort ; do not know if he was a soldier or was employed, or had an office or not ; never saw him carrying a gun in the Fort ; do not know where the body went and the box finally ; I was never told by any one ; never heard a rumour as to what became of the body ; I supposed that the body was in the box ; do not know what finally became of the body ; never heard the subject talked over among Riel's soldiers ; never said to any one that I had heard of a report as to what became of the body ; know Damase Harrison ; he is a half-breed ; can say of him as said of Lajemonière ; he was after in the Fort, in 1869 and 1870 ; believe that he lived at Point Lachine, I am not sure ; never saw him doing anything particularly at the time ; do not know if he was there when Scott was shot ; never saw Harrison on guard ; I was in the habit of giving passes to the prisoners to get out of the Fort ; sometimes ordered by Riel, and sometimes by Lepine to give these passes. (Pass handed to witness, who proved having given it.) Pass then read. It was as follows :—

"FORT GARRY, March 16th, 1870.

" Let bearers, Mr. Farmer, and Andrew Sissons, pass, if you please.

"AMBROISE LEPINE,
" Adjutant-General.

" J. NOLEN,
" Secretary."

(This pass was in French, and was read to the Jury and translated.)

I do not recollect if all the passes were given in the name of the Adjutant-General or not.

Cross-examined by Mr. Chapleau.—Heard from man Denotte that Scott was not dead when he was put into the bastion ; there was quite a crowd when Scott was shot ; everything was quiet and peaceable, and should have heard the report of the guns ; was near enough to hear ; if after the volley was fired and the body turned over, should have seen it ; the body was not turned ; knew the firing party for a long time, except one in particular, Gilmotte, who I had only known for a short time ; they appeared to be excited by liquor, with the exception of Gilmotte ; was standing about four paces from the gate ; saw Scott coming out ; Rev. Mr. Young was with him ; did not see Riel or O'Donohue coming out then ; Lepine was near there ; Duncan Nolen was there on the other side of the road ; witness on this side ; during the Court Martial did not hear the prisoner Ambroise Lepine saying one word against Scott, and he had nothing to do with the proceedings of the Court; after the vote had been taken on the execution of Scott, by the words the prisoner Lepine then used and his demeanour during the whole trial, I understood him to be against the death of Scott, and his words were, "The majority being for his death, he will have to die; "prisoner d d not order witness to write the sentence, nor did not write it himself; Riel announced what the sentence was, where and when to be executed; all the prisoner said during the whole trial, at its conclusion and after the vote being taken, was the word as described; Scott had not then been brought in; Riel sent for Scott, and when he came, the prisoner did not say a word; the only man who spoke was Riel; Edmund Turner and Joseph Delorme were witnesses; Joseph Delorme was also one of the Council; do not know what position Turner held; believe Riel was first accusator and also witness; Riel made the charges against Scott verbally; Riel was sworn to prove his charge by me; Riel was the only accuser; Scott was accused of having taken an oath not to take up arms against the Provisional Government, and afterwards doing so—also of having struck one of the guards and Riel himself; Turner was there during the trial, and gave evidence before Scott was brought in; he was sent by Riel for Scott, and was present during the time Scott was there, and heard Riel explain and translate to him his charges and the sentence of the Court; I think Turner was an Irishman; I don't think Scott asked to examine the witnesses himself; I think he said something, but do not know what he said; Riel was speaking English; Turner was speaking English; the charge of striking Riel and the guard referred to the scuffle that took place in the guard-room.

To Mr. Cornish.—I first heard that the Court Martial was to take place about three o'clock in the afternoon; I heard this from Riel himself.

To His Lordship.—I am not sure that evidence was produced as to Scott taking the oath not to take up arms against the Provisional Government; I do not know if any book was produced; the "taking up arms" referred to his coming down with the Portage party.

To Mr. Chapleau.—It was stated he had taken an oath, but do not know if it was proved.

To His Lordship.—When persons were liberated and took an oath, they signed their name to a book, but those that escaped did not.

John Bruce sworn.— Reside at St. Boniface; am what is styled a French half-breed; have lived in this country for thirty-seven years; I know the prisoner, and know Louis Riel, and all the leaders of the troubles of 1869 and 1870; remember the occasion of the Fort being taken; it was about the 2nd or 3rd of November that the Fort was taken by the insurgents; they retained possession of it, I believe, until the month of July, 1870, when the troops under Colonel Wolseley came; some time after the Fort was taken by the insurgents, some prisoners were taken; the first taken were the prisoners at Dr. Schultz's place, on the 7th December; some time after that, the Portage prisoners were taken; the Portage party was taken on the 17th February, the prisoners were kept in Fort Garry—it was said under guard of armed men; Mr. Riel was President at that time; and there were some Captains; the prisoner was the Adjutant-General; O'Donohue, I believe, was looked upon as a Captain at that time; at the time that the prisoners were taken, I heard afterwards that O Donohue had been President; was not present at the taking of the Fort; went to Lepine's room about fifteen or twenty days previous to the 4th March, and asked Lepine when he intended to liberate the prisoners; he answered, "We will release the prisoners before long, but we will put a couple to death before releasing them;" this was all that occurred at the moment; I made no reply to Lepine; previously to this, he had said the same thing, and he said it pleasantly in the course of conversation; at the taking of prisoners at Dr. Schultz's place, I had put the same question to Lepine as to whether the prisoners would be released; Lepine made the same answer; Lepine did not explain why a couple were to be put to death ; never saw Scott previous to the 4th of March ; was at the Fort on that day ; on the 4th March, in the evening, I was at my own house, and some one told me that Scott was to be executed ; did not believe it, but determined to come and see, and arrived at Fort Garry about eleven o'clock ; entered through the main gate, the gate that faces the Assiniboine River ; there were two sentries at the gate ; do not remember the names of them ; was then told by the two sentries that Scott was to be executed; then went to the Fort, and went to the house facing the main entrance of the Fort; Riel lived at the house; it was used as Riel's quarters ; walked a piece towards the small gate that opened towards the Hudson's Bay Company's stores ; as I was proceeding towards the small gate, saw a box on a pile of cordwood ; as I was proceeding in that direction, met Mr Lepine; asked Lepine what he want d to do with that box ; he said it was to put poor Scott in ; Lepine went one way, and I retraced my steps and came to see Riel ; as I was turning round to go, I went on two or three paces and saw a man coming from the direction of the office or building said to be occupied by the prisoners ; this man was proceeding towards the small gate of the Fort; he had leather leggings on and a white cloth round his cap on his head ; was excited at this sight ; did not recognize any other person that was there except Joseph Delorme, as I was surprised and excited ; Joseph Delorme was walking four or five paces ahead of the person that I saw first ; these parties were going in the direction of the small gate ; do not know if they went out, as my back was turned to the gate ; entered into the large house and went up the steps to see Riel; he was not in his room, so went back towards the small gate ; as I arrived at about the place where I had seen the man for the first time, I heard a report of fire-arms ; as soon as I heard this, I hastened my steps towards the small door of the Fort, and stepped about twelve paces outside of the small gate ; then saw the same person that I saw before, fallen down on his side ; saw one Guilmette (who I think is a Canadian, who spoke French) having a revolver in his hand, approaching where that person had fallen, and was lying a little forward and resting on his right elbow, his hands being tied behind him ; Guilmette shot, as I thought, at his head ; heard the report of the revolver ; the muzzle of the pistol was near, but cannot say how near; it was very near ; after the shot the man fell more down on his back ; then heard Riel, who was at the entrance to the small gate, call out to come and close the doors ; came in with the others through the small gate, and went out through the front gate, and went home ; did not see Lepine or O Donohue outside ; there was a crowd of people, and do not recollect seeing them ; did not see the box outside, to my recollection ; went home then ; was very much excited at what I saw; saw Lepine sometimes afterwards in the Fort ; never asked why Scott was executed ; never spoke upon the subject ; do not know what became of the body ; was told by Elzear Goulet that the body had been thrown into the river, about a quarter of a mile below, at a place called German Creek, and said that there were three persons that threw it in ; did not tell who the three persons were, nor any one of them; said that the body was conveyed in a red cutter belonging to Dr. Schultz ; had seen Dr. Schultz's cutter ; do not know if Dr. Schultz's cutter had been taken by the people at the Fort ; was never informed by anybody else but Goulet ; after the capture of the party at Dr. Schultz's, had seen the cutter in the Fort ; was told that the body had been sunk ; that it had been sunk with heavy chains ; Goulet told me this, and that a hole had been cut in the ice ; told me nothing more about it ; Goulet told me this about a week after the execution ; Goulet remained in the Fort after the execution, and was in the Fort when he told me this ; they always called Goulet by the name of Captain ; it was reported that Goulet was drowned ; he did not tell me whether the body was put in the river in the daytime or night.

To His Lordship.—Was told that the man with the white handkerchief round his head was Scott; did not know Scott.

Cross-examined by Mr. Royal.—The prisoners at Dr. Schultz's house were sober on the 7th December; at that time I was at my home; had visited the Fort several days previous, but cannot say if I had been in the Fort that day; was there the day following; it was on the 6th November that the message was sent to the English party to send twelve Delegates of the French party at the Court House to come to some understanding for the general good; it was signed, "By order, Louis Riel, Secretary;" the meeting took place at the Court House, in a building near Fort Garry, known as the old prison; at that time the public meetings in Red River did not take place in this building; there had been one meeting before; am not aware if the Government of Assiniboia objected to that meeting or not; the building was the property f the Government of Assiniboia; could not give the names of the Delegates who attended; one was Mr. Kenny, but I have forgotten the names; was present at that meeting; cannot state what was the result of the meeting without looking in my scrap-book; was President of the meeting; Louis Riel, Secretary; the result of the meeting was proffering to Governor McDougall certain Bill of Rights to use if Governor M. Dougall would accede to them; the English party said that Governor McDougall could not grant what was asked, and the English objected to the Delegates going.

To His Lordship.—The object was to stop Governor McDougall until the rights of the people were ensured to them by the Government at Ottawa; the intention of the meeting was to work for the whole country at large, as there were twelve English and twelve French Delegates; if this had been settled before the movement, everything would have been right.

The Sheriff being asked by His Lordship the decision of the Jury with reference to adjourning, and ascertaining that it was their desire to do so, His Lordship instructed the crier to close the Court, and proceedings were adjourned till Monday morning.

MONDAY, October 19th.

John Bruce, cross-examined by Mr. Royal, continued. — Perfectly well acquainted with the prisoner at the bar; was in the habit of seeing him before and after the 4th March; when witness spoke about the liberation of the prisoners at the Fort, did not go for that special purpose; this happened about fifteen days previous to the 4th March; when prisoner stated that the prisoners had to be liberated, but that one or two had to be executed, do not think he was serious at that time; had told the same thing on another occasion, previous to this, and at the time did not think he was serious; always found the prisoner to be a good-tempered and a good-hearted man; think it was about noon when arrived at the Fort on the 4th March; the persons who were accompanying Scott from the Hudson's Bay Office towards the gate I did not recognize, only Joseph Delorme specially, as he was a little forward of the others; know that there were two other persons with Scott, one on each side of him; am well acquainted with the Fort; know the relative position of the buildings inside it; stood at corner of Dr. Cowan's house, and Delorme and the prisoner Scott were coming out between Dr. Cowan's and Mr. McTavish's house; was standing at the south-east corner, next to the Hudson's Bay store, when I saw Delorme and the man with something white upon his head.

After some enquiry from His Lordship, witness stated that he believed the person with the white handkerchief round his head was Scott.

Cross-examination continued.—The time that elapsed was a little over five minutes from the time I first saw Scott until the next; Riel's office was on the first floor on the right hand side as you went in the hall; it is possible to do this distance i two minutes; took more because tarried in the building, visiting the different offices; when I returned to the shop, heard the volley, and then walked quickly; there are twenty paces to the spot were heard the volley t the small gate, and stopped ten paces outside the small gate; there was a crowd outside the door, so walked ten paces to clear the crowd and have a better sight of what was going on; do not know if inclined to the right or left or walk straight forward through the crowd; stood near the road; there were already some near Scott; the crowd was very near; do not know if there was any noise among the crowd; did not pay any attention; did not recognize any of those that were near the body except one, Guilmette; noticed Guilmette more than any one else, because he had a revolver in his hand, and because saw him fire it; know the Rev. Mr. Young; did not see him at that spot then; witness saw Guilmette sideways; do not recollect seeing the prisoner Lepine outside the Fort; attention was drawn to the person being shot; when I saw Delorme and Scott and the two persons going out of the gate, Lepine was not there; did not see Rev. Mr. Young at this time; was the first President of the Provisional Government.

His Lordship here stated that it became a matter of importance to ascertain the basis of this Provisional Government.

In reply to His Lordship, the witness stated that Riel acted as Secretary at the first meeting; do not know by whose authority; Dr. Schultz's house was taken by the prisoner; gave no authority, as President, for this to be done.

Cross-examination continued.— Used to attend occasionally the sittings of the Provisional Government after the month of November; in the month of November, I was President; afterwards held office as Commissioner of Public Works; Riel was then President; it was during the months of November and December after the taking of Schultz's house—I resigned not long after; resignation was made in writing; at the meeting, was asked to sit at the head of the table, and in taking his seat, tendered resignation; it was written down by the Committee and was accepted by them; the majority of the members of the Committee were appointed by Riel; they were composed of French half-breeds only; O'Donohue used to attend now and then; witness saw Lepine there, but cannot say if he was a member of the Committee; he was invited to take a seat when he used to come in sometimes.

In reply to His Lordship's query that the President ought to know if Lepine was one of the Committee, the witness stated that he was President in name only, but had not the powers of one; a great many things took place that he was not aware of.

His Lordship.—Who had the power and authority?

Witness.—Mr. Riel had.

His Lordship.—Do you think that that thing you have described should be called a Provisional Government?

Witness.—I do not.

To Mr. Cornish.—I resigned the Presidency of the Government; was only styled President as stated before; resigned because a great many things were done without my knowledge; the taking of the Fort was against my will; being at home when it was taken, also the taking of Dr. Schultz's house; was not a consenting party to the taking of the Government stores; was not present at the taking of Schultz's house; saw two cannon pointing at Dr. Schultz's house; think they were taken out of the Fort; they were outside the Fort; saw no person placing or in charge of the cannon; knew that it was going on; knows of no reason why the Provisional Government should have captured Dr. Schultz's house; have in possession, from McDougall, a letter dated 13th December; this was after the taking of Dr. Schultz's house; I think at this time McDougall was in Pembina; I also withdrew from my office as President, as I thought that they were going too far and doing things that I did not approve of; have already stated the things; my name was attached to things that I did not approve; first opposition was to the document that was sent to McDougall to tell him to stop at Pembina; saw the document long after, and my name attached to it without consent; his name was attached to the proclamation of the 8th December without witness' knowledge.

To His Lordship.—Do not know who prepared these documents; was not present when the Bill of Rights was drawn up; have seen the document, but have no recollection of its contents; do not know what the object or intention of it was; (the French copy was then shown to the witness); cannot say who prepared the documents for the Provisional Government; have seen Stutzman in the town; Stutzman was doing nothing; do not know whether he framed the documents or not, but saw him in company with Riel; the *New Nation* was the paper of the Government; never said that anyone had cut Scott's throat with a knife; said he had finished him; was stating facts; had it from Goulet, the person who was drowned; had written a letter to that effect; Goulet said that the body was first put into the coffin and taken into the bastion, and about twelve o'clock it was found out that Scott was not dead; there were three in the bastion when this was found out, and one of them shot him in the head with a pistol; Goulet did not name the persons; witness asked Goulet, but Goulet would not say; Goulet was the only one who informed me of this; never spoke to any other person about the matter; have written a letter giving these facts substantially the same; Goulet did not, to my recollection, tell witness that Scott had said, "For God's sake kill me, or let me out of this"; have copies of letters in French that I have written.

His Lordship here informed the witness that he would have to go home and fetch the copies of all such letters, and that he should consider it contempt of Court if he did not produce them. (The letters referred to were copies of letters written by witness to newspapers.)

Francis Charette was then called, but not being about, His Lordship informed the Court that they would take recess a little earlier than usual.

John Bruce recalled.

His Lordship.—Did you find the letters?

Witness.—Nothing is complete; my papers have been knocked about; I have not the fourth letter complete.

His Lordship here read the fourth letter written by witness relating to Scott's being placed in the bastion, and to the words being heard, "For God's sake take me out of here or kill me," and a person finishing Scott with a pistol according to some, and with a knife according to others.

Mr. Chapleau here said that he thought that this evidence of what the witness had written or had not written, was irregular.

His Lordship.—But we must have it for the Jury to judge of the witness' credibility.

Mr. Chapleau.—I think they can already judge of that.

His Lordship (to witness)—Have you those words in the French?

Witness.—I have not; there are some words in the English version that I have never written in French; it was translated by a Canadian into English, and I was afterwards told that a great many expressions were put into the English version that did not appear in the French one; the expression, "My God, my God, take me out of this, or kill me," or "son of a bitch," I never heard in the letter in French that I wrote, but Goulet told me of the expression as already deposed.

To Mr. Chapleau.—There is something in the paper that I never wrote or told any person to write; never saw or heard anything that is written there; only know what Goulet told me; at that time had nothing to do with the Provisional Government, and do not know what capacity Goulet was in when he spoke to me of the matter, or whether he held any position at all at that time; have no personal knowledge of Goulet holding any position at the Fort; he was one of Riel's partizans, and with him in the Fort.

Mr. Chapleau here objected to any evidence being taken of what Goulet said that was not said in the presence of the prisoner.

His Lordship thought that the evidence should be received, but took a note of Mr. Chapleau's objection.

Francis Charette sworn.—Have lived at Ste. Agathe for two years past; previously lived at St. Robert; remember 1869 and 1870; do not know who had possession of the Fort; believe it was French half-breeds; know it was Riel who commanded; Lepine was also there; do not know Lepine's occupation; never heard him called any name by the men; never heard him called Adjutant-General, but have seen it in the papers, the *New Nation* paper; the *New Nation* was printed in Winnipeg; do not know by whose authority; was started in 1870; do not know when it ceased to be published; the last copy saw printed was about the month of April; can't say whether it was a weekly paper or not; remember the 4th March, 1870; was in the Fort that morning; had been in the Fort for preceding six or seven days; was doing nothing in the Fort; was told that if he did not stay in the Fort, he would be taken prisoner; went there first on a visit; was told this by a Captain named Joseph Delorme, who was Captain of the men; there were other Captains there; François Poitras, Michel Dumas, jr., were Captains; can't say if Nault or Goulet were Captains; knew them, they were in the Fort; saw him among the others in the Fort; François Poitras was my Captain; sometimes mounted guard; had nothing else to do; mounted on guard at the Fort gate; do not know if there was any guard on at north gate; always mounted guard on the south gate; saw guards upon the small gate facing the rising sun; did not visit the gates; knew there were prisoners confined in the Fort, but never mounted guard over them; was never in the guard-room; saw Lepine only two or three times; saw him in the Fort and in his room; used to see him through the window of his room; the room in which I saw Lepine was about two chains east of the place where the prisoners were confined; Riel was in Dr. Cowan's building; do not remember seeing Scott in the forenoon of the 4th March; saw him about twelve o'clock; Scott was coming out of the Fort; Scott's coat was of a chocolate color; he had a white cloth on his head, his hands were tied behind his back; when I saw him coming out of the gate, there were a great number of persons around him; at this time witness was on the stone wall of the Fort, upon the top; was not on guard; when he heard that a man of the name of Scott was to be shot, went there to see; can't say if any person was with Scott, thought that he was accompanied by some one; the second time saw Scott; he was standing about thirty or forty paces from the wall towards the river side; saw Scott talking with a man; heard some guns fired and saw him falling; was on the wall all the time; came down from the wall and went to see the body, and saw the wounds from the guns; one was in his breast, and one in the shoulder; there was blood proceeding from the wounds in the breast, but not from the one in the shoulder; did not notice the back part of the body; was about two feet from the body at the time; did not see anything else at that time; saw a pistol in a man's hand; thinks the man's name was Guilmette; he took the pistol and put it into Scott's ear and fired it there; the pistol did not go off upon the first attempt to fire it; it snapped; saw Lepine, and he commanded us to go into the Fort; Lepine said, "Go in, you have no business here;" Lepine was about two paces from me when he said this; witness left and went into the Fort; at this time saw a pistol in Lepine's coat, in the inside breast-pocket; saw Lepine put his hand on the pistol; Lepine spoke to Guilmette when he put his hand on the pistol, and he heard the words uttered, "Finish him," but do not know if Lepine said this; heard the words, "Why is that pistol not in order?"—thinks this was Lepine said this *then*, and thinks so now; he heard the words, "There is one in order"; cannot say if it was the same voice or the same person that uttered these two things; when this was said, I did not make no difference; thought it was the same voice; it was at the time I saw Lepine put his hand upon the pistol, that I heard the words about the pistol not going off; after the pistol had been fired, Lepine told me to go to the Fort; Lepine's words were these, "Go into the Fort, you have no business here ; go away from here ;" witness left and went into the Fort ; Lepine put his hand on me, and touched me on the shoulder, and told me to go into the Fort ; Lepine commanded me loudly, but did not make any threat ; do not think he spoke in excitement or anger ; witness received a kick from somebody that was going in, but do not know who kicked me ; no one spoke of kicking before I went away ; the kick was close to the posterior ; heard no other person giving orders except as I have mentioned ; saw a box before, but did not see it afterwards ; saw it inside the Fort before the guns were fired, and before I went outside the Fort ; did not see it when returned inside of the Fort ; saw the box the night when they put it in the grave ; do not think it was the same night ; it was the second night after that saw it put in the grave ; have forgotten the incident completely ; can't say who put it in the grave ; these are the only times he saw the box ; when ordered into the Fort, went to the same place as had been staying before ; went with Captain Poitras to the lower part of Dr. Cowan's house ; was not on duty that day ; went into and out of the house ; heard Scott talk in the bastion and thought they had put him there ; did not see Scott ; never spoke to Scott before ; heard " O Lord, O Lord ;" do not know what became of Scott's body ; first saw the box alongside of Dr. Cowan's house ; when I heard the words, "O Lord, O Lord," did not see Scott ; Joseph Delorme heard the words and told witness ; Delorme was at the door of the bastion, and witness was on one side : believe Delorme was on guard at the door ; think that Joseph Delorme was Captain ; witness asked Delorme who was talking inside the bastion, and Delorme answered it was Scott ; nobody ever told me where the body was finally placed ; thought all the time that the body was in the box when it was put into the ground.

To His Lordship.—There might have been some inside the bastion ; heard these expressions only once ; then went away ; it was the night of the day following the day the box was put into the ground.

To Mr Cornish.—Was on guard at the south gate when the box was put into the ground ; it was put in between the south gate and Dr. Cowan's house ; there were several persons engaged in putting in into the ground ; there were only a few of the men who carried guns present, in comparison to the number in the Fort : people were going in and out of the Fort ; do not know who went in and out of the Fort.

Cross-examined by Mr. Chapleau.—After I was on the wall, came down and went through the small gate and came out ; after I had passed through the small gate, saw Scott lying on his side ; his chest and his face were partly visible ; after the pistol was fired, turned back ; saw the body stretch out ; at the same moment the pistol was fired the second time ; Lepine had his hand on his pistol in his breast coat-pocket, and I am sure that the pistol Lepine had in his pocket was not the one fired at Scott's head ; Guilmette was the man who had the pistol in his hand, and it was the same pistol that snapped ; saw Guilmette after he came back to the Fort, and believe he was drunk ; my impression is, as have already stated, that it was Lepine's voice I heard ; when Scott came through the gate where I saw him first, Lepine was not with him ; if he had been, would have seen him ; after Scott had passed, saw the six soldiers pass afterwards ; did not hear any command ; saw a man holding something white in his hand ; the man who held this lifted it up three times ; the distance I was from this man was about thirty feet ; am very sure the man who held this was not the prisoner at the bar—he was a middle-sized man ; remember the man ; saw Scott only in one position (kneeling) ; saw Rev. Mr. Young with Scott after they came out of the Fort ; did not see him inside of the Fort ; lost sight of Scott when witness turned and looked into the yard and saw the six men ; did not see Scott until afterwards as described ; heard the volley fired, and then got down in the inside of the yard and went out of the small gate ; saw Scott as described ; saw Mr. Young at some distance, seven or eight paces, standing and not speaking to anyone ; he was

5

alone, looking as if he was crying; was a couple of paces from the bastion when heard what I have stated; heard the words distinctly.

Frank Geo. Beecher sworn.—Am Private Secretary to Lieut.-Governor Morris, witness produced a document that he had been subpœned to produce; could prove handwriting of endorsement, the date on which it had been received, 10th January, 1873; (the document was handed to the Clerk to be proved, and His Lordship instructed Mr. Beecher that it would be handed back to him when it had been examined.)

Pierre Gladu sworn.—Reside at St. Vital; lived there twenty-two years; know Lepine since I have been in the country; I am a half-breed Canadian; in the month of February, was at Fort Garry; was there like all the others; was taken there with a sleigh and stayed; was taken there as a prisoner by the President, Mr. Riel; had come to Narcisse Marion's place, on the other side Red River, in the Parish of St. Boniface, and was there taken prisoner by Riel; believe it was in February; was in the Fort until spring; was pressed into the service when taken, but got free afterwards; when in the Fort became a soldier, and when ordered to act as a soldier, did so; was in the habit of mounting guard, to guard the gates; never guarded the prisoners; knew there were some prisoners confined in the Fort; heard of Scott being confined there; first time saw Scott was when they were putting irons on his hands; could not tell who put the irons on; it was done by Riel's orders; was in a room and looked through the door into another room where Scott was, and saw this; it was a room where the prisoners were; saw the irons put on Scott's hands; this was done in the evening; do not know what they did after the irons were put on; went away; did not see Scott again until saw him shot; saw Scott as he was coming out of the Fort; I was outside of the Fort, on the left hand side of the door; did not see Scott until he was coming out of the gate, there was such a crowd; do not know who was with Scott; after Scott had come out, some person led him away; it struck witness as if it had been Baptiste Lepine; led Scott about thirty paces to the north; then Baptiste Lepine got Scott to kneel down; Rev. Mr. Young was there at once; Mr. Young knelt down for a few moments with Scott; seeing that the man was in a direction with the crowd, Baptiste Lepine took him to another spot about ten paces from the first; Scott knelt at the second place; it appeared to witness that it was André Nault with the white handkerchief; after the handkerchief had been raised up by André Nault, the guns were fired; saw the man Scott fall down and heard him cry out a sort of a cry like a man in distress; witness went forward; as he approached the body, saw a man of the firing party sitting down sideways upon the body of Scott; the man's name was François Guilmette, I think they called him; then Guilmette asked for an arm to finish him, saying he was not dead; a weapon was given to Guilmette by some one (do not know who), and he put it to his head and fired; Guilmette appeared to be a little in liquor, and took some little time; after the shot was fired, Scott gave a sort of jerk as if he wanted to stretch; I stepped forward to see, and saw some blood running from Scott's face, and witness went up to put down the cloth over his face, and heard the voice of Riel saying, "Let nobody come near;" I was about three paces from the body when I heard Riel say this, so I came back to the gate of the Fort.

His Lordship here asked the Jury if they thought they could go on with an evening sitting, and upon the Foreman answering in the affirmative, instructed the Crier to adjourn the Court until 7.30 p.m.

TUESDAY, October 20.

His Lordship took his seat upon the Bench at 9.30 precisely.

His Lordship then instructed Mr. Chapleau to read to the Jury, in French, the letter of the 3rd of January, 1873, which was addressed to Lieutenant-Governor

Morris by the prisoner and Riel, professing to give the reasons of the rebellion ; which Mr. Chapleau having read,

Baptiste Charette was called and sworn.—Lives in parish of St. Norbert ; lived there in 1870; remember the 4th of March, 1870 ; was at the Fort ; knew there were prisoners at the time in the Fort ; knew a prisoner by the name of Thomas Scott ; did not see Scott on the 4th of March ; did not remark at the time well, but do not recollect seeing him ; saw a man led out to be shot that day ; believe that man was Scott ; saw Scott as he was coming out of the gate ; can't say how he was dressed ; appeared as if he had someting white on his head ; his hands were behind him ; did not pay any attention if they were tied or not ; was just inside of the gate ; went out after Scott went out ; did not notice who was with Scott ; did not notice if any one led Scott or not ; when I saw Scott outside of the gate, Mr. Young was with Scott ; before Scott went out André Nault was with Scott, and also a man named Joseph Delorme ; did not recognize any others ; after I went out, saw Rev. Mr. Young talking to Scott ; they were about thirty-six feet from the gate ; they were standing, and Mr. Young was talking to Scott ; did not see Scott kneel ; it was near the wall and nearly on the track ; did not see Scott and Mr. Young move from this spot ; saw Scott shot on that day ; did not see him shot in the same place as he was standing with Mr. Young; he was shot opposite the small gate, about forty feet from where I saw him first ; the man Scott was on his knees, and then they fired ; six men fired ; the six men were about forty feet from Scott ; the men's names were Pierre Champagne, Marcel Roy, Alexander Parisien, François Guilmette ; do not recollect the others, they were Canadians ; saw a person named André Nault holding something white in his hand, and in view of the firing party, and then the guns were fired ; he raised the white thing up with his hands ; next saw the man called Scott fall ; went up to him ; saw the marks where he was shot ; the marks were in the breast, and on the shoulder, and a third one between the two; the body was lying on its side ; saw blood coming out of his wound and out of the side of his nose ; it was the wound on the breast that seemed to bleed ; did not look behind Scott's body ; saw the man Guilmette take a pistol and fire it ; shot Scott in the ear ; the body then moved ; did not see from whom Guilmette got the pistol ; do not know if the pistol snapped ; know that it went off ; heard nobody speak about a pistol ; know that Guilmette spoke, but paid no attention to what he said ; saw the body put in the box ; cannot say who put it in ; the box was made of plain rough boards ; did not see the box carried there ; heard somebody hammering, but do not know if it was nailed down ; the box was closed up with a board ; they then took the box inside the gate ; do not know who put the body in the box, or who carried it into the Fort ; did not hear any orders given for this to be done ; was standing about thirty feet from the body ; they took the body up and put it in the box, like lifting up a person in a sleep; when the box was carried into the Fort, went into the Fort behind the box ; they that were carrying the box took to the left, and witness took to the right ; the left would be towards the bastion ; know there was a hole dug near the Hudson Bay Company's store ; it was said to be dug to put the body in : did not see the box put in the hole.

To His Lordship.—Went to the Fort ; was asked to stay, and did stay ; nobody sent word for me to come to the Fort; went there, and friends of mine there told me to stay ; sometimes mounted guard ; remained in the Fort fifteen days ; had leave from Michel Dumas, my Captain, to leave the Fort, and I went.

To Mr. Cornish.—Saw Lepine sometimes but not often ; never paid any attention to Lepine being called Adjutant-General ; never heard him called that ; people outside the Fort spoke of General, but never heard it spoken of inside.

To His Lordship.—Saw Scott walk from the small gate the thirty paces; know Baptiste Lepine ; do not know if Baptiste Lepine walked with Scott ; if Baptiste Lepine had walked with him, do not know if I should have noticed him ; my attention was drawn towards the man with the white thing on his head.

Cross-examined by Mr. Royal.—It was a little before noon when I saw Scott; there were about thirty or forty persons inside the gate; was not armed; saw only the six men armed; would have noticed if any others were armed; did not see Lepine, O'Donohue, or Riel; saw Riel outside after going out; the thirty or forty men I speak of were between Dr. Cowan's and Mr. McTavish's house; did not notice if Rev. Mr. Young was walking with Scott, or if any one was with Scott, when he came to the gate and went out; my attention was wrapped up in looking at Scott; am sure my brother François was among the crowd; was not on top of the wall; it was Ambroise Lepine who held up the handkerchief; was on the edge of the crowd in a line with the others, no one intervening, and saw very well who it was held up the handkerchief; could not be mistaken; could see perfectly well; was about thirty feet from the man who held up the handkerchief where I was; there were twelve men stayed in the room; they were guards; never saw Lepine give orders to the guard, or act in any capacity.

To His Lordship.—Did not observe anything peculiar about Guilmette on that occasion, beyond he was drunk and not in his good senses; saw Guilmette drinking.

Mr. Cornish here stated that the case for the Crown would close here for the present.

Mr. Chapleau here requested His Lordship to grant a recess of two hours, so as to allow him to consult with his colleague, Mr. Royal, as to the defence endeavouring to render the evidence for defence as short as possible.

His Lordship acceded to the request, and the Court was adjourned two hours.

TUESDAY AFTERNOON.

Thomas Bunn sworn.—My occupation is that of a farmer; have lived in this country all my life, with the exception of occasional visits to Canada; I am an English half-breed; was Secretary of Council Assiniboia, and a member of the Council in 1869 and 1870; in the end of 1869, was not an officer in any other Government; was Secretary to the Provisional Government; do not know when he or I position as such ended; never tendered my resignation, and was never dismissed; have no records, and do not know if any were kept in this Government; have certain documents referring to elections of members in this Government; was appointed by a Committee appointed by Convention to be Secretary of the Provisional Government; I was present when I was appointed; I think the resolutions of the Convention were taken down in writing, but cannot swear it; it was early in 1870 that this took place—think 25th January; think it was an adjourned meeting; it was at a previous meeting, that was called a mass meeting, on the 29th of January, that Mr. Smith was present; this meeting, as far as I know, was called by Donald A. Smith to bring out the feeling of the people with respect to Governor McDougall; got a letter from the late Governor McTavish to attend this meeting; he wrote to me in a private way; (witness could not produce this letter, as he had not got it;) attached no value to it at the time or now; the contents were subsequently asking in a friendly way to come to the meeting; said the meeting was called by Donald A. Smith, in his capacity as Conventioner of the Government of Canada; went to the meeting; Mr. Smith, McTavish and Bishop Machray were there; was a large meeting; was composed of a large majority of the English population; think Judge Black was Secretary; I was Chairman; there were no minutes kept to my knowledge; think Mr. Bannatyne was Secretary the second day; there was a proposition made for the election of representatives from both the English and French to consider the advisability of electing representatives of both; the French reserved the right of appointing their own, and there was a committee composed of five or six—myself, Bishop Machray, and others—to consult over the manner of appointing the English representatives; Bishop Machray was then a member of the Council Assiniboia; the English Committee subdivided their part into twelve electoral divisions; the first Bill of Rights was drafted at the first meeting on the 16th of November; delegates, both French and English, were chosen, twelve of each; delegates differing about the manner of securing these Bills of Rights, the delegation was not appointed; the twelve French and twelve English Delegates said that Governor McDougall could not grant the Bill of Rights, could only lay it before the authorities; in consequence of this no English deputation was appointed; about this time the proclamation of McDougall and Colonel Denis was issued, and the meeting of the delegates came to an end; have the Bill of Rights; it is the one that was passed; this Bill of Rights was supposed to be the basis of the conditions in which the people would enter into the Confederation with the Dominion of Canada; after the issuing of the proclamation, the meetings dissolved; there was a deal of confusion at the time, and the effect of the proclamation was to confuse people a little more than they were before; it had no effect at all on the Governor and Council of Assiniboia; practically the Council of Assiniboia were not acting at that time, in my opinion; it was on the 25th of January, 1870, I think, that the Provisional Government was formed.

To His Lordship.—There was no meeting appointed by the people to establish for this country an Independent Government.

To Mr. Chapleau.—The first meeting for that purpose was on the 25th of January.

To His Lordship.—They had no previous expressed authority from the people for that purpose.

To Mr. Chapleau.—It was not on the 25th January that the Provisional Government was formed.

His Lordship here informed the witness that he would have to look over the archives, as he a moment ago had stated that a Government *had* been formed on the 25th of January.

To Mr. Chapleau.—Believe that a Government called the Provisional Government was formed on the 25th of January by the delegates arranged to be elected at a meeting of the people; on the 19th or 20th of the same month, a committee was appointed by the Convention to nominate officers of a Government; do not recollect the names of all the committee; I was one; the committee was composed of six or eight, half French and half English; I recollect James Ross and O'Donohue; do not recollect the names of the others; I was reported for Secretary of State, and O Donohue as Treasurer; John Bruce, Minister of Public Works, as I think; James Ross, Chief Justice; A. G. B. Bannatyne, Postmaster General; my duties as Secretary were never defined; I did duties, wrote certain letters to the Hon. Joseph Howe, Secretary of State for Canada; I refer to the letters accrediting the delegates chosen by the representatives of the people to go to Ottawa to negotiate with the Canadian Government; the delegates were appointed by the Convention of the 11th of February; I think Riel was elected President on the 25th; was present when Riel was elected as President; he was elected by a large majority of the Convention; I think the Convention was composed of twenty-four; Riel was elected long before the Delegates were appointed; I think it was on the 11th February that the Delegates were appointed; (witness here produced a number of letters [copies] sent by him to each of the Delegates); what was called the Legislature of Assembly passed laws (witness produced Bill No. 4, presented by Hon. Dr. Bird, which was passed by the Assembly. The bill produced was entitled "An Act to Indemnify Members"; there was not any public works to my knowledge, but think there were; there were some members of Council Assiniboia who were Delegates; in the latter part of February, there were general elections in the English parishes; there was a burst of the Delegates elected on the 25th of January, about the 17th of

February, by what is known as the Kildonan movement; I now produce the return of the elections; I was re-elected; there were twelve chosen for the English; do not know if there was a re-election for the French; knew they had twelve; the elections were promised by Donald A Smith, Archbishop Taché and Bishop Machray to save Bolton's life; these elections were made with the consent of the Assembly. (His Lordship here asked the witness how the Assembly could give the consent after the Kildonan affair, as he had already stated that the affair had burst it up.)

To Mr. Chapleau.—There was a popular feeling that a new election should take place, because it was considered as the best plan to get out of serious difficulties; Governor McTavish did not oppose the meeting of the Assembly; knew that he was very ill at that time; it was publicly known that Donald A. Smith was a Commissioner of the Canadian Government; Donald A. Smith was then also one of the officers of the Hudson's Bay Company; I think he was living at the house of Governor McTavish, and was in communication with him; the Conventions were public proceedings and actions all through; there was never any protests made by the Council of Assiniboia to the sittings of the Legislative Assembly.

Cross-examined by Mr. Cornish.—Think that the object of the elections was to save Bolton's life; assembled after this election on the 9th of March; think the English twelve assembled; could not tell who was from the Portage; resolutions were passed on 9th of March; written resolutions; Archbishop Taché was before the Council on that day; one resolution was an expression of loyalty to the Queen; can't tell how long the session continued; was for some days; can't tell of any other resolution; the expression of loyalty was "part of a resolution;" don't recollect the remainder; this session might have met to meet Archbishop Taché; did not know he had arrived at all; there was a notice sent to me; the session took no action in the matter of Scott's being shot; the powers of President were never defined; Riel was President; never resigned as President of State; never got my pay yet.

Archdeacon John McLean sworn.—Was in this country in 1869 and 1870; was present as last witness stated; assisted D. A. Smith in promoting the elections which took place as stated; I went with D. A. Smith, soon after Bolton was condemned to death, down the Red River, to induce the people to elect representatives; witness here proceeded to give his own experience; one day I received a note from Captain Bolton asking me to come and see him, as he was condemned to be shot and executed that evening at twelve o'clock; that evening I went down and was taken to Captain Bolton's room, which was in the building afterwards known as the prison; I found Captain Bolton handcuffed and ironed on the legs, reclining on a buffalo robe, in the room; he then told me he had been condemned to die; I asked him if he believed it would be carried out; he said he did; I then immediately went and saw Mr. Riel; he told me the man must die; he was very much displeased; I spoke to Mr. Riel on the subject as well as I could, and went back to Captain Bolton and said I was afraid that it was only too true; I then entered into religious conversation with him; I saw Mr. Riel again, and asked his permission to get the material to administer the Holy Communion; this was done; Captain Bolton gave me an account of the transactions, and his last message to his family; he wrote on a bit of envelope that he had, what his position with the Portage movement was; as the time drew near I was very deeply distressed, more in fact than he was, as he had shown great Christian fortitude; I went to Mr. Riel and implored him to spare the young man's life, and to postpone the execution till the next day at noon; I went home and Mr. Riel promised he should be safe until I came back; I came back about seven; by this time many leading people had knowledge of the facts, and came and implored Mr. Riel not to execute Captain Bolton; I think, if I remember right, it was again postponed; I then thought that in all probability he would escape; it was at this time that Mr. D. A. Smith took a very active part in endeavoring to save Captain Bolton; during the time I was in the room with Captain Bolton, Riel came in, and burst into tears, and stated in excited tones that he could not help this matter—he was sorry; afterwards he came to the door and knocked at it, and asked me to come out, and said that the Captain's life would be spared; that night I was in Fort Garry until midnight; afterwards I was told that the reason was that Mr. Riel was sending some men down the river, and he did not want me to get out until the men were off; this enabled me to hear a conversation between Mr. Donald A. Smith and Mr. Riel; Mr. Riel strongly urged Mr. Smith to remember what he had done in saving Captain Bolton's life, and to try and get the English delegates to come up, for he could not answer for the lives of the other prisoners unless they came; this made a great impression on my mind; I had been under serious alarm that blood might be shed, after I had heard the Canadian prisoners express themselves very much; I should have done it had I been in their places, and I tried all I could to keep them quiet; I was afraid of conflict between them and the guard; taking all these things into consideration, when Mr. Donald A. Smith called and asked me to accompany him, I thought it was my duty to do so, and I did so; we went down the Red River and were very well received, and we stated to the people that any delegates that might be sent was on account of present distress: we told the people that by and by the Canadian Government would come in and set everything right; one thing I wish to say in justice to Mr. Donald A. Smith, he repeated what I said about the Canadian Government coming in, and made it stronger than what I did; we came back to Fort Garry and went into the rooms of the prisoners; I addressed them and spoke to them of the danger of us all, and they unanimously voted that I should go with Donald A. Smith; all held up their hands; we went up the Assiniboine and found that the parishes had elected their Delegates before we went; at the first address I made to the prisoners, there were two or three who did not hold up their hands, and I told them that if they did not so, I would have nothing to do with it; then they all did so; I told the prisoners that I thought they were in danger of their lives, and it was very probable that it might have influenced them; I must say this in justice to the prisoners.

To Mr. Royal —Had very often visited the Fort; had to make a request to Riel personally to see the prisoners; used to see Governor McTavish—he was sick, and attended him; one of the nights I was with Captain Bolton, Mr. Riel asked me if I would take something to eat; had been from home all day and was much fatigued; was brought into a room in the Fort and had some supper there; there were two persons there, but do not recollect them; Mr. Riel was there and treated me with civility all the time I was in the Fort; I am not very sure of seeing the prisoner; Mr. Riel appeared to control everything; he certainly controlled me at all events; he never allowed me to go in to the prisoners without an interpreter; he told me I was only to pray, and I was not to read any part of the Scriptures, or I should be sure to talk politics to them; I went to Governor McTavish's without getting permission of the guard; am not sure if there was any guard stopped me from seeing Governor McTavish or not; think there was a guard, but do not think it gave me any trouble; for the greater part of the time, I was almost refused permission to see the prisoners, but after Captain Bolton's case there was hardly any difficulty at all.

Hon. A. G. B. Bannatyne sworn.—Was in the Province during the latter part of 1869-70; was a member of the Provisional Government; was elected a delegate by the people of Winnipeg and St. John's on the 19th of February; I was nominated by that Convention as Postmaster; was brother-in-law to the late Governor McTavish; remember the meeting on the 16th, of members of the Delegates sent to Fort Garry object of that meeting was to take into consideration the state of the country; the authorities were not notified that Colonel Dennis was getting up a party to admit McDougall; I am not positive that the

Bill of Rights was accepted or not ; they sat for several days ;[the Governor and Council of Assiniboia advised Governor McDougall to remain where he was for the present, owing to the unsettled state of the country ; there was a reply.

(The letter was here read in full.)

Was then a member of the Council ; was not a member of the Convention ; saw the original of the letter to Governor McDougall from the Governor and Council of Assiniboia, sent on the 30th October ; an answer was received by Colonel Dennis ; there was also a report by Colonel Dennis since he came into the country, and which stated the hopelessness of getting the old settlers to help him to the country ; a meeting was held after the letter was sent, and a Bill of Rights adopted ; there was a counter-movement made by Colonel Dennis, Dr. Schultz and others, principally strangers ; it was kept quiet for a while ; it was afterwards an armed movement, not authorized by the Hudson Bay Company or the Council of Assiniboia ; they armed men in Lower Fort Garry ; excited the Indians to rise and join against the old settlers ; there was a party who were armed in Dr. Schultz's ostensibly to protect private property, but I have Colonel Dennis' own letter to show that he did not consider it in danger; believe that it was fterwards taken by the Provisional Government; Colonel Dennis issued a proclamation on the 4th of November ; Snow and McArthur met the French party to ask them to leave the house of Dr. Schultz, which was surrounded by armed men led by Riel ; on the 1st of December, Colonel Dennis brought into the settlement a proclamation purporting to be from Governor McDougall ; that proclamation was doubted ; then there were proclamations issued by Colonel Dennis to kill and burn down houses, and slaughter, and conserve the peace ; there was another proclamation about that time by Riel ; proclamations at that time were very numerous ; the Bill of Rights was assented to.

(The witness here stated that he had the authority of Colonel Dennis in writing to say that his proclamation was not legal.)

The day on which it was issued, the prisoners were taken at Dr. Schultz's house ; the Schultz party did not apply to the Governor in Council for assistance ; we considered ourselves wiped out of existence after the proclamation was issued ; the Governor in Council did nothing afterwards until late in the summer ; up to the arrival of the troops,the only Government was the Provisional Government ; on the 19th of January, there was a mass meeting ; on the 25th there was a Convention ; think there were twelve from each side appointed ; they were requested to meet to make known to the Commissioners the wants of the people ; met again on the 26th of January; it was at the meeting of the 19th of January that Riel, Richot and others spoke ; the mass of the people at that meeting was favorable ; for some days the delegates met ; they requested Mr. Smith to be with them ; said it would be better to frame their Bill of Rights themselves, and then they could send the deputation to Ottawa ; Mr. Smith also handed in his papers and commission from the Canadian Government ; Judge Black was elected Secretary, and Riel was elected President about the latter part of February; protests were made against my own election ; the present Bishop of Saskatchewan was chairman of the meeting ; was styled a member to serve in the Council Board in the Provisional Government ; the Council sat and passed laws and made public works without protest ; the Council met in February and adjourned till March after Bishop Taché's arrival ; public Bills were passed by the Assembly.

WEDNESDAY, Oct. 21.

A. G. B. Bannatyne—cross-examination by Mr. Cornish.—I suppose the persons I spoke of were British subjects ; it was understood that Colonel Dennis was a surveyor and head of the surveying party said to have been sent by the Dominion Government ; this afterwards became an armed movement; at first it was quiet ; it became an armed movement when they enlisted men at the Stone Fort ; this was you may say a counter-movement to another armed movement ; would not be positive which movement was organized first ; in the fall of that year there was considerable talk among the French to get up a movement to keep McDougall out; about this time, Colonel Dennis commenced going around among the English settlers, to see whether they would unite with him and bring in Governor McDougall, should the French party oppose him by force ; at this time I do not remember any assemblage of persons at Stinking River ; at this time there was no barricade on the road between Pembina and Winnipeg ; there was a difficulty about the surveys, and immediately after this, Colonel Dennis commenced getting up his force ; I have nothing by me to refresh my memory as to dates except the official documents ; Lusted, I think, was a resident of the country ; Schultz also; Franklin was an old settler ; Mulligan was an old settler; Franklin was taken prisoner at Schultz's ; Drever joined the counter-movement and was also an old settler ; the others also joined the counter-movement ; cannot tell who were the strangers ; recollect Dr. Lynch, Mr. Farmer, Dr. O'Donnell, Bubar, Chisholm, and could recollect others if I had time ; they were strangers in the sense that they had not been in the country for very long ; the movement was, I believe, to prevent McDougall coming in, not to prevent the surveys ; was not a member of the Convention when Riel was elected ; was appointed a member of the Provisional Government ; we had no law ; the only law was swept away by McDougall ; this Government was got up to save anarchy and strife while arrangements could be made with England or Canada ; Judge Black sat as a Delegate on that Convention, and he was Judge of the land at that time ; I went to Scotland in June to bring my family back, and returned early in the fall ; am a native of the North of Scotland ; at the time of the publication of the *New Nation*, and the first issue was coming out, it was altogether American ; I heard from Riel that he would never work for annexation to the States ; I saw Mr. Coldwell, who was connected with the paper, and told him that Mr. Riel had told me that the next issue would be stronger than the previous one, but that it would be the last ; Mr. Coldwell said if he could do that he was an abler man than he believed him ; immediately after the editor was put out of place, and another editor put in, and the tone of the paper was changed ; Riel said he was willing to take assistance from all quarters, but as soon as he was strong enough he would repudiate the American element ; Mr. Robinson was the responsible editor, and said he was both proprietor and editor ; Mr. Coldwell was hired by the day's wages ; know that Stutzman came down from Pembina about this time, and shortly after was sent away by Riel on short notice ; was frequently at the Fort when Riel was there ; was not there on the 4th March ; had heard of what was to take place, but did not go down ; during my visits to the Fort have seen Lepine ; Lepine seemed to be one of the party, and was appointed by the Convention of the 25th January, by both English and French, as Adjutant-General, and acted as such in the Fort ; am not aware of what became of Scott's body ; never had any conversation with Riel on the subject of the disposal of Scott's body.

To His Lordship —I did all I could to prevent the execution taking place ; the Fort was closed on the night of 3rd of March.

Charles Nolin sworn.—Reside at Pointe de Chêne ; was born in the Province ; was in the Province in 1869 and 1870 ; know perfectly well when Thomas Scott was said to have been shot ; unhappily I did not know him under favorable circumstances ; first became acquainted with Scott in the month of August, 1869 ; Scott was working on the Dawson Road ; he was a laborer on the road ; one day the laborers were at work, Scott was at work in the bush ; he appeared not to like the eatables that were given him ; he objected to the food furnished ; witness was certain it was good, as witness furnished it himself ; Scott and fifteen men revolted against the Superintendent of the Government works, Mr. Snow, and Scott was the leader of the fifteen men ; to the best of witness' 'knowledged, they struck work for three days; know that I need good provision, beef, and sometimes tea and sugar; might have happened that provisions were badly cooked; what I mean by revolted is they struck work; the men came over to the office, seventeen miles from where they struck work, with a flag, and wanted to be paid for the time they had worked, and the time they had struck work; Mr. Snow was willing to pay them for the time they had worked, but not for the time they had struck work; Scott and the men wanted to get the pay by force; knew Scott; the other fifteen were all strangers in the country; Snow was also a stranger.

His Lordship stated that he would stop this evidence, as it appeared to be merely a little difficulty amongst strangers.

Witness continued.—Saw Scott at the time of the troubles, and I arrested him and made him a prisoner in the Ferry-boat; I did this on the authority of the Hudson Bay Company; this was the latter end of August. (This was ruled out by the Judge.)

Witness was at the Fort when Riel was elected President; was representative from Pointe de Chêne; had been elected by the electors of Pointe de Chêne; there were forty-eight members, twenty-four French and twenty-four English; was present all the time; there was only one member who would not vote, that was Mr. Boyd; everyone else voted for Riel; believe Mr. Boyd's constituents had told him not to vote for Riel; do not think Boyd was personally opposed to Riel; was not at the Fort on the 4th of March when Scott was shot, but came there towards the evening.

Cross-examined by Mr. Cornish.—Personally Mr. Boyd did not object to Mr. Riel being elected; there was a good deal of discussion over the matter, as to whether the Hudson's Bay Company still existed, before they elected Riel as President; four were sent to ascertain this—Lepine, John Frazer, John Sutherland and Xavier Pagé—and report; after they had come back and reported, I think Judge Black withdrew; after Riel was elected, he vacated his seat as President, but remained in the Convention; the vote was not taken before receiving a report from the four messengers; after Riel's election there was some speaking, and Mr. Frazer rose and said, " This is no more a Convention, as we have elected a President ;" then Judge Black rose and vacated his seat as Chairman, and Riel took it as President; think that the country was well represented at the time of Riel's election; cannot say the number of people that were present; am pretty well satisfied that the great majority of the English Delegates were present; cannot say if Taylor, of Headingly, was there, but think he was; the votes were taken by a Secretary, and every one used to rise and give his vote; the Secretary wrote the proceedings of the Convention; know Taylor, of Headingly; if Taylor did not vote for Riel, he did not object to him, as I think; the Chairman took the motion for the election of Riel as President; each member rose and voted " Yay " or " Nay," and as he did so his name and vote was recorded on ordinary foolscap paper; Mr. Taylor came afterwards and did not object to Riel; cannot say if Taylor voted or not; the Bill of Rights was under consideration at the time; on the road to the Fort, heard of Scott's execution; was in the Fort about a fortnight previous.

Xavier Pagé sworn.—Remember the election of Riel as President; it was about the beginning of February; was a member of the Convention for the parish of St. Francis East; think every one voted for Riel, with the exception of Mr. Boyd, who did not; do not think Mr. Taylor was present when the vote was taken; some of the English members were afraid of doing something that was not right, so they proposed to send to Governor McTavish; Mr. John Sutherland proposed to send the deputation, and asked to go himself; the four were: the prisoner and witness, John Sutherland and John Frazer; went and saw Governor McTavish; there were no soldiers on guard at the door; Governor McTavish offered the party seats; Mr. Sutherland said they would not be long, only came to get some information from Governor McTavish;

Governor McTavish enquired what it was, and Mr. Sutherland asked him if the Government of Assiniboia was in existence or not; Governor McTavish said, "No!" Then Sutherland said, " Would it not be advisable to establish a Provisional Government?" The Governor said, " Not only it is necessary, but for God's sake establish one; we shall have no peace in the country until one is established;" Sutherland or Frazer asked Governor McTavish, "And your power as Governor?" he said, "Leave me alone, I am a dead man; you work for the people;" nothing else was said, but bade the Governor good evening, and he saluted us in return, and we left: witness and the other three returned to the Convention-room; the two English representatives, Frazer and Sutherland, explained to the Assembly the result of their mission; there was no excitement about the report in the Convention, and we thereupon decided to elect a President, a Provisional Government being spoken of, but I cannot say any subsequent resolution was passed to that effect, and Riel was then elected as President of the Provisional Government; I understood by what was then done that a Provisional Government was then established with Riel at its head.

To Mr. Cornish.—When we went to Mr. McTavish's, Mr. Sutherland spoke in English; witness understood English sufficiently to know the words; was not at the Fort on the 4th March; was not present at the shooting of Scott at all; knew there were prisoners in the Fort on the 10th February; at the time of the establishment of the Provisional Government, the English asked them to release the prisoners; we said, " We are now strong and united, and these people could do us no harm," so advised to let them go; this was after Riel's election that it was spoken of; it was spoken of before also; they had kept the prisoners, as they were afraid they might raise trouble if refused; it had never been spoken of publicly before this, only privately; I mean privately among the members of the Convention; it was not stated privately among the Convention that if they agreed on the election of a President, that then the prisoners might be released; do not recollect having heard this mention; it was only talked among ourselves; some said if they were released there would be some disturbance, and they generally all agreed.

Narcisse Marion sworn.—Resides at St. Boniface; knows the prisoner Lepine well; saw Scott when he was shot; was present when some guns were fired on the 4th March; was about a hundred yards from the place the firing party were; I was with another man named Andrew Anderson; I was coming from the town when I passed near the Fort; was told it was Scott when he was shot; cannot say who composed the firing party; was too far to notice the men; did not notice who gave the signal to fire; saw a man carrying a sort of a white flag; don't know who it was; am sure it was not the prisoner; it was a man of middle size; on that day did not see the prisoner Lepine; think I should have noticed him if he had been there; I then returned home; saw a man falling and some one moving, as I understood to finish him, but did not stay; I walked off on my way and did not recognize who this person was; I did not enter the Fort.

Cross-examined by Mr. Cornish.—Was about hundred yards from Scott when the guns went off; was beckoned to go on one side and keep clear, (witness here pointed out his exact position on the plan of the Fort which had been used for the purpose during the trial); noticed a man by the name of Deschamps, because he was drunk and tumbling about; after the shooting, passed right straight along and took no further notice of what took place; to the best of my knowledge, I counted six men in the firing party; did not notice a man named Guilmette in the firing party; do not know Guilmette; did not notice André Nault; know André Nault; know Rev Mr. Young; did not see Rev. Mr. Young there; know Elzear Goulet; did not see Elzéar Goulet there; know Riel very well; did not see Riel there; know O'Donohue; did not see O'Donohue there; there were a good many people there; they were from all directions, from up the river, and down the river, and from all places; had heard before I came over, that morning, that Scott was to be shot; is was a rumor; do not remember who told me; lived about twenty chains south of St. Boniface Cathedral; am a blacksmith; could not say where I heard the rumour; was not near enough to see if Scott was dead; the man who had the white flag witness saw him bringing it down, (witness here motioned in imitation of the act); when it was brought down the guns were fired instantaneously; thought afterwards that this was a signal for the firing of the guns; the guns were fired, the man fell, and then I thought that it must have been a signal.

Michel Dumas sworn.—Know Lepine, have known him for many years; have always known him to be a man of good character, and of peaceable disposition; on the 4th March, 1870, was in Winnipeg; was present at what was called the execution of Scott; was not there when Scott came out of the Fort; saw Scott when he came out of the building that served as a prison, inside of the Fort; saw him coming down the stairs outside of the building; Scott had a white cloth on his head; was in the house when I saw him pass; was in John McTavish's house; saw Scott through the window, and saw him till he reached Dr. Cowan's house, and afterwards saw him when he came in sight again to the corner of the house in which witness was; went out to see him again, but could not see him on account of the crowd; I saw two men leading Scott as I took it, walking on each side of him, and I am sure neither of those two men were the prisoner; I then followed the crowd that was going out, and saw when the guns were fired; when I proceeded to go out of the gate, and so I reached the small gate, there was such a crowd there that I could not get out; I did not stand there; there were a few others with me that could not see, so we got an old sleigh that was there and placed it against the wall, and by means of this we got on the wall; as we reached the top of the wall, we heard the report of the guns; immediately after the discharge of the guns, heard a man shout; this shout resembled the cry of a person who had been struck; among the crowd of people who were there, heard a man say, "Didn't you promise me to finish him;" as he was saying these words, the crowd got thinner, and he heard a man answer, "Yes;" then saw a man whom I knew to be Guilmette, firing at the man Scott with a pistol; it appeared to me as if he fired at the head of Scott; witness then came back into the Fort; saw something in the shape of a box lying on two benches, but it did not look at all like a coffin; did not occur to witness what it was for; appeared to be a case that guns are carried in; it was large enough to hold the body of a man; do not know anything else relating to Scott or what became of his body; if the prisoner Lepine had been near the body of Scott, or near there, would have known him as well as if it had been witness' own father; Lepine was not there when I was on the wall.

To Mr. Cornish.—I know Francis Charette; did not pay attention whether I saw him there; on the spot did not see him, but did see him afterward; the prisoner is not a neighbour of mine, neither are the Charettes; know four Charettes (father and three sons); but do not know them by their names; did not see Charette there; there were plenty more besides witness on the wall; in consequence of the excitement, did not notice any one in particular; know Baptiste Charette; did not notice if he was there or not; knew Guilmette; only recognized him as being near the body; it was Guilmette who said, "Will you promise me to finish him?" and some one whom I did not know said in answer, "Yes;" when Guilmette asked this, the man who answered was at a distance in the crowd; Guilmette wore other clothes than those generally worn; did not see Auguste Parisien there; was so troubled and excited that I did not notice even who were the two persons next to me on the wall; was soldier in the Fort; knew Scott by sight; had seen him two or three times; knew that Scott was a prisoner; heard it after Scott had been made a prisoner; heard from people that were moving about the Fort, that Scott was to be shot; it was not stated what Scott was going to be shot for; do not know if there was any meeting in the Fort the morning Scott was shot ; do not know if there was any preaching ; if anybody preached, the witness was not present ; do not recollect seeing the prisoner that morning in the Fort ; did not see Riel ; witness endeavoured to see some of the leaders to get permission to go home, but could not find any of the leaders, so was obliged to stay in the Fort ; did not go to the officers in Dr. Cowan's building ; do not know if the prisoner had any other name except Ambroise Lepine ; heard it from this one and that one the term Adjutant-General, but did not know that it referred to Lepine ; thought it was one of the leaders they referred to, but did not know who ; always addressed him as Mr. Lepine, and Riel as Mr. Riel ; was soldiering in the Fort about two months ; left the Fort quick, and after leaving it did not go near the Fort for two months.

Rev. Father Richot.—Am Curate of St. Norbert ; have been in the country twelve years last June ; was in the country in 1869 and 1870 ; was absent in the winter of 1869, but in the spring of 1869 was here ; was here in the spring of 1870 ; am aware what movement took place in 1869 in this country ; was not present at the meeting of delegates of the 16th of November, held in the Court House ; was present at the meeting at which D. A. Smith's papers were produced ; do not remember the date ; was present at the meeting of the 19th of January ; John Bunn acted as president, Judge Black acted as secretary ; Mr. Bunn was president for the two days of the meeting, but do not know it ; Mr. Black acted as secretary for the two days ; Mr. Smith represented himself as a delegate from the Dominion of Canada to give communication to the people of certain powers given him ; he said he had not these papers in his possession ; this is about all that transpired on the first day ; many speeches were made, but no official documents were produced ; did not see in the papers any report of this meeting ; the meeting next day was very short ; the meeting opened in the afternoon ; prominent members present proposed that twenty English delegates should come and meet twenty French delegates ; the meeting was very large and agreed unanimously to this proposition ; this was all that was done at that meeting ; was not present when Riel was nominated as President ; was appointed as a delegate jointly with Mr. Scott and Mr. Black as delegates to the Dominion Government ; these three delegates were appointed by the President of the Provisional Government, and the document was signed by Mr. Thomas Bunn, as Secretary to that Government ; the letter produced is a copy of the instructions I received ; also received a document of appointment as delegate ; never understood that the convention formed part of the Provisional Government ; understood that the Council of Assembly was composed of a number of members elected by the people, and that the President chose his advisers ; date of the letter of instructions is the 22nd of March, 1870 ; the delegates were also bearers of a list of demands ; the delegates left immediately for Ottawa. The witness then gave an account of the delegates' visit to Ottawa, and was stating the time that Sir John A. Macdonald commenced to negotiate officially, and his conversations, when His Lordship objected, saying he could not go into any discussions that took place between Sir John A. Macdonald, Sir Geo. E. Cartier and the Delegates, but would allow any official documents to be read.

Mr. Chapleau urged that the conversations should be taken as evidence, but His Lordship decided they should not, and at Mr. Chapleau's request filed the same.

The Court was then adjourned until 10 the following morning.

THURSDAY, Oct. 22nd.

Father Richot's deposition continued.— Witness knew as a fact that the Provisional Government was composed of the President and a certain number of special advisers who were elected from the members chosen from the people ;

do not know how the special advisors were taken; only know that they were taken, but do not know by what process; according to my understanding the Government consisted of the President (Riel) and his Councillors, who I know were certain persons chosen to advise with and consult on the affairs of the country; this Council was composed of Francis Dauphinais A. Lepine, Thos. Bunn, André Nault and some others, whose names I do not now recall to mind; always understood that I and the other delegates were appointed by the President of the Provisional Government; witness here produced an appointment, dated February 12th, 1870, "By nomination of the President of the North-West Territories, as a Delegate to the Government of the Dominion of Canada, jointly with Mr. Black and Mr. Scott;" witness also produced the French copy of the Bill of Rights; I do not know if they were printed as part of the proceedings of the House; the Manitoba Act comprised the substance of the Bill of Rights; the Bill of Rights was then read to the Court, and the witness stated that the English version was delivered to the authorities at Ottawa by the Delegates; I now look at a copy of a letter written by me to His Excellency Lord Lisgar, dated 20th April, 1870, at Ottawa, and also at His Lordship's reply; I wrote the letter and received the reply; the reply is dated 22nd April, 1870; the Manitoba Act was mostly framed according to the Bill of Rights; I asked for the whole of the articles of the Bill of Rights, in my capacity as Delegate; witness produced a copy of a letter which he addressed to Sir Geo. E. Cartier, dated 18th May, 1870; these documents were fyled; the negotiations commenced from 26th April and were continued until the last part of May; they were not put an end to and have continued since, and are still in continuation, as the promise, or demands, have not all been granted.

Mr. Chapleau.—Have you in your possession any official communications from the Canadian Government or any member of it, as to the course the Provisional Government should pursue in the interval of the military forces entering into the North-West Territory?

Witness.—Have no written official documents to that effect; all that I received was only verbally from Sir Geo. E. Cartier and Sir John Young, now Lord Lisgar; I made a written report of my mission to Ottawa to the Provisional Government on the 24th June; on my return from Ottawa I found the whole population quiet, and there was no disturbance; the same provisional manner of conducting business was as when I left for Ottawa, and it continued in this way until the arrival of Colonel Wolseley, which was some time in August. (Letter from Thomas Bunn to witness read, requesting him to make a report of his mission to the Provisional Government.) The reason the three delegates were chosen was to represent the whole community, Mr. Black as a Scotchman, Mr. Scott as an English, and Father Richot for the French; witness knows, since his return, that Lepine and Riel and some others, have been in actual correspondence with the Canadian authorities here in this country, viz., the Lieutenant-Governor of this Province.

Mr. Chapleau proposed to produce these letters. His Lordship refused to prove them.

Witness.—Was well acquainted with the members of the Council of Assiniboia, and also the late Governor McTavish; had an interview with him; asked him if the Government of Assiniboia existed; the Governor looked somewhat embarrassed, and said he preferred not to give an answer; this was all that was said on this subject; witness said to the Governor, "If you give me no reply, I can make no report;" witness remained about an hour there; the Governor kept himself on his guard, but was forced to admit that the affairs of the country were in a strange state; the Governor was well this day; had been ill previously; this interview took place between the 27th and 30th of October; had another conversation about the beginning of December with the Governor about the subject of the proclamation of Governor McDougall, which Governor McTavish complained of from the beginning, and declared himself completely powerless to remedy the evils of the country; I had a knowledge of the whole commotion of the colony and also of the beginning of the commotion; this was because of the great dissatisfaction of the population here on account of the conduct of the first employees of the Canadian Government; their orders appeared not to be specific enough to appease the people as to their intentions; I think that nobody in the country knew what these surveyors had come here for; nothing was explained to me.

To His Lordship.—Never asked Governor McTavish about the surveyors and their power; know as a fact that some of the surveyors were working on the property of some of the settlers here, and were brought before the authorities here, and the authorities decided that the surveyors had no right to do this; I understand this was tried before Dr. Cowan and some members of the Assiniboia Council; have always known the prisoner as a man of a very peaceful temper, and although of great physical strength, he has never abused anybody.

Cross-examined by Mr. Cornish.—Was not at the Fort frequently before the month of March, only some times; heard of the shooting of Scott on the 20th of March; about the beginning of March, heard of the rumour in St. Norbert, from a neighbour; went to the Fort when it was a question of Captain Bolton's affair; do not know what time it was; do not think I was at the Fort since then and Scott's affair; Mr. Riel visited witness seldom : in October, there were many meetings in St. Norbert, and in the beginning of November the people had a meeting; witness addressed the people at certain meetings; the object of those meetings at St. Norbert was concerning the arrival of Governor McDougall, and the people accompanying him, as I understood; was not at the first meeting; addressed the people on occasions; Riel was present at the general meeting, and was not at some of the other meetings; I told the meeting what duty and prudence advised me to say of the danger they incurred, but did not lay down any law or rule to them; do not consider myself obliged to answer the question as to whether I had advised the people to let the Canadian party come in peacefully; did not give such advice; there was a party assembled from the 20th to the 22nd of October on the road; do not believe they were armed; do not know if those that took the Fort were armed; after the 20th of October, many had guns; do not know if there were any men at Scratching River guarding the road; during the autumn of the year the guards were distributed through different parts of the country; there was an armed guard at Stinking River, and saw a fence put across the road; I should say there were about hundred men there, some few having guns in their hands; some persons were stopped, two turned back, and some permitted to go on; some carts were stopped; I am not aware that any carts containing goods said to belong to the Canadian Government, were stopped; there were some goods going to Winnipeg in carts; they were stopped and taken on my property; there were about twenty carts stopped; have no knowledge of any of Schultz's goods being taken on the road; know nothing of it personally; part of the party left beginning of November, and the others in the latter part of it; they came to Fort Garry, and I suppose they got into the Fort; did not follow them.

Paul Proulx sworn.—Know the prisoner at the bar; was in the Fort on the 4th of March; saw a man (which was said to be Scott) going out of the house where it was stated the prisoners were kept; saw him going towards the gate and out of the gate; had something white round his head; was accompanied by two or three men, one of whom was Rev. Mr. Young; quite positive that the prisoner was not one of the men who accompanied Scott; saw the firing party firing; know two of them, Guilmette and Parisien; at that time was not excited and looked on quietly, and am sure Lepine was not near the party firing; know the prisoner for fourteen years; his reputation was that of a good and quiet man.

Cross-examined by Mr. Cornish.—Was standing at the door of Dr. Cowan's house facing the small gate of the Fort, when I saw the man they called Scott;

pass by me as he was going to the gate; when Scott had passed, I followed; saw Scott stop on the road, about the length of the Court-room; was moved from this place to another; cannot say who moved him; when Scott was moved, the firing party stood near the gate in a line with me; after Scott was moved, did not see the firing party change their position; did not see any person with a white handkerchief in his hand; did not hear any word of command given to fire; did not see any signal given to fire; after the firing, Scott fell on one side and leaned on his right shoulder; did not observe if Scott had his hands tied behind him; did not see any one firing with a pistol after the volley; after Scott fell, did not move up to the body; was standing about the length of the Court-room from Scott; do not know what was done with the body; I saw a box outside of the Fort, near the wall of the Fort; did not see it moved from there; it was a large box made of rough boards; I sometimes was a soldier in the Fort, and sometimes not; I mean sometimes acted as guard; when I wanted to mount guard, I did; had no Captain; was not an officer; was in the Fort altogether more than two months; did not see Lepine at all that day; saw Riel in the evening; did not hear any one say, "All that are here go into the Fort;" saw O'Donohue that day, in the morning, inside the Fort; know André Nault; saw André Nault inside the Fort, about five o'clock in the morning; he came to my room; know Francis Charette and also Baptiste Charette; did not see any persons that day inside the Fort that I now mention, except Rev. Mr. Young and Guilmette; do not recollect seeing Goulet.

Hon. John Sutherland sworn.—Was one of the Delegates of the Convention of the 19th of January, 1870; was one of a deputation that went to see Governor McTavish; Mr. John Frazer was the other one; know Mr. Pagé and the prisoner at the bar; the delegation was to enquire if Governor McTavish was Governor, or continued the Government of the country; either myself or Mr. Frazer spoke to Governor McTavish; do not recollect very well; we went by the consent of the Convention; our question was in this sense, " Was Governor McTavish still Governor of the country, and would he continue it;" the answer was, " Form some Government for God's sake, I have no power or authority;" this is the only answer, to the best of my recollection, that we got; the prisoner was with us; he came as I understood to conduct us; probably Pagé might have been; Pagé and the prisoner were members of the Assembly; it was the English members, as I understood, wanted to ascertain the point; a feeling existed that it would be necessary to ascertain if the Government existed, which, as we understood, was the Government of the country, and did not like the idea of establishment of any Government opposed to that of the Hudson's Bay Company or of Governor McTavish.

Cross-examined by Mr. Cornish.—It was discussed as to the propriety of forming any other Government to that of the established one of Governor McTavish and the Hudson's Bay Company; it was discussed among the English members outside of the Assembly; one special reason for myself going to the Convention was on account of the country being in a very troubled state, and we were sent there by the people, to meet from all parts and to come to some understanding for the public good; do not recollect for what purpose the mass meeting was assembled; the Convention, if I recollect well, was in the latter part of January, or early in February; saw some difficulty about the producing of Mr. Smith's documents; was not present when Riel was elected as President; there were some armed guards came in on the day before when the subject was spoken of; about this time a guard was put over Governor McTavish's; I understood the prisoner went with me to Governor McTavish's to get access to the room; the door was guarded; Governor McTavish was very weak indeed at this time; think the expression, "I am a dying man," was an addition to the reply; think he referred to his bodily power as being such that he had no physical power left in connection with his want of civil power; heard that Donald A. Smith was a prisoner at that time, but could not say if he was; could not say if the prisoner had any special authority or not; he was said to be Adjutant-General, as I heard it; never saw him exercise any authority over any military force.

To Mr. Chapleau.—This Convention was sitting a day or two days at farthest, if I recollect, after our visit to Governor McTavish; know nothing about the second Convention to my own personal knowledge.

Modeste Lajemonière sworn.—Know the report that Thomas Scott was executed; know Lepine well; it was not the prisoner who was with Scott as he was coming out of the gate; Elzéar Goulet and Mr. Young were accompanying Scott at the time, to the best of my recollection; was one of the party who carried the box into the Fort; do not know what it contained; it was taken in by the order of Goulet; two men carried in the box; do not know the other man's name; we were the only two; the box was put near the bastion; I was put as a guard to prevent people coming near; as I was on guard and unarmed, a man named Hupe came near against my will and went to the box; witness carried the box, and while I carried it, and while on guard did not see any blood coming from the box, and did not see any blood on the snow at the place where we took the box; do not know if the box was taken from the place where I guarded it and put into the bastion; from personal reasons, can say most positively that the prisoner did not give the signal or command the men to fire.

Cross-examined by Mr. Cornish.—At that time had been in and about the Fort quite a while; should say about six weeks; was Riel's servant; did not mount guard at all; did not know a Captain in the Fort named Lajemonière; was standing at the attic window of Riel's house when Scott went out that morning, and I saw him go out; looked at him as long as I could through the window; from where I was could not see the gate of the Fort; Captain Gray was with witness; was talking to Captain Gray and saw somebody else behind; this was after Scott had passed; Mr. Riel was behind witness; Lepine was also behind witness; I went up there to see Scott brought out; do not know if Riel or Lepine came up there to see Scott, or whether Gray went there for that purpose; nothing was said to my knowledge, while we were there, by any of the party, except I heard Mr. Riel or Lepine say, "It is then God's truth, they are really taking him down;" heard nothing else said.

His Lordship.—Did they rush out to stop them from taking him down?

Witness.—I left before they did; I was nearer the door; I passed and went down-stairs first; I mean I left Riel, the prisoner and Gray there; I went then to the south gate; saw only the guard that was stationed there; remained there about four or five minutes; heard no firing when I was at the gate, or on that day; I thought that everything was over, and advanced towards the east gate; went out of the gate and saw a box; about twenty-five or thirty yards distance; think I saw one man standing near the box and another one nailing it; did not go to the box then, but turned back; saw a good many people around; no one could have passed through the gate without my observing it; I turned back and walked a few steps; I then stopped and spoke to Elzéar Goulet; Elzéar Goulet said, "Shall we not find a man to take in that coffin?" witness said, "I can take it in through charity," and ran to the box and took hold of it; do not know if anything was in the box; ran to the box and said, "Let us take it in;" to the best of my knowledge, think it was Guimette who assisted me to carry it in; did not notice if any one followed us; did not see Lepine and Riel up to this time since I left them in the room; did not calculate the time it took me to come down from the room; went to the large gate, and stayed there four or five minutes, and then came to the small gate; when Hupe passed me as I was guarding the box, I was about twenty-five paces from the box; Hupe stopped at the box; saw Hupe coming near the box, and put one knee on the ground and kneel against the box; Hupe was at the box long enough to listen well, and then turned back and passed me into the court-yard, and I lost sight of him; this was before dark; about this time heard Riel calling to the people inside of the Fort to come in; Riel was up-stairs at the attic window. Riel said to the people, "Fall in by ten;" this was done inside of the Fort; as I came near to the people, I saw Lepine; Lepine was walking about through the ranks, and speaking with his brother; Lepine had no command at that time, for Riel was commanding.

To Mr. Chapleau.—Riel collected them to make a speech; Lepine, while he was talking to his brother, was leaning against the house; Lepine was listening to what was said while Riel was speaking.

Atalance Hupe sworn.—Know about the shooting of Scott; have seen a box being brought into the Fort by two men; the box was near the bastion; about three-quarters of an hour after the box was put there, I came from the mess-room; while I was in the mess-room some one came in and said, "We hear some talking inside of the box;" witness then went outside to the box near the bastion; it was in the same place I had first seen it; Modeste Lajemonière was there as a guard; I leaned one knee on the ground and leaned over the box, and heard a voice inside distinctly articulate, "I say, I say;" the wood of the box was not quite joined; a man of the guard came to the witness and sent him off; I might have said to Lajemonière some one was speaking in the box; know I have said it to several persons; do not know how the box was disposed of; did not see it afterwards; know that a grave was dug in front of Dr. Cowan's house, but do not know if the box was put in.

To Mr. Cornish.—Saw the shooting of Scott; did not see Scott taken out of the gate; saw a man kneeling by the roadside; they fired at him, and the man fell; went up and looked at him, but saw no blood or nothing else; his hands were tied behind his back; he fell on his side; saw a person about him with a pistol; a Canadian named Guilmette; Guilmette was very drunk; could not see exactly, but think he shot him through the head; the body did not make any motion when the pistol shot went off; it lay still; immediately went into the Fort; do not know who ordered us to go in; some one was crying out, "Go in, go in;" who cried out I do not know; did not know any of the parties immediately about there; saw Riel that day; saw Riel in his house in the attic room when he was making a speech; did not see Riel at the time of the shooting; saw Riel several times that day in his quarters at Dr. Cowan's house, and passing in and out; did not see Lepine all that day; do not recollect having done so.

To His Lordship.—Did not know who the firing party were.

To Mr. Cornish.—Did not see André Nault there; saw Elzéar Goulet, but did not see him outside the gate.

To His Lordship.—Do not recollect seeing any one in particular, except Guilmette, at the time Scott was shot; all of our people were there, but I recognized no one in particular.

His Lordship.—I understand that this is all the witnesses for the defence, except the Archbishop of St. Boniface.

The Court was accordingly adjourned until the following day at 11 o'clock.

FRIDAY, October 23rd.

Archbishop Taché sworn. — Was here in 1869-70; came here 10th August, twenty-nine years; was a member of the Council of Assiniboia since 1857; the Governor was merely President of the Council of Assiniboia; the members gave their opinions on equal footing, and the measures were passed by the majority; the Governor had no veto right; this right was exercised by the Governor and Hudson's Bay Company in England; the measures took effect from the moment they were proclaimed; the nominations and appointments were made by a majority of votes; although the President, the Governor took part in the deliberations of the Council. Witness was here asked who were the members of the Council of Assiniboia at the time of his departure in June : Bishop of Rupert's Land, John Black, John Frazer, John Sutherland, Dr. Bird, Boyd, Bannatyne, Thomas Bunn, Dr. Cowan, Solomon Hamlin, Paschal Breland, Emileon Genton, William Dease, Roger Goulet, and the witness, James McKay; these are all I remember; the meetings were not at stated times ; at the time of the departure of the witness, there was no question of any political changes; the members of the Council of Assiniboia were not notified of any political changes ; was acquainted with Governor McTavish ; he was in the colony at the time of my departure for Rome ; I came back to the Province on the 9th March, 1870 ; I returned to the Province at the request of the Ottawa Government from Rome ; the demand of the Government was on account of the troubles that had taken place during my absence ; at the time of my departure for Rome, the difficulties were foreseen, but had not taken a definite form ; it was because I had foreseen these difficulties that I had proceeded to Canada in the month of June, so as to put the Canadian authorities on their guard ; they did not pay any attention to the representations I felt it my duty to make ; when in Canada, I received a letter from Governor McTavish ; before my departure for Canada, I had several conversations with Governor McTavish on the subject ; at the same time that I went to Canada, I was on my way to Rome ; the letter of Governor McTavish to the witness was published in the Report of the Committee of the North-West ; the letter was dated 4th September, 1869 ; I copied that part of the letter which referred to the troubles, and sent it to Sir George Cartier ; Sir George Cartier replied that he had provided for everything, and the next day, I read in the Ottawa papers that arms and ammunition were being forwarded to Governor McDougall ; I returned from Rome at the request of the Canadian Government ; on my arrival at Ottawa, I was immediately introduced to the Privy Council then sitting ; they informed me as to the condition of affairs at Red River ; the witness' opinion is corroborative of this, because when he had anything to do with the Government, I was always referred to Sir John A. Macdonald and Sir George E. Cartier; the time I had interview with Sir John A. Macdonald, he handed me a letter which stated that the letter I received from Mr. Howe was official ; with the exception of a letter from Mr. Howe, dated 4th December, to Vicar-General Thibault, the rest are published in the North-West Committee's report ; witness here produced a letter from Sir John A. Macdonald dated 6th December, marked private; the Government of Ottawa requested me above all to put myself in communication with the leaders of the movement, and I did so upon my arrival ; they also requested me to communicate with Mr. McTavish, Mr. Salaberry, Father Thibault and Mr. Smith ; I saw Rev. Mr. Thibault at once ; I saw Mr. Smith, who was about to depart for Canada and who said he did not want anything more to do with the matter ; I communicated several times with Mr McTavish, ex-Governor ; on the 8th March I received a letter from Governor McTavish, which I can produce, in which he speaks of a proposed loan; during the intercourse with Governor McTavish that I had, I came to the conclusion that the letter was written on the full possession of his mental vigour and faculties, and that he was not biased by bodily fear or otherwise ; am satisfied that his bodily sickness did not affect his intellect—that the letter I have produced was written of his own free will ; that he was not forced to write it ; he repeatedly expressed to me his satisfaction at having been able to come to that agreement.

To His Lordship —It was expected that the Ottawa Government would pay the debts of the Provisional Government, and I so told Governor McTavish.

(Mr. Chapleau here insisted upon proving and putting in a document purporting to be an agreement for a loan between the Hudson's Bay Company and Governor McTavish.)

On the 1st of May I addressed a letter to the Hon. Mr. Howe ; this letter is published in the Report of the North-West Committee; I received answer to that letter from Mr. Howe; it is also published; I appeared once before the Legislative Assembly of Assiniboia; think it was about the 14th of March; remember the names of some of those who were there; Dr. Bird, Dauphinais, O'Donohue, Lepine, Bannatyne, Bunn, Hay, Spence; those are the only names I remember; this Assembly was presided over by Riel; I appeared before the Assembly at the request of Riel, but I do not know whether it was an official request or not; on my arrival here I heard that the Convention had appointed three Delegates for Ottawa, but it was, however, rumored that they would not go to Ottawa; I believe that the answers were given on account of the political state of the country at the time, and not from any bodily or physical suffering at the time; he was in full possession at the time of his faculties and vigour; Governor McTavish told me he was acting in the best interests of the country, and he stated this often; after my arrival here and after my explanations, matters seemed to take a different turn; on the departure of the Delegates, the prisoners were released and tranquility appeared to have returned; shortly before the departure of the Delegates, Governor McTavish spoke to me of a proposition made by the Provisional Government to borrow money and chattels belonging to the Hudson's Bay Company, and at that time, unknown to Mr. McDougall; I had several communications with Governor McTavish in March; Governor McTavish recognized the existence of a Provisional Government, and recognized it because the proclamation of Governor McDougall, which he had previously thought to be legal, had led to his own abdication, for at the time I was talking to him, Mr. McTavish admitted there was no other Government in the country except the Provisional Government; he (Governor McTavish) himself counselled the strengthening that Government in order to maintain peace and order; before my departure to Canada, I again wrote to Mr. Howe, on the 9th of June, 1870; this letter is also published; I received a reply some time afterwards; the letter is dated 4th July, and is published on page thirty-four of the blue books; two of the Delegates returned, the third died before his return; my return to Canada was in consequence of my mission; I returned on the 27th of June; know the prisoner at the bar; have known him for seventeen years; he bears a good character; know him to be of a peaceful disposition; he lived with me two years; have known the prisoner for the last four years; so far from his having been a fugitive from justice, I had great difficulty in inducing him to absent himself a short time from his home at the urgent request of Sir John A. Macdonald.

This closed the evidence for the defence.

And the Court adjourned until three o'clock, in order to give Mr. Royal, Junior Counsel for the defence, an opportunity to prepare his address.

At three o'clock, the Court met pursuant to adjournment, and after routine Mr. Royal said :—

May it please your Lordship and Gentlemen of the Jury,

There are many reasons which will prompt my remarks on this subject. You have sat for many days listening to the evidence before you, and really I hope that the same will be done for you that was recently done in England for a jury that sat nearly two hundred days on the Tichborne case, who were paid five dollars per day. We have sat until eleven o'clock at night, and it is time we came to an end. It is now my duty to address you in the English language. In doing so, I will not be able to do so with the same ease as I could in my familiar tongue. However, this is the peculiarity of our state trials. In all the trials that have taken place with respect to the Red River country, the trials have been very lengthy, occupying sometimes twenty-seven or thirty days. The first state trial has been long enough to tax your patience. As I told you, I will be very brief. I will summonse the evidence taken before you, which you will have impressed on your minds, and I will leave to my senior Counsel the task of raising the legal points and discussing them. Now, gentlemen, what says the indictment against the prisoner at the bar?

"The Jurors for the Court of Queen's Bench, on oath present that Ambroise Lepine, on the 4th of March, in the year of Our Lord one thousand eight hundred and seventy, at Upper Fort Garry, feloniously, wilfully and of his malice aforethought did kill and murder one Thomas Scott, against the form of the Statute in such case made and provided, and against the peace of Our Lady the Queen, Her Crown and Dignity."

Well, gentlemen, it is the duty of the Crown prosecutor to prove all the material facts that are mentioned necessary to constitute the crime as laid down in the indictment. I will summonse the evidence taken before you on both sides. Here, gentlemen, are the facts that the prosecutor for the Crown has depended upon to make his case out. Who was the first witness? William Farmer, he who made the information against the prisoner. Mr. Farmer, unfortunately for himself, was selected as a Grand Juror. However, it is a duty to his country which, I suppose, he thought according to his conscience. Mr. Farmer was among certain parties from the Portage who were arrested by a party from Fort Garry on the night of the 17th of February, and was amongst those brought into the Fort. When he was asked who was the leader, he says he does not know. When pressed he says, " Riel, Lepine and O'Donohue were among the parties who came out to arrest the Portage party." He says it was discussed whether they were to be taken to the Fort or let go, and that the prisoner was in favour of their being let free, and O'Donohue took the opposite side. It seems O'Donohue was the commanding authority there, but the Crown prosecutor has tried to impress upon your minds that Lepine was the leading mind. However, Lepine was in favour of letting them go to their homes. But this evidence from Mr. Farmer will not have any great weight upon your minds. The mind cannot be trusted too long. The prisoner at the bar, whenever he appears upon the occasion, appears to be lenient and on the side of humanity. Of course, I will go from the ground that relates to their being arrested at their stopping at Headingly and Kildonan. These facts have combined to show what was the reason of these meetings. Now, gentlemen, after O'Donohue had succeeded in having the Portage party brought to the Fort, what was done? They were searched. When the question was put whether Lepine took a prominent part in having them arched, it is denied that he did. You must bear in mind that three or four names have been placed before the public. The names of Riel, Lepine and O'Donohue have been discussed in the public newspapers. These facts, it must be borne in mind, have an important relation with the case. You must also bear in mind that Lepine was with a crowd of others; that he never took part in the search of the prisoners. This is the burden of Mr. Farmer's evidence. Upon being asked in the cross-examination whether the prisoner had addressed himself angrily or in any rash words to the prisoners, he says, "No." He says there was another dictator in the Fort; there was somebody else. These are among the chief points in Mr. Farmer's evidence. The second point in this summary is the evidence of Mr. Newcombe. Mr Newcombe was the second witness. He was examined at the preliminary investigation which took place last fall. He was one of the Portage party. On being asked whether the prisoner at the bar was there when he was arrested, he says he does not remember. Mr. Newcombe is very intelligent, and yet he cannot say whether the prisoner was with the party who arrested them or not. He says he does not remember whether he was there or not. It is a remarkable fact that a man like Mr. Newcombe does not remember. Certainly an intelligent man like Mr. Newcombe would have noticed whether a prominent man, known to be such like the prisoner, was there. We have this fact on oath that Newcombe does not remember having seen Lepine there. However, Mr. Newcomber remembers that they went over to the Fort. There were only forty men, half of them on foot. If Lepine had been there, he would have seen him He remembers very well the fact of their being searched. He said he did not see him give orders at any time. When he was liberated, when he had come to a certain room where the prisoner was seated at a desk, he took a certain oath, not an oath of allegiance, but an oath that he would not take up arms against the existing authorities. When asked if he saw the prisoner give any orders or directions there, he says, "No; I saw him only sitting as his desk." When he is asked whether he saw the prisoner at the bar under other circumstances, he says, "Yes; I have seen Lepine in the guard-room and in the yard." The evidence, gentlemen, given by Mr. Newcombe, like that of Mr. Farmer, is more favorable to the prisoner than against him.

Now I come to that given by Mr. McPherson. His evidence seems to bear upon the accusation more than the two others. He states he was at Winnipeg in 1869 and 1870; that when he was taken near the Prairie Saloon, there were about four or five hundred with those who took him. (Mr. Cornish here corrected Mr. Royal, stating that McPherson had alluded to the force in the Fort, and Mr. Royal accepted the correction) Mr. McPherson's mind appeared to be very much at rest. I believe so little was in fear, that both he and Scott made up their minds to go down town from the Fort and have a drink, for as soon as they were searched, Scott said it was a very cold day. "Come down and let us have a drink," and on going they were stopped. When Scott was being led to the spot where it was arranged that he should be shot, he (McPherson) said, "I was at the window, I could see in the yard what was going on; I saw the Rev. Mr. Young and Scott going down to the eastern gate; there was one person coming behind them, it was the prisoner at the bar; I saw Lepine coming behind Mr. Young and Scott." If the credibility of this witness had not been shaken by the testimony of others, it would certainly have a very great bearing upon this case. We have grounds for the belief that Mr. McPherson was not under favorable circumstances to see. He was looking down from the window; there were double windows; he was looking from the inside; whether or not there was frost on the glass it does not appear, but at any rate he saw the prisoner. "I saw a well-built man"; he saw him only from the back, he never saw his or Scott's face either. The procession was going out when he saw it. When asked if Lepine was the only man well built, he said Lepine (the prisoner) had brothers, and that some of those brothers were as fine-looking as the prisoner. I do not say anything against Mr. McPherson personally or against his motives. It is a very careful man who ought to swear to what Mr. McPherson tells us he saw. On his cross-examination, Mr. McPherson gives us a bit of history at that time. He says, "I was a constable of Colonel Dennis." It appears that others as well as the Crown swore in constables. There were three or four governments too. Dennis had one. Schultz had one. It seems that Mr. McPherson was one of the guards who were supposed to protect or guard Dr. Schultz's property. It seems that the guard kept on Schultz's house was not very effective. He says that one morning he was allowed to go to the post-office to get letters for himself and the others, and that he did not return again to Schultz's because the party there were taken prisoners. When asked who were the officers of the movement with which he was connected, he said the officers were not elected or appointed, but took command spontaneously. It is for you, gentlemen, to take his evidence and see what amount of credibility you are to put upon the evidence of Mr. McPherson.

We come to the evidence of Mr. Young. A great deal of importance is paid to his evidence; he, perhaps, is a man that saw what passed and took place at a certain moment. He was there. He told you that he was in Scott's room giving him the consolation of religion. While he was there, there were a great many parties in the guard-room and hall. While there, he must have recognized everybody, especially some of the prominent parties, but he saw nobody. If the prisoner had been there, we must come to the conclusion that Mr. Young would have seen him. Mr. Young said he did not see the prisoner at the bar. When Mr. Young was coming down-stairs, at that time Mr. McPherson swears that Lepine was with them. Mr. Young did not see him; Mr. Scott did. Surely Mr. Young was noticing what was around him. When Mr. Young and Scott came to the eastern gate of the Fort, it is said that both paused there. Mr. Young does not say this; he says, "We went along to the first spot where Scott knelt before he was killed." This fact you must bear in mind, because some other witness says they stopped. Mr. Young was with Scott the whole time. He was with him and had him by the left arm when they both went around to bid good-bye, and when they came down-stairs When they proceeded to the first spot he was with him; he was with him when they proceeded from that spot to the second one. We now come to this part of Mr. Young's evidence when he saw him after the guns were fired. In his cross-examination, on being asked whether he lifted the body to examine it, to see if it had life left, he said it was dead. He could not understand what Scott said; it was only a shriek or moan. He did not observe whether Scott was breathing or not, he did not touch the body, but he said the distance that he was from it then was eight feet when the pistol shot was fired at Scott's head. He said he remarked from the position he occupied at the time, he did not see any hole or holes in the front of Scott's dress, and he remarked to the Chief Justice that it was difficult to state accurately occurrences that took place some four or five years ago. It is very probable that Mr. Young may have been mistaken. The position that he occupied is not according to the one stated by others. He states that he saw the bullet holes in Scott's coat; they were at the back. Other witnesses have told you that there were scratches on the shoulder, as if the bullet had passed through. Mr. Young said he saw the marks a little lower down, the traces of a bullet. You, gentlemen, are natives of this country, you know what kind of a hole a bullet makes in passing through woollen cloth. It remains with you to decide whether Mr. Young can swear that this hole was made by a bullet or bullets. When a man's life is at stake, it is a very doubtful thing to swear that a certain hole is a bullet hole. I do not wish to cast any reflection on Mr. Young's evidence. These are facts that the jury as well as anybody else can determine. Well, from the distance Mr. Young occupied at the time, was it possible for him to swear that those scratches were caused by a bullet hole. It is for you to decide. When more than one witness will come before you and say that they have seen the holes in the chest of the man who was said to be shot, you will be able to say which is correct. Mr. Young has seen Mr. Lepine under two circumstances. The first, when he came himself in his efforts to prolong Scott's life, and when he came to Mr. Riel at Mr. Young's request. He saw him before sending Campbell to Smith; Smith was then living in the same house with Governor McTavish; he himself went to Riel on the same errand. Riel does not understand any more English than Mr. Young understands French. On being asked does he understand French, he says no; he may have picked up a few words here and there, because he has lived for a short time in a mixed community; but remember this, he would not go far enough to say he understands even a little French Indeed he states he does not understand French. What does Mr. Riel say? He says, "It is not my duty, it is not my business; I am very sorry the case has been decided. I will send for Lepine." Lepine comes, and what takes place before these three men? Mr. Young gives in his information this inference. He says the conversation was in French; Lepine did not say a word, but he shook his head and said no. Mr. Young, being there, ought certainly to know, but Mr. Riel or Mr. Lepine might have said anything else that was in his mind at that time, and could Mr. Young from his own admissions know what it was? The witness could not state anything giving even the sense of the conversation that then took place. On the second occasion when Mr. Young went to ask for the body of Scott, there was the very same comedy or a repetition of the same fact. Riel sent for Lepine. Certainly it was most kind of Mr Young to make this request, but, gentlemen, you will notice that the person who exercised the chief command was Mr. Riel and not the prisoner at the bar. These are two occasions on which Mr. Young saw the prisoner. When Mr. Young was accompanying Scott, he never saw Lepine; he may have seen somebody else less renowned, less known than Lepine; however, he gave the names of those parties he had seen. Surely he would have seen him if he had been there. He noticed O'Donohue, but he did not see Lepine.

Gentlemen of the Jury, in the cross-examination Mr. Young stated that he had seen Riel in the guard-room where he did not see Lepine. He has also seen some one else, a man by the name of Goulet, and he afterwards saw O'Donohue, but he never saw Lepine. When, after the firing, he asked Mr. Young what took place, he said this, "I heard a voice saying, Put an end to his misery." It was said in English. Mr. Young is the only witness who has stated this. The most important part of Mr. Young's evidence is what he saw when he came down with Scott to the last place. He also defined the position of the body.

Now we come to Campbell's evidence. Campbell had a good opportunity of seeing what was going on. He is in fact a kind-hearted man and was allowed to go into the Fort and bring provisions, food and even luxuries to the prisoners, and he was permitted to hold conversations with them. It is well for you to remember these facts. Liberty, gentlemen, is the sweetest thing in the world, and it is best appreciated by prisoners. You must remember that these prisoners had opportunities of meeting. The Bishop of Saskatchewan was allowed to go and make speeches to them; he mentioned one case of their holding public meetings among themselves. Campbell had excellent opportunities of going to the Fort; he was allowed to go to it to bring things to the prisoners. We next find that on one occasion he was stopped by one of the guards and refused permission to enter; he was told to go and get special leave from the Adjutant-General Lepine, who was then one of a Government composed of delegates from all parts of the country, and he had been chosen unanimously to act in the capacity of Adjutant-General. The position was never well defined. He was then Captain of the Guards, and he was, on the occasion referred to, coming to the gate, when Mr. Campbell requested him to be allowed to pass, and Lepine said: *Pass*, in French to the guard, and Campbell was allowed to proceed. Campbell says he does not understand French, but the English word *pass* is much the same in French, and from this it is inferred that Lepine was in command then. This is the only conclusion that can be derived from that fact. I do not see that anything more can be deduced from that fact. Campbell remembers the 4th of March; he remembers Mr. Young; he described the prison in full. He did not see Lepine in the guard-room. Like Mr. McPherson, he went to a window to see Scott go out. Did he see Lepine, the prisoner, come after the prisoners? No. He states that he saw Lepine at a distance; that there was a large guard at a distance; that Lepine, Riel and O'Donohue were there. How is it that they can be in the same place at the same time? This man Campbell, so it appears, has not given likely evidence. He states that he saw through the window, he saw Mr. Lepine while he was going out; he states, moreover, that he was with three persons together. I believe he is the only one who has stated that; two or three other witnesses state that O'Donohue was not there. Looking from the distance he was, and as he admits he was excited, could he see correctly? However, these parties are always before his sight. He recognised them among a guard of men. Some of you have been in the Fort, and you know the topography of the place. Place yourselves in that position, and from that window in a diagonal way, some hundred and twenty feet if you can, in the guard-room, and do you think that you could recognise anybody sufficiently to swear to his identity? He says, "I lost sight of them at once." Strange thing! What does Campbell next see? he sees a box carried by six men. He tells you the direction in which it was carried. You must remember how the carrying of that box was done. Was it by two or six men? Remember. Campbell swears it was carried on the shoulders of six men. Another witness, one of the carriers, comes and tells you it was carried by only two men and in their hands. There is very much contradiction. You are the judges of these facts. On Campbell being asked if he saw the prisoner at any time afterwards, he says, " Yes, I saw him in the gathering on the occasion of the hoisting of a flag Riel was ordering on that occasion." When asked what position did the prisoner hold, he says he was only one of the guards. Did he make a speech? No, it was somebody else that made a speech. The fact that the prisoner was seen now and then should not weigh against a man who is being tried for his life. It seems that Campbell saw the prisoner under some other circumstances, and he relates them. What does he say of Hallet's affair? Hallet had some trouble with his guards. Lepine was there; he did not appear to be exercising authority; it was somebody else that commanded the guard. Hallet had been ordered to be put by himself on account of some rash words he had used. The prisoners resisted on Hallet's behalf, and the Captain of the guard took Lepine by the shoulder and drew him away, and the prisoner did not resist on that occasion, showing that he submitted to the orders of the Captain. It has been attempted to prove that Hallet suffered so much from his confinement that he died from it. In the cross-examination, it was elicited that poor Hallet had undertaken a Government contract, and that he lost heavily and in a moment of temporary insanity he committed suicide. This is all that comes out of Campbell's evidence. It is for you to state how far and how much it implicates the prisoner in the death of Thomas Scott.

We now come to the evidence of the Rev. Bishop Machray. This gentleman gives the part he has taken in the matter, and in his cross-examination he says that John Bruce was at the head of affairs. Of course, he can only state this from hearsay. He states, moreover, that he used to visit the Fort for the purpose of seeing Governor McTavish. He states that the question of any other authority existing was asked Governor McTavish, and besides he states that that gentleman was dangerously ill during the troubles. He states that at the meeting of the Council of Assiniboia, he was the only one who suggested the employment of force to put down the movement. He admits afterwards that this advice was not prudent, because if acted upon it would have brought the two classes of the settlement into conflict, and this is what he wished to avoid. He states that the Council of Assiniboia, through Governor McTavish, issued a proclamation ordering the people of the movement to disperse, and that this proclamation was published in both languages. He says at that time the meetings of the Council of Assiniboia came to an end by the rash and false proclamation of Governor McDougall, dated the 1st December, 1869. When asked concerning the powers and authority of the Council of Assiniboia, he says the Council was not executive, it was only legislative, though the Governor generally sought the advice of a few of the members. It strikes me that there was then no definite Government in existence. Certainly it is for you, gentlemen, to say. When questioned as to the body of Scott, this witness does not differ from what was already said by Mr. Young.

Next we have Chambers; he was before you; he was there on the morning of the 4th of March; he saw something he describes with a certain amount of accuracy, the distance the firing party was from the man Scott, who was said to have been shot. He says the firing party were standing only about eighteen feet [20 yds] from the man to be shot. The soldiers were armed with rifles [trading guns], that they appeared to be under the influence of intoxicating liquors. When Chambers is asked who was in command of the firing party, he states it seemed to be Lepine. When pressed for the fact, he says it was a man named Lepine, but he says I cannot identify him as the prisoner; however, the man's name was Lepine. He told you that the man in command of the firing party was Lepine. Well, gentlemen, you have heard it stated from other witnesses that it was another man that commanded the firing party. When he saw Lepine, he was sideways, he saw his side only. You have also this other fact that when Chambers went to the body, he saw what other witnesses did not see; then he saw some blood on the man's face. You have other witnesses who state that the white cloth covered his face. Here is another contradiction on which you have to judge. Chambers is a gunsmith; when asked if he saw marks on Scott's coat, he says he did not observe anything, but the blood on the white cloth. He is asked what he next saw. He says he saw six men drawn up into line. Now, how can a witness, if not in line, especially when he is sixty or seventy feet away, swear positively as to who was or who was not there? Chambers was near the gate when Scott and Young came out. He observed Mr. Young and Scott, but did not see Lepine. His evidence that Lepine was in command of the firing party is contradicted by four or five other witnesses. Here is another witness, Alexander Murray, who saw something from the key hole; he is very precise in his description. He saw something not seen by other witnesses. For instance, he swears positively that when Scott went around to see his comrades for the last time, it was Mr. Young who said, "Good-bye, boys." Scott only bowed his head. Gentlemen, here is a contradiction. Mr. Young states that it was Scott that said, "Good-bye, boys;" he does not recollect having seen anybody with Scott at that time. When asked if the prisoner was there, he says, "No. Saw Lepine on that day, but it was some time after the firing." Murray was a very intelligent witness. When he is asked what was the popular feeling in the settlements along the Assiniboia, he says that Governor McTavish could have crushed out the movement. He says that if the Governor and Council of Assiniboia had sworn in a number of special constables, no troubles would have taken place. He says the people of the Portage rose and took up arms to release the prisoners. During the course of the evidence, the learned Judge also stated his opinion that this would have been the proper course to pursue.

Duncan Nolin has seen something; he states that on the morning of the 4th of March, he came to the Fort and saw Scott; he did not see Mr. Young, but he saw Lepine leading Scott to the place where he first knelt down. It is only there that he saw Mr. Young. Strange thing for this witness! However, you have gathered it in the evidence. Lepine was not seen at the spot. Nolin himself says he was very much excited. When he saw Scott coming out, Lepine took him by the arm and led him out. He saw Riel on the spot with O'Donohue walking about, but he did not see Scott on the first spot. Whatever weight you place upon that, you must remember that this evidence is that Lepine was not there. The same witness goes as far as to tell you that it was somebody else that led the party.

Now I come to the most important evidence for the Crown. I come to the evidence given by Mr. Joseph Nolin. He swears that he was Lepine's private secretary, and as such he called the Council of War that took place on the night of the 3rd of March. He tells you that this Council of War was presided over by Lepine, the prisoner, and this evidence is not contradicted. Lepine was there by the authority of these men. What share did he take? It is true he presided; after, Riel came and made a speech, and made the accusations against Scott; some witnesses were heard; when the votes were taken, two dissentient voices were heard, Lajemonière who preferred to see Scott executed, and Baptiste Lepine who said, No! he was not in favor of the sentence of death. Did the prisoner at the bar vote or say anything in favor of the sentence? No. All he said was that the majority are in favor of death and he will have to die. He did not say anything else. He merely said that the majority being against Scott, he will have to die. If in connection with that fact we take the evidence of Modeste Lajemonière, who was in the north attic window of Dr. Cowan's building, and who declares that he heard either Riel or the prisoner, who were then behind him in the same room, say distinctly, "Then in God's truth, they are bringing him down," you will have to put these two expressions together in order to get a correct meaning. Are these the words of a man who is guilty of the act for which he stands accused? I do not believe it. I need not remind you that the only inevitable fact from the evidence of Joseph Nolin as put before you was the connection of his being President. You must remember that this last deed, this one deed I do not pretend to contradict. This is the only fact we do not contradict. He is no more *participes criminis* than I am, or the hundreds of others who were engaged in the movement and who invested him with the office he then held. We have the evidence of John Bruce; with this you are well acquainted. You must take his evidence as being very imperfect. He says, "I have seen the prisoner; the first conversation I had with him was in December; I asked him whether he was going to release the prisoners?" He says that Lepine said he was, only that he intended to shoot a couple of them before doing so. When asked if he was in earnest, he says "No, I think the prisoner was merely joking." Now what of Mr. Bruce and his evidence? When he writes letters to the papers he states certain things, and when, under oath, he is asked if these things are true, he says, "No ! I wrote the French of them, somebody translated them into English" (and did not do them justice), and this is the kind of a witness that the Crown has thought fit to bring before you.

However, if that witness varies, his variations are not against the prisoner at the bar. He understood that the prisoner was not in earnest when he spoke. He never saw him acting in any capacity, and when asked if he would have seen him on the occasion of the shooting, he says, "Yes, I would have seen him if he was there." He saw the box that morning, and asked Lepine what it was for? Lepine says it is to put poor Scott in. If this question is to be considered, you know very well how to consider it. You may judge by his actions if not by his words. He gives you names, but he did not see the prisoner. He saw Joseph Delorme, and here is another contradiction. He states what Goulet has told him with reference to the body, but all this was ruled out by His Lordship as only hearsay evidence.

We come to François Charette, the fourteenth witness. He said he was looking from the wall. You will remember that when Bishop McLean was giving his evidence about the occasion of the visit to the Stone Fort, how he saw one man with a very long pistol, and another with a very long gun; how excited the witness was, and how he saw things that did not really happen. Charette swears this, "I saw Scott standing about thirty paces from the wall; I saw him talking with a man, and the next thing I heard some guns fire and saw Scott fall; I came down from the wall and went towards the body, and saw the wounds on the body; one of the wounds was in the breast, one was in the shoulder, and another was between the two." He says blood was oozing out of the wound in the breast, but the shoulder was not bleeding;" although only two feet from the body, I did not notice wounds or bullet holes in the back of the coat." He saw a pistol in the hands of Guilmette, and he thinks that it was Guilmette that fired at Scott's head. And now he states a new fact in the case; he says the pistol did not go off at first; it snapped. Then he saw Lepine for the first time. "Somebody said behind me, You have no business here, you must go into the Fort." You must remember that Charette was a guard. However, he says he saw a pistol inside Lepine's breast-pocket. Nothing very extraordinary, I suppose, at that time. He heard some one say, "That pistol is not in order." He is not certain who said it. When he is pressed by the Crown to repeat the words that he heard, he says, "I heard the words, Here is one in order, finish him, but I cannot say who said so." It is astonishing that when something is likely to be in favor of Lepine, he does not remember it. He swears positively that it was like Lepine's voice that he heard. He states this fact that at the same time that he saw Lepine put his hand to his pistol, the pistol went off. We must give him credit for this, because it is utterly from the evidence to say that Lepine furnished the pistol. The one that snapped was the one that was fired, another chamber having been used. This, gentlemen, is an important fact. He says, "I was not looking at Lepine." He says, "I only looked at him after I came into the Fort." He says, "I was kicked." This is also another important fact. He then says, "My curiosity was aroused; I was not certain that Scott had died from the wounds of the guns." He says, "I believe there were five or six men in the firing party." He saw the box when it was carried into the Fort, I suppose when it was placed near the bastion. He says, "I heard a voice saying, O Lord, O Lord." Of course, when asked if he knew Scott before, he says, "I did not know his voice, but I distinctly heard these words coming out of the box." He says he did not personally know that it was Scott's voice, but Joseph Delorme told him it was Scott's voice. "Delorme was on guard at the eastern bastion; when I heard those words, I asked who was there; Delorme answered, Scott." He says nobody ever told him how they finally disposed of the body. His opinion is that the box was put in the ground that evening. He further says in his cross-examination, "I saw a man with a white handkerchief or cloth in his hand give the signal, but I swear positively that the prisoner at the bar is not the person that gave that signal." You remember what Chambers swore. He says, "I was not more than thirty feet from the man that gave the signal. He saw also Mr. Young; he says Mr. Young was not more than eight or nine feet from the body. I contend that this man's evidence is contradicted by others.

Baptiste Charette swears most positively that it was André Nault that gave the signal to fire. This is a flat contradiction. Baptiste Charette's evidence is very favorable to the prisoner. He saw Scott as he was coming out of the gate. He says he was inside when he met him; he does not say that Lepine was leading Scott. The next thing he saw was Mr. Young talking to Scott. He stood near the door at that time; from the position he was occupying, he could see the firing party. When he is asked, "Did the prisoner at the bar give the signal?" he says, "No! it was given by another person." Baptiste Charette when near the body saw three wounds. You must remember that Mr. Young did not come very near the body. He saw only some blood, he saw bullet holes in the back. I do not see how they could see wounds when Scott's coat was buttoned up. When he is asked in his cross examination if the prisoner took any active part in ordering the firing party, he says, "No! I saw the party come out of the gate; saw them in such a position; saw Mr. Young and somebody else." He swears positively that he did not see the prisoner that morning. Now this closes the evidence on the part of the Crown. This evidence I have gone over. I have left out everything foreign or irrelevant to the question.

The prisoner at the bar stands accused of having feloniously and wilfully killed a man by the name of Thomas Scott. It is for you to say what connection he had with it. The prisoner was selected by the people of the country who had formed a certain Government to take the place of the one that had been wiped out by the false Proclamation of Governor McDougall. I do not deny it. It is a matter of public notoriety, that he was nominated by a Convention composed of Delegates selected from all parts of the country, to the post of Adjutant-General with very undefined duties. If he has had any participation in the act, so has the whole population of the Province who rose and supported him at that time. If he is guilty of treason, so are they. If he is guilty of murder, so are they equally guilty. Lepine, you have seen, was only one. He presided at the Council of War. I believe there are doubts in the case, especially when it is remembered that this man had no interests in the deed perpetrated on the morning of the 4th March—no interests except the interests of the people who commanded him and the Government that then existed. There were some parties conspiring against that Government. A party was on its way to release the prisoners in the Fort, and it is for you to say if you can on the evidence that was brought by the Crown, if the prisoner is *participes criminis* in the perpetration of that crime. If he is guilty, so are four or five hundred others who took part with him; if he is to be punished for the accusation against him, not only there are a few others who are equally guilty, but every one who took part in the movement at that time. If the evidence of the Crown does not bear strong enough in favour of the prisoner, I believe I can state through witnesses that this man was not at the so-called execution. You will be able to come to the conclusion that sensible people ought to do. I will now recall to your memories a few facts that were adduced for the defence.

Bunn's is the first. It relates to the organization of the Government and the action he took and the position he took. His answers were clear and definite, and the fact is a credit to the country. From his evidence it is easy to see what the path is.

Bishop McLean told you the part he took in advising the parishes to send Delegates, &c. The Bishop of Saskatchewan is not clear on this point. The third witness for the defence does not know anything immediately connected with the case. His evidence is limited exclusively to the troubles, and the causes which led to them, and the different phases of the movement. You then have Charles Nolin's evidence. I may here state that it is by Bannatyne's evidence that we know that the prisoner was elected Adjutant-General. Nolin's evidence is short. He was not present on the 4th of March, and he does not know anything immediately connected with the case. Nolin was one of the Delegates elected to attend the meetings in January. He was present at the election of the President. He swears that the prisoner was one of the four Delegates that went to Governor McTavish. Mr. Sutherland was the one who reported. He states the same thing in the same words. There are three witnesses whose case is immediately connected with the case in hands. The first is Paul Proulx; we have also Father Ritchot's evidence, but it is not immediately connected with the case. Proulx was there on the 4th of March. Of course he was well acquainted with the party in the Fort. He knew Lepine perfect'y well. He saw Rev. Mr. Young and Scott. He swears positively that Lepine was not there in command or taking any action; he was in no way or kind connected with the procession. Moreover, he saw the firing party. He swears positively that if Lepine has been there doing anything, he would have seen him. "I swear positively that I did not see him do any act on that morning. I saw who gave the signal : I swear positively I did not see Lepine doing it." He states that he was close to Dr. Cowan's house, and that he followed with the crowd.

When asked if Lepine was there, he says, No ! He stood in a good position to see what was going on, and he describes the position of Scott to the firing party. He saw the box ; he never saw it afterwards. He saw Riel, O'Donohue, Goulet, Delorme, but did not see Lepine, the prisoner, at all. Here is a man who is not excited ; he had been there for eight or ten weeks, he went out to see and saw something. This is corroborated in the main by the evidence of the Crown. I come to the last three witnesses, Lajemonière, Hupé and Archbishop Taché. The prisoner at the bar is accused, that is to say, Scott died directly through the hands of the prisoner at the bar. You have it from the mouth of the Rev. Mr. Young and Chambers, that Scott was dead when they left him, and Mr. Young did not lift up the body, but Mr. Young swears that Scott was dead. You have Charette's evidence that he heard him shout in the bastion, " O Lord, O Lord." Here is Modeste Lajemonière who was Riel's servant ; on the morning of the 4th of March, he was looking out of the attic of Riel's room, when he saw Rev. Mr. Young and Scott coming down. He saw Riel and Lepine behind him, on the same flat and in the same room. This is very strange. He did not see Lepine and Riel coming down with the party. No ! he did not see them there. He heard the prisoner say, "In God's truth they are bringing him down," meaning are they in earnest. He left and went down-stairs, leaving Riel, Lepine and Gray there ; went to the main or south gate, and after all was over he went to the eastern gate. It was there that he stopped by Goulet, who asked if there was nobody to take in that coffin, and he hastened towards the spot himself with another man. There were not six of them, there were only two of them that carried the coffin to the bastion, and he (Lajemonière) was placed as a guard over the body. There was another guard in front. His orders were to allow nobody to come near the box. However, a man broke the orders and rushed past the other to the coffin; that man came to the coffin, knelt down and listened, and heard two words repeated, " I say, I say." When asked if he put the box in the ground, he said he did not. As Huppé passed him, he said, "That man is not dead, he still speaks." The next thing was to bring Hupé to corroborate this evidence. He tells a similar story. He says his curiosity was aroused while he was in the mess-room; he heard a man say Scott was not dead, because he was heard to talk. He had the curiosity to see for himself, and he describes minutely the position, and he says, " I heard a voice in the box shout, I say, I say." On being asked if he saw Lepine do any act on the occasion, he says, " I did not see him."

This is the last witness that the defence had to bring. We had another witness of course, His Grace Archbishop Taché; he told you very clearly a great many of the events that took place in 1869 and 1870. He has produced to the Court official documents. His words were not merely words, they are based upon written papers. These papers have been produced. It is now my province to tell you of him. Gentlemen, the evidence that was brought by the Archbishop is most conclusive, because he had not words to say, but he had official documents. Every declaration was supported by official documents, and these documents will tell you whether the opinion of the people in the settlement was that their liberty was in danger. If there were dissensions and troubles, they rose gloriously for their lives and their liberties. This rising was shared in by the people generally. The people gave them credit for their deeds. As I told you when I closed the evidence for the prosecution, if this man is to be found guilty by you of murder, if that man is to be sent to the gallows, I say that three-fourths of our population must be sent to the gallows too. The part that the prisoner took at that time, that part was taken by the voice of the people who nominated him as Adjutant-General. You know that in that capacity he presided. Legal points are to be raised in the accusation in this case. You will hear important rules of evidence, and also you will hear that one of the best authorities states that while there is presumptive evidence, if the body has not been found, there can be no conviction. Facts have been told of men being found guilty by a jury, of murder, and the person said to be murdered turning up living after many years. I might recite three or four examples where innocent persons have been sent to the gallows for crimes that were never committed. You will see as well as others that the greatest care is required and that the most attentive examination is necessary to prove that the man is dead. The Crown has never proved that Scott is dead from the trading guns of the firing party by drunken men at a distance of sixty or seventy feet. I believe that the Crown prosecution is bound to prove all the facts that are material to prove the murder of which that man stands accused. Has that man wilfully murdered Scott? Has that man killed Scott? You have the evidence. It is for you to meet the discrepancies and contradictions which appear in the evidence. I have tried to summonse the evidence. There is much of it that is political. Your minds have been distracted by these political features. I have limited myself to the evidence. It is for you to say whether this man standing there was connected with that fact because he was in a position at that time which was conferred upon him by the people. It is for you to say that the part he took in the affair is remote or not. It is for you to say so. You, who are natives of this country, have to bear in mind these other facts that poor Parisien, Sutherland, Turner and Goulet have met their deaths. They have died! If it is to be said that the fifth man must die, that responsibility rests on you. On a calm consideration of the case you must decide that the prisoner at the bar is no more *participes criminis* than the guard who was in the Fort until the 23rd of August, 1870. The case is in your hands, and I hope that you will be able to agree upon the facts, and that the verdict of your consciences will be that the prisoner at the bar is not guilty of the crime of which he is accused.

M. Royal spoke until six o'clock, when the Court took recess. After recess, he resumed his speech, speaking upwards of an hour and a half.

Mr. Chapleau then followed in French, his speech lasting from half-past nine until midnight, when the Court adjourned.

"J'ai entendu plaider M. Chapleau dans la cause de Lépine et dans celle de Nault, et je vous assure qu'il a droit d'être fier des succès qu'il a obtenus, sinon sur le jury, du moins sur l'esprit de ceux qui sont à portée d'apprécier le talent. Il ne se trouvait pas dans la meilleure position possible pour faire ce que les gens du métier appellent une bonne cause. Il est arrivé ici à peine six jours avant l'ouverture de la Cour, presque sans renseignement sur la cause dont il s'était chargé, et cela, quand il s'agissait de refaire l'histoire de notre Province pendant quatre ans. Dans l'impossibilité de rien connaître de la preuve qui pouvait être faite par la poursuite ou par la défense, il a dû procéder, je ne dirai pas à tâton, mais avec une extrême prudence, et en sondant chaque pouce du terrain sur lequel il avait à se mouvoir.

"Pour un avocat habitué aux succès les plus sérieux de la Cour d'Assises, on s'imagine bien un peu qu'une foule de petites ficelles sont mises en jeu pour amener le jury où l'avocat veut le conduire, ou du moins pour l'écarter tellement de son chemin qu'il ne puisse jamais en venir à une entente unanime. Mais, pour cela, il faut connaître le jury, son éducation, ses habitudes, ses opinions, ses traditions, il faut savoir quel souvenir attristant le fera pleurer, quelle joyeuse allusion le fera sourire. Il faut un peu flatter ses caprices, ses ambitions, ses vanités ; il faut le grandir dans sa propre estime, afin qu'il résiste aux appels de la poursuite qui va démontrer tout à l'heure que si l'accusé n'est pas condamné, la société est perdue à tout jamais.

"Il n'y a pas jusqu'aux juges qui n'aient leurs côtés faibles et qui ne puissent être, avec une diplomatie suffisante, amenés parfois dans une impasse qui profite au client.

"Mais tout cela ne peut réussir, ne peut même être essayé que lorsque l'avocat possède la connaissance et l'habitude de son monde. Sans cela, ses plus beaux mouvements se heurtent à l'indifférence générale, ses mots les mieux trouvés tombent à plat s'ils ne frappent pas absolument à faux, et ces petits échecs répétés finissent souvent par influer sur la cause d'une manière désastreuse.

"M. Chapleau se trouvait malheureusement dans ces circonstances défavorables. Il venait plaider une cause qu'il ne connaissait que très peu—judiciairement parlant—devant un juge qu'il n'avait jamais vu sur le banc, devant un jury et devant un public dont il n'avait jamais eu l'occasion de connaître les idées ou les tendances. Ajoutez à cela toutes les fausses informations qui furent prodiguées et qu'il n'avait aucun moyen de contrôler, toutes les réticences mises dans les quelques renseignements qui lui furent donnés, les préjugés qui surgissent toujours plus ou moins contre les étrangers, le fort courant d'opinion constamment entretenu contre les accusés dans une classe nombreuse de la population, et vous aurez une faible idée des difficultés que M. Chapleau avait à surmonter dans cette cause.

"Son seul moyen de succès, dans les circonstances où il était placé, était de s'en tenir à la preuve, et d'aller droit devant lui absolument comme s'il eût plaidé sa première cause ; il avait à mettre de côté toute son expérience du jury, pour ne s'appuyer que sur son talent d'avocat.

"Un nouvel écueil à craindre, et qu'il ne pouvait éviter qu'avec la plus grande prudence et la plus grande délicatesse, résultait de la nature même de la cause et du côté politique qui en formait les principaux traits. Un avocat de la position de M. Chapleau, ex-Solliciteur Général, Conseil de la Reine, ne pouvait pas prôner dans les mêmes termes qu'un autre l'héroïsme et la grandeur d'un soulèvement dont l'origine était certainement illégale, et, pourtant, autour de ce point tournait toute la cause.

"La Cour, on doit le dire, avait accordé à la Couronne toute la latitude possible pour sa preuve, et toute l'histoire du gouvernement provisoire a été faite. En écoutant l'interrogatoire des témoins, on oubliait souvent que Lépine subissait son procès pour la mort de Scott. On avait l'air de s'occuper avant tout des faits et gestes de la population française durant ces malheureux troubles de 1869-70. C'est le juge lui-même qui a dirigé les procédés, et c'est lui qui a voulu chercher à élucider le pourquoi et le comment de ces malheureux événements. La défense s'est trouvée autorisée à faire une contre-preuve, à démontrer la signification de l'attitude de la population anglaise.

"Puis venait ensuite la conduite des gouvernements anglais et canadiens, divers actes du gouvernement de la Baie-d'Hudson, de l'hon. M. Archibald alors qu'il était lieutenant-gouverneur de cette Province, les promesses et surtout la nécessité d'une amnistie. Cela faisait partie des questions de droit plutôt que de faits, et elles furent plaidées en anglais pour le juge en même temps que pour le jury.

"C'est avec cette preuve que M. Chapleau a fait sa cause en s'aidant des lacunes de la preuve de la poursuite. La cause se divisait naturellement en trois parties : 1o. Scott a-t-il été tué ? 2o. Si oui, Lépine est-il responsable de sa mort ? 3o. Si Lépine est l'auteur de la mort de Scott, n'agissait-il pas comme membre d'un gouvernement aussi régulièrement organisé que les circonstances le permettaient, et doit-il être tenu pour responsable d'un acte que toute la contrée, par le fait de son adhésion au gouvernement provisoire, aurait refusé de condamner ?

"Voilà les trois points qu'il y avait à discuter, et je puis vous assurer qu'ils l'ont été de main de maitre. M. Chapleau a pris la preuve de la poursuite point par point, témoin par témoin, et il en a fait voir les contradictions et les lacunes avec une vigueur d'argumentation irrésistible.

"Il est une chose bien certaine, et tout avocat ne pourra manquer d'admettre, c'est que la poursuite a été très-faible, négligée surtout, dans sa preuve. Les faits qui se rattachent à la mort du malheureux Scott sont tellement connus de tout le monde, qu'on a paru vouloir se passer des minutieuses exigences de la preuve légale. Des témoins ont prouvé que Scott avait été blessé, mais personne n'a prouvé qu'il était mort. Il a été démontré, au contraire, qu'il était encore vivant plusieurs heures après ce qu'on appelle son exécution. Et aucune information n'a été donnée sur ce qui s'est passé plus tard. Bien plus, aucune démarche n'a été faite pour recouvrer le cadavre, s'il existe ; on n'a rien fait pour mettre les tribunaux en demeure de dire que réellement, légalement, judiciairement, la mort de Scott était prouvée.

"Quant à la part que Lépine a prise dans ce triste drame, elle se réduit à ceci : il présidait la cour martiale. A-t-il exprimé son opinion en faveur de la condamnation ? Non. A-t-il insisté pour que la sentence fût exécutée ? Non ; au contraire, il a témoigné la plus grande surprise en apprenant qu'elle devait avoir lieu. Il est vrai qu'il occupait une position éminente dans le gouvernement provisoire, et il n'y a pas de preuve qu'il ait usé de l'influence dont il pouvait jouir pour empêcher la perpétration de cette regrettable erreur. Mais qui donc peut se vanter d'avoir fait plus que lui ? Qui donc a fait la moindre démarche sérieuse, légale pour empêcher l'exécution de Scott? A-t-on essayé les moindres démarches devant les magistrats ? A-t-on des preuves des plus légères tentatives d'évasion ? Non ; au contraire. D'après les témoins les plus intéressés à pallier leur coupable indifférence, il y avait plus de deux cents personnes présentes à l'exécution de Scott, et personne n'a dit un mot, n'a fait un geste pour empêcher que ce sang fût versé. Tout ce monde-là n'est-il pas aussi coupable que Lépine ? Celui-ci n'a fait que suivre l'exemple de toute la population en laissant agir comme ils l'entendaient ceux qui avaient à cette époque la direction des affaires de cette contrée. Il n'a pris aucune part directe à l'exécution ; ce n'est pas lui

FRANCIS E. CORNISH. CHIEF JUSTICE, HON. E. B. WOOD. STEWART MCDONNELL.
HON ATTORNEY GENERAL CLARK.

qui a tiré les coups de feu, ce n'est pas lui qui a donné le signal, il n'était pas même sur le lieu de l'exécution. A plus forte raison n'y a-t-il rien de prouvé sur le dernier acte du drame, lorsqu'on présume que Scott a réellement été mis à mort, puisque les premières blessures n'avaient pas été mortelles.

" De quel droit les vengeurs de Scott viennent-ils aujourd'hui demander la punition de Lépine, lorsqu'il n'a fait que ce qu'ils ont fait eux-mêmes ? Pourquoi la justice fait-elle le procès de Lépine pour un acte public que les représentants de la justice n'ont pas même essayé de prévenir lorsqu'il était de leur devoir de le faire ? Pourquoi fait-on déclarer à la Reine que *la paix et la dignité* demandent la condamnation de Lépine, lorsque les représentants de la Reine ont eux-mêmes aidé à l'établissement du gouvernement qui a mis à mort l'infortuné Scott ?

" Mais le côté principal de la question, le côté qui intéresse le public étranger, c'est la reconnaissance du gouvernement provisoire comme gouvernement *de facto*, et la promesse implicite d'une amnistie accordée à tous ceux qui en ou fait partie. Le juge Wood, président du tribunal, n'a autorisé que la production des documents officiels, et a refusé l'admission des lettres privées de Sir George E. Cartier, de Sir John A. Macdonald et d'autres personnages qui, ou ne peut cependant pas le nier, avaient pleine autorité de parler et d'écrire comme ils l'ont fait, et de promettre ce qu'ils ont promis. Malgré cette lacune dans la preuve de la défense, il y avait suffisamment dans les *blue-books* pour démontrer que le gouvernement de Riel avait été reconnu comme ayant une existence *de facto* par le gouvernement canadien et par les autorités impériales ; que les délégués de Riel avaient été invités, après l'exécution de Scott, à formuler leurs demandes, et que le gouvernement canadien les avait accordées sur les ordres formelles du ministre des colonies. Cela ne vaut-il pas autant, ne vaut-il pas mieux qu'une promesse verbale ou écrite d'amnistie ? Et de plus, toute la population de la Rivière-Rouge n'a-t-elle pas accepté le gouvernement de Riel ? Le Gouverneur McTavish lui-même ne l'a-t-il pas autorisé ?

" Si ce gouvernement n'était pas légal, ni régulier, il n'est que la manifestation d'une usurpation de pouvoir qui devrait être soumise aux tribunaux d'une manière différente. Si le gouvernement de Riel n'était pas un gouvernement établi d'après la loi et la constitution, tous ceux qui en ont fait partie, tous ceux qui l'ont soutenu, tous ceux qui l'ont toléré sont coupables de haute-trahison et devraient être poursuivis comme tels. Le crime de haute-trahison est le plus grand crime connu à la loi anglaise ; pourquoi l'ignorer, pour ne s'arrêter qu'à un acte isolé d'homicide ?

" Mais on sait très bien que la Reine elle-même a pardonné la rébellion et qu'elle a oublié la révolte dont certains de ses sujets se sont rendus coupables contre son autorité. Toutes les mesures ont été prises pendant trois ans pour empêcher les poursuites contre les chefs du mouvement de 1869, et ce n'est que l'automne dernier que Lépine a été arrêté par le fait d'une poursuite privée. Le mot a été dit en pleine Cour. S'il y a du vrai dans toutes les protestations de loyauté, et de la sincérité dans toutes ces dénonciations contre les ennemis du trône, ne devait-on pas poser la question carrément, bravement, comme elle doit l'être devant les tribunaux et devant le public ? Cette manière d'éluder l'esprit de la loi, de s'autoriser des lacunes des documents officiels, de prendre avantage des préjugés d'une partie de la population pour arriver à un simple fait d'homicide ; lorsque pas moins de six personnes ont déjà perdu la vie par suite de ces malheureux événements, et qu'on demande encore la vie d'un égal nombre, cette conduite, dis-je, n'est-elle pas illogique au suprême degré ? Ne porte-t-elle pas avec elle sa propre contradiction ?

" Il y a eu dans toute cette phase de transition du gouvernement de la Baie-d'Hudson au gouvernement canadien, une série d'erreurs, de bévues commises par tout le monde. Pourquoi n'en demander compte qu'à ceux qui étaient les moins en position de ne pas se tromper ? Pourquoi vouloir que des hommes absolument ignorants de la loi et de la constitution aient observé, dans leurs procédures, toutes les formes de la jurisprudence ? Pourquoi les condamner pour avoir suivi les instructions du gouverneur McTavish qui leur conseillait fortement d'établir un gouvernement ? Pourquoi leur demander d'avoir été plus loyaux que le Secrétaire d'Etat, qui écrivait à M. McDougall qu'après le 1er décembre, le gouvernement de Riel était le seul en existence *de facto* dans cette contrée ?

"Si le gouvernement provisoire n'a pas eu d'existence légale ou *de jure*, et il ne pouvait pas en avoir sans qu'il s'en suivit une révolution dans la Confédération, on a du moins reconnu les Métis comme belligérants, on a traité avec eux. Ils ont donc droit aux immunités accordées aux confédérés du Sud, aux insurgés de Crête, aux "raiders" de St. Albans, aux révoltés de Cuba, aux soldats de Don Carlos. Ceux qu'on prend les armes à la main, on les juge comme révoltés, si on croit que ce soit de bonne politique de le faire ; mais après avoir traité avec eux, après avoir demandé et obtenu une suspension d'armes, on ne leur fait pas un procès pour meurtre ou pour incendiat.

"Je ne prétends pas exprimer mon opinion sur la valeur de ces arguments ; c'était aux jurés et au juge de les apprécier. Je ne fais que présenter un tableau très en petit de l'argumentation de M. Chapleau dans cette cause, laquelle marquera certainement dans nos annales judiciaires comme une de nos intéressantes *causes célèbres*.

"En écoutant ce long plaidoyer—long seulement par la multitude des faits et des événements qu'il embrassait, car il n'a duré que deux heures et quart—je me prenais à regretter, au point de vue de l'art, que cette cause n'eut été portée devant un tribunal composé de trois ou cinq juges choisis dans Ontario ou Québec, devant un jury d'hommes brisés à ce genre de questions, et devant un public plus capable d'apprécier l'importance de la cause et le talent de ceux qui l'auraient dirigée.

"Malgré le trop peu de temps que M. Chapleau eut à sa disposition pour préparer sa cause, il eut de beaux succès oratoires. En plus d'une circonstance, on sentit un frisson parcourir tout l'auditoire ; même ceux qui ne le comprenaient pas étaient émus par cette voix sympathique et expressive qui rend si bien tous les sentiments et toutes les émotions."

SATURDAY, Oct. 31.

After routine, Mr. Chapleau said :—

May it please Your Lordship, Gentlemen of the Jury :—

In the evidence given in this case there are certain points raised. First as to the evidence objected to, I say that in the case *per se* evidence has been allowed which should not have been permitted. I refer to the evidence given by Bruce from Goulet. (His Lordship the Chief Justice here stated that on a second consideration of the matter, he had struck out all of Bruce's evidence in connection with Goulet's statements about the final disposition of Scott's body. If the evidence had been given while the deed was being committed, it would be regular, but it was told some time afterwards.) The second point is the proving of Scott's death. I want to quote a few authorities before the Court. We know the great maxim produced by Sir Matthew Hale as being the safest rule to follow. It goes to say that there is no murder if there is no death. There is a want of evidence in consequence of what is alleged, inasmuch as no one has stated that he has seen Scott dead, and no one has stated what has become of the body. The last edition of Archibald, 7th edition, page 271 and page 238, in 622, states that it must also be shown that the deceased died of wounds or other injuries given him, and within a year after he had received them, because if he had died after that time, it is fair to presume that the death might have proceeded from some other cause. I quote from Taylor on Evidence, page 199. After having spoken of some cases, the presumption of death of a person long missing, he goes on to say, " If the person has not been heard from for seven years, the presumption of death is permissible." I also quote Taylor on Evidence, page 613 : " A jury should not condemn if there is the shade of a shadow of a doubt." No court or jury has a right to act upon presumptive proof of the death of a party. In the same author on page 640-41, the same rule from Taylor is mentioned ; the statement of absence from the country is only presumptive of death. These cases have been general. I will quote about circumstantial evidence. In a case which occurred in the reign of Queen Elizabeth, the circumstances showed that the party was guilty, the jury could not find that the man was not guilty, the evidence was only presumptive that the man had really died. But the party did not die. I will quote from Phillips on Evidence, the case of Miles Scales — a case in which the captain of a vessel had been beaten by one of the mates in the presence of the sailors; blood was found on the deck, but the body was thrown into the sea, death could not be proven, no body had been found it turned up some years afterwards that the man was still alive. The author says the rule that the body must be found is absolute. I also maintain that the best evidence must be produced by the Crown. I maintain that the ruling of Hale must not apply strictly, and I must submit before the Court that the best evidence in this case has not been produced. The act was proved to have been done, that the man received wounds, but it has not been proved that these wounds caused death. It has not been proved that these wounds produced by bullets at twenty-five or thirty yards, fired from trading guns, caused death. At any rate it is open to question whether at that distance the man was shot by these trading guns. The best evidence should have been adduced. The evidence of that witness has not been received. The opinions of medical men are absolutely necessary. They rather than others, are prepared always to establish the cause of death. The Crown should have produced one medical man. This would have had more weight than the testimony of any one who was in the crowd. I maintain before the Court that the firing of a pistol does not convey positive evidence, unless a medical man's report was received, and why ? I just put the question to the Rev. Mr. Young if death could have followed from the firing. When I put the question, whether in some cases that bullets might have traversed the body, of course he would not answer. I quote from Taylor on Medical Jurisprudence as to the effects of bullets in the use of firearms. The author quotes a case where the deflection of the balls did not produce death. It is only a few months since a case occurred in Montreal. A young man attempted to commit suicide by shooting himself in the breast. The bullet was fired in such a way that if it had gone in the usual way it would have produced instant death. Three weeks afterwards that man was walking in the streets as if nothing had happened. It was discovered that the bullet had deflected and lodged in the back. I put this case before the Court and before the jury. The same rule also applies in the case of gun shots.

I come to another point ; it comes from the fact that the prisoner at the bar at the time of the shooting was then acting in his official capacity as Adjutant-General. I maintain most respectfully before this tribunal, that in a case of wilful homicide, or manslaughter, or assault, if he is guilty of anything, he is guilty of murder. Assault does not apply to his case.

I maintain that in the case in question that the prisoner acted in his official capacity in the so-called Provisional Government, by circumstances arising out of other circumstances which are termed by the authorities under the authority of a Government de facto recognized by the sovereign authorities and their representatives. I also maintain that the prisoner at the bar should have been tried for high treason and not for murder, if tried at all. In execution of the decree of the de facto Government, if amenable at all it should be high treason for which he should be first tried, if tried at all. (Mr. Chapleau desired that it should be understood in all these proceedings he does not wish it to be understood that he waives or considers the question of the liability of this jurisdiction overruled by the judgment, but reserves to the prisoner that right if he desires it. In support of this he quoted a proposition laid down in evidence, though it is only submitted *en passant*.) I will quote from what may be termed the classical rule in the laws of nations, page 67. (M. Chapleau here quoted the passage.)

I wish to put it to your Lordship, the conversations given by Archbishop Taché as to the state of a'arm and disturbance the country was in at that time. I wish to put in as a record a letter then written by Governor McTavish, dated the 4th September, 1869, in which the Governor has plainly stated the condition in which the colony was left. He certainly understands that the sovereign authorities and the Canadian representatives understood that the acts committed before the transfer would be excused. The letter of Archbishop Taché and the conversations he had, form what I now maintain. At the same time I refer to the report of their public acts and the report made by the Privy Council to the people of the mother country, the first dispatch between the Council and the authorities in Canada. I state as a proposition in this case that the movement was raised in a rightful way. I maintain before the Court that these proceedings and acts were carried out under lawful authority ; that these men who came into the country under Gov. McDougall and Col. Dennis did not come in a lawful manner, and their acts were not done in a legal and lawful way. The first rising and the meeting of the 16th November were a perfectly lawful movement. The then declarations of Gov. McTavish must be taken into consideration. The armed movement which was raised by Col. Dennis in this country, and the arming of the people, were for unlawful purposes ; that this movement was of such a nature as to justify the rising of the people then. The proclamation of Gov. McDougall on the 18th December was not sanctioned by the proper authorities in Canada and the sovereign authorities in England, and it has been proved to be illegal. It is not necessary for me to prove that the commission given by Gov. McDougall to Col. Dennis gave him the powers of a Lieut.- General for the North-West Territories. That commission gave him power to disturb the public peace, to burn down houses, to kill and destroy. I maintain that this proclamation was sufficient to justify any uprising of force to resist its provisions being carried on in the colony. I mean now to refer to the proclamation of the 8th of December. I say that proclamation was in effect the recognition of the rights of the people. It was issued at a time when there was no authority to justify it ; at the time it was issued, the Hudson's Bay Company had no rights in the colony. At that time, in the month of December, there was in fact a recognition by the authorities of the Hudson's Bay Company, and it was well understood among the population and generally known that the Hudson's Bay Company did not assume power in the country, and did not afford protection to the citizens. That state of things continued up to the 25th of January. I maintain that the authorities were so much out of existence, that executions, judgments or writs of any kind were not issued. Jails were broken into and complete isolation throughout the country was known to be the case. In the month of January there was a kind of a convention of the whole people which continued to the 25th of January. That convention agreed to a certain Bill of Rights. I do not speak of the proclamation of Riel. In the first Bill of Rights which was drawn up there is a certain perfume, I may call it, which I do not sustain or admire. The Bill of Rights then framed is certainly a Bill of Rights which the settlers of this country had a right to present at the convention in January, and before they proceeded to the election they had a right to do so. We cannot act on presumptions. Before proceeding to the election of a President, they asked the advice and opinion of Gov. McTavish. One witness says he declared himself favorable to the election of a Government. Mr. Sutherland declares that the condition he was in rendered him powerless. I also maintain that during that time not one single writ or act of prosecution was issued against anybody. No one took legal proceedings against any one ; no single writ of information whatever was issued. I say that these abstentions from executive authority are sufficient to prove that there was no law or authority in the country ; that the declaration of Gov. McTavish was given in view of that state of affairs. It will be remembered that the 9th or 10th of February was the time when the declaration was asked from Gov. McTavish, and I find that just on the eve there was constituted a kind of Assembly ; that on the same day the people saw that they wished the difficulties in the country would come to an end ; that that Convention was recognized by all parts of the population, afterwards by the Government of Canada. The Adjutant-General was appointed by a regular authority, because it was understood that at the time of the election of the President that the power of the Hudson's Bay Company was at an end ; that the movement of the other parties was to upset that authority ; that the cause of the movement of the 17th of February was the Kildonan affair. It will be said that that movement dispersed itself. It will be argued that the people were going to their homes when on the 17th of February they were arrested and brought to Fort Garry. I maintain that their detention in the Fort was a right acquired by reason of the authority possessed by the Provisional Government. That in the present case the law as laid down in Weedon, page 36, applies. I insist that there was a Government recognized as a *de facto* Government, and that the armed movement in support of it was according to the authority of the then existing Government. I must now proceed to the detention and to the action of the Government during that time. The arrest was made in February. The delegates were chosen not only by the President and Council of that Government, but they were chosen by the Convention itself to go to Ottawa. *En passant*, I may observe that during all these meetings Judge Black was the chairman of the Convention, and left his seat only when he saw that Riel had been elected. Delegates were appointed to go to Ottawa at that meeting. There were as members of that Convention four or five persons who were members of the Council of Assiniboia. The delegates were appointed to go to Ottawa by the Government. I must regret the treatment that the prisoners received while they were in the Fort. In times of war and revolution, there is no help for these things. What have we seen in other countries ? Instead of the lives of four or five, we have seen revolutions sweep away the lives of four or five hundred. While we have wars and insurrections these things must last. During the time the delegates were sent to Ottawa, there occurred a fact that is the strangest of all which took place during the whole of the troubles. When people come from a country and are not familiar with constitutional law and practice, these men should have been treated as negotiators ; it is the law at least among civilized nations that they should receive the same treatment which is given to barbarians. They were dealing with a Government in complete fairness. When the delegates arrived in Ottawa, when they presented their papers, they were acting according to their papers, which had been given to them to act in their capacity as delegates, as negotiators on behalf of the Provisional Government. I know it will be argued that the Government of Canada never recognized them except as representatives of the people. I will maintain that when the negotiators went to Ottawa, the Government saw their credentials, that they were introduced to the Executive Council and formally received and recognized.

(Mr. Cornish here asked if this was another speech to the jury.)

I say that this recognition was a matter of fact, was a matter of good faith between the parties, that they passed treaties, and that they and the Government have been recognized by the letter and answer from Hon. Joseph Howe, Secretary of State for the Provinces. I know that the answer was given them to say that the Governor-General representing Her Majesty and the Privy Council in Ottawa, received these delegates. I know that that recognition was not a complete one. I have seen the letters of Sir Clinton Murdock and Lord Lisgar, and it would be against my duty to say that this should be doubted. They acted in good faith and were led to understand that they were in the full capacity of ambassadors. If there is blame upon some one, surely it is not upon them ; we have the evidence of the extraordinary Commissioner, Archbishop Taché. I am sorry to see that the Crown has not brought complete evidence in this matter. The evidence of Mr. Donald A. Smith was not brought because the Crown was understood to say that these meetings had no other reasons that the explanations of his instructions from Ottawa.

(His Lordship here said that if Mr. Chapleau had given the slightest hint that Mr. Smith was necessary, he would have had him summoned.)

After the delegates had gone, there is also proof of those delegates then being in Ottawa. Archbishop Taché was asked to come as an extraordinary Commissioner to settle the difficulties in this country. He was appointed the special messenger of the Ottawa Government to come and settle the troubles, and he came armed with a Commission and invested with power and authority to do what was best for the country, and empowered to make promises which he was assured would be carried out. As to the court martial and the proceedings of the 4th of March, I maintain it was the action of a Government *de facto*, and it was necessarily a military Government. The court martial was recognized by those Governments. The documents, papers and records of that Government have been destroyed ; the records of that court martial are not to be found, and I know that it will be argued that the trial was a mock trial. I maintain that the members of that court martial could not be supposed to know everything about law as if they were experienced jurists, but it appears that they were not entirely ignorant of it. I maintain that the court martial was entirely composed of military authorities. It has been said that witnesses were not called and the French language was only spoken ; witnesses were called and were sworn. Scott was tried on three different accusations ; the first was of having taken up arms against the Provisional Government, and that he had struck the President of the Government and one of the guards. Evidence was produced and those charges were sustained, and the sentence of death was pronounced by the Court. Now, gentlemen, we have the evidence of Modeste Lajemoniere to prove that the prisoner was not present at the time of the execution, and have also the evidence that after the body was put in the bastion, one of the witnesses swore he heard the words "O Lord, O Lord," and that he believed those words came from Scott who was in the box. I will pass to the evidence of Baptiste Charette, and you will recollect that Chambers swore that it was Lepine that gave the signal with the handkerchief. This man swears positively that that signal was given by André Nault, and that man will have to bear the responsibility of the act. It is for you to say whether the prisoner was actively engaged in the proceedings of that day, if he was *particeps criminis* in the accident said to have been committed. It is true that the prisoner was at the court martial. When there is doubt more or less, it is reasonable and just that the prisoner should receive the benefit of those doubts. The great maxim is clear upon this point. It is better that ninety-nine of the guilty should go unpunished, than that one innocent should be sacrificed. I maintain that this man throughout has shown himself to be a British subject, loyal to the Queen and his country. He has been dragged from his home and from his family to answer a charge of which he is no more guilty than four or five hundred others who acted with him at the time. I have come more than two thousand miles to defend him, and I believe that his cause is a just and righteous one. I appeal to your sympathies, to your sense of justice. Four or five lives have already been lost in this unfortunate affair, and is the cry to be still blood ? I appeal to your manhood, and to your honor, and to your sense of fairplay, and I maintain that the prisoner at the bar is not guilty of the accusation against him, and that you will render a verdict of acquittal, and that it is your duty as well as your interests to see that this settlement continues to become a flourishing colony.

Mr. Cornish then addressed the jury and spoke for half an hour, after which the Court took recess, Mr. Cornish resuming his address on the Court re-assembling. He said :

May it please your Lordship, Gentlemen of the Jury:—

I am sure that all of you have sat with a great deal of patience listening to the facts and evidence in this case, and I may be permitted to say that you have exhibited throughout these long two weeks that patience and attention which should ever characterise jurors and juries. Gentlemen, I can assure you that these facts speak volumes in your favour, for they prove that the attention which you have bestowed upon this case was deep and absorbing. You have shown by your deportment that you appreciate and respect the responsibilities that your oaths have imposed upon you, and that in order to come to a just verdict it is absolutely requisite that every word that has been uttered by the witnesses—nay their very manner and actions—have not escaped your searching attention and enquiry. What have we, gentlemen, in this case on which you have sat night and day for two long weeks? You know the indictment, and you have heard evidence on both sides. You have seen, the counsel for the defence have employed every means within their power to refute the evidence which the Crown has placed before you, and which was extracted from not very willing witnesses either. The chief ground on which the defence rest their case is that the killing of Thomas Scott on the 4th March, 1870, was the act of a regular government, duly empowered and acting under the constitutional authorities of the country. When did that government become *de facto*, and who gave it authority? By some means or other that government has become defunct. What has become of it? Do they mean to say that it was a *de facto* government because it elected a president and because it had a council, and armed men to carry out its decrees? I can tell you that that government was only a government of physical power, and that this was used to enforce its will. But that time has passed away, and those notions that justice, slow-footed as she is, would never overtake the murderers of poor Thomas Scott, are dissipated. The time has come when the law will be enforced. It is in accordance with that law that you are here to-day. One of the points raised by the defence in their special pleading is that it is necessary to prove that Scott is dead. If Thomas Scott is not dead, no one better than the prisoner knows where he is. If Scott did not die, the prisoner and his accomplices are the people best able to give us the information where he is. Would to God that Thomas Scott were not dead, and that he could stand here in this Court to-day; would not every man raise a shout of satisfaction, and the prisoner at the bar would he not stand gloriously acquitted? But unfortunately Thomas Scott did die, that must be the conclusion of every man who has heard the case. Yes, everyone of you must come to the conclusion that Thomas Scott was killed and murdered by the prisoner at the bar and his accomplices. It is a principle in British law that all persons who participate in the taking away of life deliberately and without authority are guilty of wilful murder. Another special plea is that there was no evidence given as to Scott's death by a doctor or a surgeon, but I trust that you will not permit such a weak and absurd idea to lead you astray. In order to arrive at a just and sensible conclusion, you are to judge from the evidence, and if you think that evidence justifies you in believing that Thomas Scott is not dead, then there was no murder. We have the evidence and the witnesses to say that they saw a number of men drawn up in a line with double-barrelled guns, and then discharge them into Scott's body, and we have the evidence to show that the prisoner at the bar was ordering and directing these men on that occasion. It remains with you to say whether the prisoner at the bar was one of these men who were present on that occasion or not. They say there is positive evidence that Scott spoke after he was put in the box. Perhaps in the agonies of death he may have called upon his murderers to release him or put an end to his agonies, and though the prisoner was there with all his generous instincts, there was no one to go to poor Scott's relief. There can be no question that the poor man died of these gunshots and the wounds they inflicted. Yes, for no crime whatever, for the evidence does not go to say that any charge was proved against him at that mock trial. Poor Thomas Scott was taken out of the Fort in the light of noon and butchered by fiends in human shape—slaughtered by the authority of a court martial presided over by that man at the bar, acting under the directions of the Provisional Government! Gentlemen, some of the arguments used by the defence do not need to be refuted. They contradict themselves. I am sure you will admit that the prisoner has had every allowance and latitude given him. In order to bring you to a proper conclusion, it will be necessary to take you to the time that he was arrested with the Portage party on the 17th of February, to the fatal 4th of March. He was proceeding homeward to the Portage; he had a right to travel on with others. We find by the evidence of Mr. Farmer that on the night of the 17th of February, he saw a number of men proceeding from Fort Garry. We find that Lepine, the prisoner, was one of that party and in authority. On that occasion some conversation took place between a man named Panquin, of the Portage party, and who enquired what Lepine and followers meant by their demonstration of force. I feel here that it is my duty to state that as soon as I heard this man's name, I despatched a messenger with a subpœna to that man who I was informed was residing at the Portage, and that messenger returned stating that Panquin was out of the Province, beyond reach at Fort Pelly. The Portage party were surrounded, and a man by the name of O'Donohue and the prisoner at the bar appeared to be in command. They were arrested and taken to the Fort. Thomas Scott was one of that Portage party. They did not suppose that anything was wrong. They were mistaken. The party that was taken were imprisoned there, and poor Scott was kept there until the 4th of March, when he was taken out to be murdered. It has been proved by credible and reliable witnesses that the prisoner at the bar was there present at that slaughter, acting under the orders of the so-called Provisional Government. Alex. McPherson, one of the witnesses, said that Lepine was behind the party that led Scott out of the prison to be shot. Alex Murray tells you that he saw him that day actively moving about the Fort giving instructions to the armed guards. Murray also tells you that at the time they were taken prisoners, the prisoner being asked if he was in command of the Fort party, made his bow in assent to the supposition. The next thing we hear is that the prisoner is in command of the insurrection, giving orders. And what can you say of the Hallet affair, of the treatment that poor man received at the hands of the prisoner, who, there is no question whatever, was an active participant in these proceedings? We proceed to the 3rd of March. For some reason or other, it may be that Louis Riel's words are true that he was going to teach the Canadian Government that he was in earnest, by taking the life of one of Her Majesty's subjects. This is the only reason that we have heard alleged during the whole course of the trial and investigation as to the cause of the murder of Thos. Scott. It was necessary to slaughter some one to help the cause. We find on the 3rd March poor Scott was taken into a room and informed by the chief witness in this mock court, presided over by the prisoner, that he is to be shot. The same opportunities for defence which have been given freely, nay abundantly to the prisoner at the bar, now on his trial, were denied poor Scott. He had no counsel to come two thousand miles to defend him, no jury of his countrymen to examine the evidence, no chance to show that he was innocent of the crimes charged against him. The man before you presided at that court which in less than two hours, in a language foreign to their victim, decided to take his life in order to teach the Canadian Government that they were in earnest. Yes, a victim must be immolated to baptise the Provisional Government with his blood, and that victim was poor Scott, and one of his murderers is the prisoner at the bar. What was the pretext for the justification of this bloody deed? That Scott had struck Riel and beaten one of the guards, and that he had broken his promise or oath that he had taken to the Provisional Government. I tell you there is no proof that Scott ever made any promise or took any oath to the Provisional Government. Examine the testimony of Joseph Nolin, and what does he say? He tells you he was told at three o'clock in the afternoon of the 3rd of March that Scott was to be brought before the Council and sentenced to be shot. Murray tells you in his evidence—and Murray is a most credible witness—that on the night of the 3rd of March, about eight o'clock, while he was looking through the keyhole of his prison door, he saw and heard Scott in an altercation with his guards, and that Riel, O'Donohue and Lepine were present, and that there was a scuffle. Now recollect what Joseph Nolin says; he states that three or four hours before that scuffle took place, and consequently before Scott had struck the guards, or the captain, or Riel, they had made up their minds to try him and sentence him. Now I want you to put together what Nolin says and what Murray says, and see if you can't see that the court martial and the sentence were not contemplated long before the alleged striking could have taken place. These charges of striking the Captain and Riel were mere pretences, unsupported and not proved. It is murder, cold-blooded murder and nothing less. Will you follow the evidence for a moment? What says the President of that mock tribunal—the prisoner at the bar?—" The majority only want his death, and he shall die." The evidence goes on to show that four were in favor of his death; one was in favor of exiling him; and one, Baptiste Lepine, was opposed to the sentence. The records and minutes of that court have not been placed before you; they have been destroyed. On the morning of the 4th March, Nolin swears that the prisoner came to his room at five o'clock in the morning. What did he come there for? To see that the minutes of the proceedings of the night before had been correctly recorded. It appears that Riel called that morning at Nolin's room to see if the *procés-verbal*—the minutes—had been properly recorded, and we find by the evidence that they were altered by Riel, though Nolin states that the alterations were only with reference to the form. There has been a great deal of evidence with regard to the complicity of the prisoner. Take the evidence of McPherson. He swore that Riel was one of the men who accompanied Scott to the place of execution. Take the evidence of Murray. He says that he saw Lepine and saw Mr. Young. It is true that there is a discrepancy or rather an apparent contradiction with regard to the person who said " Good-bye, boys," when Scott and Mr. Young went around to say good-bye for the last time. It is a matter of perfect indifference who said these words. Some of the witnesses say that it was Scott who said the words. Murray swears that it was the Rev. Mr. Young. It is easy to account for the difference. Mr. Young may have said, " Here is Scott come to bid you good-bye, boys," and then Scott did so, but I am sure you will not permit yourselves to be misled by so trifling a matter as this. We all know what followed. The defence have attempted to surround the case with mystery and doubt, but it is a sad reality. The men who are detailed to do this bloody work are first made drunk by the prisoner and his associates, in order that they may in their drunken orgies make sure of their victim. It appears that on the occasion of the murder, the Rev. Mr. Young was the messenger of peace; that when that good man, whose name must always bear an important part in the efforts that were made to prevent his butchery, anxious to do his utmost to prevent the bloody deed, waited upon Riel, the President of this so-called Provisional Government, to ask and implore him to stay the murder, if not to prevent it at all events to postpone it. Riel sends for his Adjutant-General Lepine, the prisoner. He comes and is informed of Mr. Young's request. The prisoner shakes his head emphatically, gives the gesture of dissent, and turning upon his heel walks away and leaves the room. We now come to Mr. D. C. Campbell's evidence. He was in the Fort. He was in the habit of visiting the Fort with provisions; he did so purely out of friendship and warm-heartedness. On one occasion he was stopped from going out of the Fort by one of the guards.

He sees Lepine, the Adjutant-General, coming and he represents the matter to him. Lepine gives the order to the guard to allow Campbell to pass. There can be no mistake, the prisoner was a person then in authority. The next witness is John Bruce, and some are apt to speak disparagingly of John Bruce and his evidence. You know what Bruce said; you remember Lepine's observation to him with regard to the shooting of a couple of the prisoners before they should be released. You remember what was said to Murray a long time after the affair of the 4th March, when Murray went to obtain £60 and his gun and pistol, which he had delivered up in the presence of the prisoner. You remember what the prisoner told Murray on the occasion: "You had better keep quiet, for the Fenians are coming," and it is a matter of fact that the Fenians did come. We have the evidence of Duncan Nolin who saw Scott shot on the 4th of March. We have the evidence of Joseph Nolin, Lepine's private secretary, and you will admit that he did give his evidence with a firmness and a clearness that was becoming, and which, more than all, has not been contradicted.

It being one o'clock, the Court here took recess.

After recess, Mr. Cornish resumed :—I was going to refer to the testimony of François Charette, who is a man who knows Lepine well and who lived near him for some time. You all know what Charette says in his evidence. He was on the wall, and came down after the firing and saw the prisoner, and saw him with his hand on his pistol in his breast-pocket, and saw Guilmette fire the pistol at Scott's head. He heard and saw what passed, saw the prisoner there, and heard a voice say to him, "You have no business here, go into the Fort," and he received a kick which he believes was administered by the prisoner. It appears that when one chamber of the revolver had snapped, the prisoner's voice was heard to say, "Why is not that pistol in order? Here is one in order," and that moment Charette swears that the prisoner laid his hand upon his pistol in his breast pocket. Charette also tells us that that night he heard a voice utter the words, "My God, my God," from within the bastion. Charette swears that it was Nault who gave the signal with the handkerchief to the firing party. Chambers swears that it was the person known as Lepine. Charette also swears that the box was put in the ground on Saturday night or Sunday morning, but he cannot identify the parties who were doing it, or swear that the body was in the box at the time. Charette also swears that it was not Lepine that gave the signal with the handkerchief, that it was André Nault. This is an apparent inconsistency between the testimony of Chambers and that of Charette himself, but I think it is easily explained. It is within our power to prove that there were two parties giving signals on that day; one was to the party in charge of the firing party, and the other was to the guard itself. The evidence given by Baptiste Charette has satisfied you that it came from a most unwilling witness. He saw the Rev. Mr. Young there. He saw André Nault there, and he saw all that was going on. It appears that the Rev Mr. Young was instrumental or rather was the cause of a delay of nearly two hours. Poor Scott was condemned to die at ten o'clock, but it was noon before the slaughter commenced, and Riel and Lepine became impatient about their victim. What was the conduct of this man when applied to by the Rev. Mr. Young and Bishop McLean for the body? Was it not proved that Riel promised the body on condition that there would be no demonstration made about its burial; and that afterwards he had to recall his promise because the prisoner as Adjutant-General refused to give up the body, and claimed that body as his? Was that the conduct of a man of such generous instincts as have been ascribed to him by the learned Counsel for the defence? To refuse the clay of poor Scott the last rites of the Christian Church, was an act which must impress upon your minds the character of the prisoner at the bar. And if we are to believe the records, Scott was not the only one condemned to die. Major Boulton was condemned to be shot at twelve o'clock in the night, and his life was spared only on conditions which were extorted by threats and a display of powder, shot and guns. And you must put the story of the cutter going out at night, and the entire disappearance of Scott's body, together and draw your conclusions. And next we have the evidence of Rev. Père Ritchot, and what does it prove? Why, it proves that there were others behind the scenes, misguiding and misleading those whom they should have been teaching and instructing. Yes, it may be before we get to the end of this question that others may be drawn in who have escaped under the garb of sanctity and religion. In the evidence of Modeste Lajemoniere, we are given to understand that the prisoner, together with Riel, was in the attic of Dr. Cowan's building looking out of the window when Scott was passing out on the morning of that fatal day of March, and that one of them was so surprised that he said, "In God's truth they are bringing him down," as much as to say that they were surprised. Are you to be misled by such shallow pretences as these, manufactured for the occasion? Who, I ask, was in command there at the time; and if the prisoner was opposed to the execution, why did he not rush down and say, "Halt, return that man to his quarters, you must not take away his life." No, it was the prisoner who pronounced the sentence of the court, "The majority want his death and he shall die." The body in the box confirms that of Lajemoniere, and can we believe that, while poor Scott was lying there in the fearful agonies of death, there was no one either to put an end to his miseries or to relieve his pains? It is not unlikely that when he was carried into the bastion, a knife or a pistol was used to cut the last thread of existence; but the long time that poor Scott must have suffered the agonies of death is known only to his torturers and to Him who is the avenger of all crime. It is a rule of law that no man on a jury should prevent a just verdict because of prejudice or in spite of proof. I trust that you have come to the conclusion that the so-called Provisional Government was not legal, or lawful: this, you are aware, must not determine your verdict. It is upon the immediate facts of the murder of poor Scott that you must decide. The learned Counsel for the defence has appealed to your sympathies, because the prisoner at the bar has a weeping wife and family fearful of the issue. I tell you poor Scott had a mother, and that mother had a son, who according to the evidence which has been given, was foully and cruelly murdered by the prisoner at the bar and his associates on the 4th of March, 1870, and that even the last rites of Christian burial were denied the poor clay of Thomas Scott, and the body was spirited away by the prisoner and his associates, and to this day it is a mystery where that body is. I am sure that there never was a clearer case, and it is your bounden duty to record a verdict of guilty against the prisoner at the bar.

Mr. Stewart Macdonald, junior Counsel for the Crown, then addressed the jury in French as follows, closing the case :—

May it please Your Lordship,

Gentlemen of the Jury :—

After hearing the able and long addresses delivered to you by the learned counsels for the defence, and also the able and elaborate address by the leading Crown Prosecutor, I as junior counsel for the Crown address you with some reluctance. The thought struck me, while I was listening to the many legal points raised by the learned counsel for the defence, whether or not they were admirable as reasonable objections in justification of the foul deed committed on March 4th, 1870; in carefully examining the evidence and giving every possible doubt to the prisoner at the bar, you will find that the great mass of testimony, both for the Crown and the defence, goes to show that the prisoner Lepine was a participator to the crime of which he is charged, and which he is proved to have been directly concerned in the killing of that ever-to-be-lamented loyal victim of illegal power, Thomas Scott.

You have now reason to say that he was loyal to his Queen and country, and this loyalty he has sealed with his blood, as has been proved by over thirty respectable and intelligent witnesses. When we recall to mind the insurrection of 1869 and 1870 in the Red River Settlement, it is with feelings of horror that I refer to the crime which was committed in open day, and which has been so mildly termed "error" by the leading counsel for the defence. But, gentlemen, while addressing you I feel that you have that conscious dignity of your position as men of respectability and your responsibility as jurors between Her Majesty the Queen and the prisoner at the bar, that will lead you to respect the oath you have taken and the allegiance which you owe to her and to society. It has often been remarked that mixed juries seldom agree upon their verdicts, in consequence of party spirit and prejudice being admitted into the secret circle. To men whose minds are well disposed, such as you appear to be, it is to be trusted that you will manly and nobly unite in the verdict on this important trial, thus showing to the world that notwithstanding all the influences brought to bear on your minds, that you came into this Court as jurors armed with that free spirit of determination to do justice which characterises every honest man, and as such you are asked as a right to agree upon your verdict. It is needless to tell you that the eyes of the world and of this community in particular are upon you in so critical and important a moment as the present, awaiting with breathless interest the results of your deliberations. It is now your duty to weigh carefully all the evidence you have heard during this long trial, and if the evidence for the defence is found wanting, it will be a duty incumbent on you, both individually and collectively, and after a calm deliberation, to declare to this honorable Court that you find the prisoner at the bar, Ambroise Lepine, guilty of the crime of which he is charged in the Bill of Indictment found against him somewhat over a year by your peers the Grand Jury, and for which up to the present time he has been awaiting his trial. You must discard all feelings of fear, favor or prejudice from your minds, and concentrate all your ideas upon the evidence which has been laid before you, and if a reasonable doubt arises in your minds as to the guilt or innocence of the prisoner, you are bound in justice and law to give him the benefit of that doubt. But that doubt must be well founded, not simply a doubt for an excuse to throw aside a simple duty, but that which will plead fairly and justly in favour of the prisoner. The case now under your consideration is without parallel in the history of British America. The result thereof will be echoed all over the civilized world, and whatever decision you may come to, it will be final and will be handed down to posterity. The learned counsel for the defence has endeavoured to show you that the so-called Provisional Government of which the prisoner was a member, was a legal Government, by way of a plea for the justification of the crime of which the prisoner is accused. Admitting by way of argument the legality and existence of such a Government, is there any reason that the powers of that Government should have been prostituted? Scott's blood had no right to be shed, or his death compassed by men whose whole power was of both doubtful and illegal tenure. That blood now calls loudly for justice, and you are the chosen instruments of the law for this purpose.

Three objections in particular, amongst many others, have been raised by the defence.

First—That Scott is not proven to be dead, because two witnesses heard the words, "I say, I say," and, "My God, my God," spoken from the rough box called a coffin in which Scott's body was placed when it was taken into the south-east bastion of the Fort. To that objection I would answer in this way. The Rev. Mr. Young, although not a medical man, has told you in his testimony that Scott could not survive after receiving three bullet wounds in the breast and shoulder, and also a revolver shot in the head. If after this evidence the defence can say that he (Scott) is not dead, and can prove this statement by the production of his body alive and well, why then this charge of murder against the prisoner falls to the ground. There can be no two opinions with regard to this, the whole testimony proves the fact that he is dead, but to life only, and not to justice.

Second—That if Scott is dead, the body was or has not been found, and no coroner's inquest held to determine the manner of his death. To this I will answer: The guilty parties have secreted that body, to which Christian burial was refused, and now try to shield their inhuman act by the admission of Scott's death in their second objection, but denying it in the first. I will leave it to you to say, for you are better able to judge, is Scott's chained and manacled body lying beneath the dark waters of the Red River, or is it not ? Evidence has been given to warrant this conclusion.

Third—That the prisoner was President of the Council of War which condemned Scott to death, and that he only performed a military duty under an acknowledged Government of the country at that time. What answer can be made to this objection, and to the mock trial, for mock trial it was. Why, Riel was the accuser, the chief witness, the prosecutor and the judge, and it was at his request that poor Scott was sentenced, whilst he was denied the right of presence at the tribunal which ordered his death in twelve short hours. Of whom did this so-called Court Martial consist ? Why, gentlemen, it was composed of seven men who had been duped by Riel to imagine themselves a court of justice, and of this would-be court the prisoner at the bar was the leading spirit. Was it civilized justice when Scott was refused to have the evidence against him made known to him in his own language before he was sentenced ? Was it the acts of righteous judges to refuse his petition in this respect, or was it the act of men who had coolly and deliberately planned the death of a man of whose fearless character they stood in awe ? The prisoner at the bar unlike Scott has had a fair trial, has been defended by able counsel, and if he has to meet his inevitable fate, he will, unlike that of poor Scott, be given ample time to reconcile himself to his Maker, and implore for that forgiveness for his crime which cannot be given him in this world. If the prisoner stands in the felon's dock, you must bear in mind that it is not through a spirit of mere vengeance, but for the vindication of that law which says, "Thou shalt not kill," and for the future peace and prosperity of this Province and of the whole North-West Territories. And now, gentlemen, let us in a few brief sentences see how the evidence implicates the prisoner in this heart-rending crime.

First—He appears as Adjutant-General, showing a little brief authority on everything that his perverted and tyrannical mind dictated.

Second—The prisoners were released by his authority, and passes given them by his private secretary on his order to that effect.

Third—He presides at the so-called Court Martial and pronounces the doom which brings the thread of Scott's life to an untimely end.

Fourth—He sternly despises the requests and earnest solicitations of Scott's warm friends to spare his life a few short hours longer, that he might prepare for that terrible change from whence no traveller returns.

Fifth—He takes away that life, but not yet satisfied with shedding blood, he denies Christian burial to the remains of the victim of his unrighteous passions.

After doing all these, he now wants to plead justification and innocence. So do all criminals when they are brought face to face with their crimes and the Majesty of the law consequent upon their committal.

The day of retribution has come at last. Justice has been tardy, but sure no justification offered can be of any avail for the prisoner. The law will have to take its course, and a felon's crime must meet a felon's doom.

It is true a commutation of sentence may be granted, if the prisoner is condemned to death, but this rests with Her Majesty through the Governor General and Council of the Dominion of Canada, should they be inclined to show that mercy which the prisoner denied his victim.

It is needless for me to recapitulate the whole of the evidence, for during a long and patient investigation you have had the whole of it laid before you, and the attention you have given to the trial is worthy of the highest praise. His Lordship the Honorable Chief Justice for this Province will deliver his charge and explain to you the law in all such cases, and to him you will give that earnest attention which has characterised you throughout this trial. I now conclude in the full confidence that after retiring and duly deliberating amongst yourselves, you will have no difficulty and no delay in agreeing to a verdict of "Guilty" against the prisoner at the bar.

It being five o'clock, the Court adjourned until Monday morning at ten o'clock' when His Lordship said he would deliver his charge.

MONDAY, November 2nd.

On the Court meeting pursuant to adjournment, after routine,

His Lordship delivered the following charge in English, sentence by sentence of which was translated to the Jury by Mr. Carey, Clerk of the Court :—

THE CHIEF-JUSTICE'S CHARGE.

In giving my charge to you, in consequence of some being on the Jury who do not understand English well, I propose to speak to you as shortly as I possibly can so that you can hear every word. Mr. Carey shall translate into the French language the words that I wish to speak to you. First, I remark that in the trial of criminal cases as well as civil cases, it is highly important to hear the most learned and able men as Counsels in the cause, to aid and assist the Court and the Jury. At the same time the Jury must not be misled. It is the province of the Counsel to argue and collate facts and circumstances of law, but never to give opinions—opinions as to facts are conclusions which the Jury must draw from the sworn testimony of the witnesses in the box, and the law must be pronounced from the bench for which the Judge is responsible. The old maxim is, the Jury are responsible to the facts and the Judge to the law. I shall discuss the questions raised on this trial on the record under two heads : First, whether a homicide was committed on the 4th of March, 1870, if such an occurrence constitutes murder, and whether or not the prisoner at the bar was so implicated in that killing as to render him guilty of the crime charged on this indictment. Second, was there any act committed under the circumstances as to make it murder, and was it more or less intentional ? Are there any facts detailed before you on this trial which would justify that killing or that murder ? Was it done by such an authority and having cause under that authority which in law would make it justifiable homicide ? I shall speak to the latter proposition first, and in doing so I shall assume that the homicide did take place on the 4th March, and I shall pass briefly over the history of events which led to that killing, always keeping within the limits of the evidence given in the witness box at this trial, not going out of it. We know as a matter of public record on our state books that in 1868, the Imperial Government, the Hudson's Bay Company and the Canadian Government made arrangements for transferring the North-West country and Rupert's Land and the Indian Territory to the Canadian Government. As to the policy of that arrangement we have nothing to say on this trial. It was intended that the transfer would take place and would be consummated on the 1st December, 1869, but circumstances transpired which we know from the witness box, that it was not then done, and it in fact did not take place until the 15th July, 1870. It is said before the month of October, 1869, certain persons in connection with the Dawson Road had some small difficulties with some of the natives, but not worth speaking of. Whatever was the result of it, the design of the Dawson Road was in the interests of the people here. Of course I refer to the road between this and the North-West Angle. We next learn from Father Ritchot that there were some troubles about the transfer and the introduction of Canadian officials. It appears that the people at that time were armed with arms and guns with the object and intention of preventing the introduction of the Canadian officials. The Jury heard what he said with regard to the barricade at the Stinking and Scratching Rivers and the distribution of guards in different parts of the country, also the interruption of the commerce of the country, the taking of twenty carts of Government stores, all of which was done about the 20th of October. About that time it would appear from the evidence there were some Government stores in the town, deposited in Dr. Schultz's warehouse. The result was, the first act was the taking of Fort Garry ; it was taken as I recollect about the 1st of November. From that it would appear that Col. Dennis was collecting forces down in the settlements on the west side of the Red River with the twofold object of forcibly introducing Governor McDougall and the protection of Government property at Schultz's. The next event was the surrounding of Dr. Schultz's house and the directing of ordinance and cannon so as to reach the premises. They surrounded the building and took forty-seven prisoners. These prisoners were taken to the Fort. It does not appear from any statement of the witnesses that Scott was among the forty-seven, it would rather appear that he was not taken along with them, but by himself, and he was put in the Fort as a prisoner at the same time. The next event that I shall call your attention to, from the statement of the witness, was the Convention of the 16th of November. That convention was convened by a proclamation or public notice proceeding from the leaders of the movement, and called upon the English population to choose twelve delegates to meet twelve from the French population to deliberate on the affairs of the country. Just before the meeting of that convention Governor McTavish issued that proclamation which you have heard read (it is the one in which he states that they have taken public property and interfered with the mails). That convention met on the 16th of November, and after deliberating they adopted the Bill of Rights ; we may call that for distinction the first Bill of Rights ; it was proposed to present that Bill of Rights to Governor McDougall, and demand a concession of those rights. I refer to the evidence of Thomas Bunn. We do not know precisely from the witnesses the reasons which prevented the delegates from going to Governor McDougall. It is stated that the reason was that some of the English delegates said that the Governor could not grant these himself ; another party contended it must be secured with the solemnity of an act of Parliament before they were to be permitted to come into the country, so nothing was done and the resolutions of the convention itself fell to the ground. That disposes of that convention. Gentlemen of the Jury, you must be very patient while I go through ; and that the utmost patience and caution are necessary I need not say. The next thing we hear of in the evidence is the meeting of the 19th of January. That meeting was called by Donald A. Smith for the purpose of explaining his mission and to lay before them certain documents, among these the Queen's proclamation, all of which documents are here fyled, and most of them you have seen in the public prints. That meeting of the several speeches made on the 19th was adjourned over until the 20th. It was said by the witnesses to have been the largest meeting that they ever saw in the colony, and apparently at that meeting the utmost harmony and good-will seemed to pervade the entire body. On the 20th they met in the afternoon. Father Ritchot says at the instance of some of the leading men in the meeting, a resolution was adopted in these words : Mr. Bannatyne moved that twenty representatives shall be elected by the English population of Red River to meet twenty other representatives from the French population on Tuesday, the 25th instant, at noon, in the Court House, with the object of considering the subject of Mr. Smith's commission read, and to decide what would be best for the welfare of the country. Now observe the power to be given to the gentlemen here chosen, and in observing the power you must understand that the object of the meeting was to hear Smith's exposition, that is to consider the subject of Smith's mission, and consider what would be best for the welfare of the country. That resolution was unanimously carried by the meeting, and the delegates, the forty delegates were chosen, and they met on 25th of January and continued their sittings down to the 9th or 10th of February. The prisoner among others was one of the delegates. From the evidence it would appear that the convention went to work to frame a new Bill of Rights without hearing Mr. Smith on the subject of his mission, intending as they said to hear him after they had completed that work. That convention, according to Mr. Bunn's evidence, appointed a committee of which he was one to report officers of what was understood to be a Provisional Government. They did report, another convention adopted that report, and Thomas Bunn was appointed Secretary of State; Mr. Bannatyne, Post Master General; Mr. Ross, Chief Justice; and I think John Bruce was to be Minister of Public Works. I am not positive as to the last, but the convention did not define what should be the authorities and duties of these officers. After this was done they adopted a Bill of Rights, they had an interview with Smith, and finally they came to the great question of the election of President. Down to this time Judge Black was Chairman. Mr. Bunn says that the subject of President was referred to the same committee as elected the officers, and they reported that Riel should be President, but still that had to be confirmed by a vote of the convention. It appears no public discussion on the question, that is no speeches took place, but there was a great deal of private talk amongst the members. The English portion seemed very reluctant to take the step, alleging that the Hudson's Bay Company, with McTavish as the Governor, were the only legal authorities in the land. Then you recollect the interview with Governor McTavish and in which Mr. Sutherland says Governor McTavish said his authority was at an end, that McDougall's proclamation of the 1st of December had extinguished him and his Government, and he told them, Mr. Sutherland says, and they all agreed who where present as to that, " Establish a Government for God's sake, act for the interests of the country, I am a dying man" or "a dead man." It is but right that you should recollect that Governor McTavish must have known at that time that McDougall's proclamations were premature, and that by the law of the land, I mean the law of the Empire, the only legal sovereign in Rupert's land, and I do not include the Indian Territories of which the Red River Settlement is part, was the Hudson's Bay Company and their officers. I tell you in this connection that Governor McTavish had no more power than you or I had to divest himself of his legal authority, or to throw his mantle upon anyone else. It is but right that I should further state that Governor McTavish had over him at that time a guard, that he was a prisoner in his own house, and that his health was anything but sound. It has been observed in reference to Governor McTavish, at that time or some time after that he was weak in body, nevertheless he was clear in his intellect. Now I will leave this question for your cogitation, and in the solution of which you may be aided by your own personal experience or from possible experience; is a person who is diseased and weak in body likely to exercise that stern iron will in obedience to his judgment that he would were his physical frame sound and vigorous? Upon the result of the interview with Governor McTavish, the Convention decided that Riel should be President; that would be either the 9th or the night of the 10th of February; at that time seventy or eighty persons were then within twelve or fourteen miles of Headingly, some say hundred miles, in arms, with the avowed object of forcibly releasing the prisoners which had been taken at Dr. Schultz's house. On the 15th or 16th of February at Kildonan, some six hundred or seven hundred persons, more or less armed, were congregated apparently with the same object. The jury heard what the witnesses have stated as to the dispersion of that force. It is important for you to know and consider these facts in connection with this fact, whether anything like the unanimous assent by the great body of the English-speaking people was given to that thing called the Provisional Government. That Convention did not define the powers or authority of the President. All we know is that before his election Judge Black acted as Chairman, and after his election, Judge Black vacated his seat and Riel took the seat as Chairman or President. Now I ask you, ha l Riel, because he was elected, any more power than Judge Black had, who previously occupied the seat as Chairman? If he had, where did he get it? Who gave it to him? Did the people give it, or did that Convention give it to him? Was that Convention elected for the purpose of giving him any power, or was it elected to consider the commission of Mr. Smith, or was it only to consider the best interests of the country? I ask you to cast in your own minds if Riel, by what then took place, had the power of life and death in his hands? Who gave him that power? On the contrary, if he succeeded Governor McTavish, if that inference should be drawn, had he any more power than Governor McTavish? Had he any more power than the whole of the Hudson's Bay Company? Had he more power than the Queen herself? If he did possess the power of life and death, was it exercised with any regard for the law, military or civil? If the meaning was that this party should carry on civil government in this country, the meaning was that they should carry it out according to law. Did they do it? This is a question of fact for you. We are told by the witnesses that this Convention was burst (by Bunn I think) by the Kildonan affair, was put an end to. The Convention selected delegates on the invitation of Smith to take a list of their rights to go to Ottawa and present them to the Parliament and Government of Canada, the Parliament then being in session. On the 17th February, some forty eight persons were taken prisoners out on the prairie. Among these prisoners was Thomas Scott, who had, while in the Fort before that as a prisoner, escaped and come to the Portage. You heard the witnesses state, and I shall not detain you just now by going over the facts that transpired on the taking of that Portage party. It is asserted by the witnesses that they were taken in bad faith, in fact that they were led into a trap. It does not make very much difference whether it was so or not, but it is worthy of your attention that after Riel or the leaders knew a large party was at Kildonan, they released the prisoners they had then in the Fort, and the release of which the Portage party swear was the only object of their coming down. Why, then, did Riel release these prisoners when a large number of people were assembled at Kildonan, and turn around and take forty-eight new prisoners? It is supposed in all warfare that the honor of human nature is always respected; even brigands have some sense of honor in respect to their movements. What then are you to infer from what transpired on the 16th and 17th February? Do you find in these leaders a combination of cowardice and treachery, or do you not? I think it proper that all the facts which have been detailed should be presented to your minds. An unfortunate circumstance transpired at Kildonan, and the circumstances surrounding it, as I gather from the witnesses, divest it in a great measure of the features which would otherwise surround it, but which called for the strongest condemnation. You have heard how poor Sutherland came to his death; he was shot by a person named Parisien. Parisien was taken by Farmer, supposed to be a spy. In all military movements spies are liable to be put to death. I do not mean scouts or advanced bodies of men in military movements, but I mean a person who pretends to be your friend, simulating friendship and ingratiating himself into the confidence of your party for the purpose of giving information to your opponents. Parisien was supposed to be such a person, although no one has said that he was one. It has been suggested

8

that he was a partizan of Riel's ; however that may be, it is a matter of very little importance except as to the treatment he received, because he should never have been subjected to the harsh treatment that he received even if he was really what was supposed. Parisien in trying to get away, saw Sutherland coming up the river on horseback. Parisien in his escape had snatched a double-barreled gun, and as he was running to go to the other side of the river, Sutherland was coming across on the beaten track and they met. All the witnesses state that Parisien was very much excited, to such an extent as to lead him to act impulsively and without sedateness that takes away that responsibility that would otherwise attach to it. He may have supposed that Sutherland was heading him, he may have supposed that if he got the horse he could jump upon it and get away. His only motive may have been to make his way, or he may have distrusted him, and from the impulse of the moment drew up and shot him ; but he fired two shots, the first took effect only slightly. He shot the second barrel and shot away his life. The parties in pursuit of Parisien then went after him into the woods and brought him back, but some one, whether before or after Scott was shot, had wounded Parisien. I think that it was after. He was brought back in such a way as no human being should have been brought back. There is no doubt he resisted and struggled to get away. No one had a right to restrict his liberty at all, 1 mean in the first instance. Of course, after he had shot Sutherland, any one had a legal right to apprehend him. Some allowance must be made for the flush of excitement on seeing a human life taken away like that of Sutherland. The jury heard what was said with regard to Parisien's hands, that they were tied and his hands frozen ; that when he was brought in, medical men were appointed to attend him, and that he was taken down to the lower settlement. Then we lose sight of him. Now, gentlemen, it was argued by the Counsel that wanton disregard of human life was exhibited at Kildonan in reference to Parisien's life. It is for you to say whether it was one of the results of this unfortunate trouble not contemplated by any of the parties at all. In the same connection it is said that Goulet is dead. I do not know positively at this moment by what means or other his death was caused. No witness in the box gave any information on this subject, but it was long after the great event that took place on the 4th March. If anything improper was done by any person in connection with Goulet, let these persons be brought to justice. It will be found by this that the first person who undertakes to take law in his own hands, that the law will be too strong for him. It is very seldom that the commission of one improper act or crime can justify or palliate the commission of another crime, and one does not see how an event that transpired four or five months after the matter we are investigating can have any relation to it, I mean as to its justification. It may be that for the death of Goulet justice will overtake others as well as those engaged in the killing of Scott. From the 17th day of February, the time that the prisoners were taken on the prairie, I shall pass over until the 4th of March with the exception of one leaf in the history of these times. We are told by the witnesses that Major Boulton was condemned to be shot I think at twelve o'clock at night, Boulton being one of the Portage prisoners. I think he was condemned in the day, and I think he was to be shot in the night. Now you will always recollect that I have given you a portion of what was alleged to be the offices of the Government. Bannatyne was Postmaster, Bunn was Secretary of State, Bruce was Minister of Public Works, and Riel was President. As to the other officers of the Government we are left in the dark, and the convention that created these officers was dissolved and an end put to it by the Portage movements, on the 19th or following days of February. I will recapitulate the evidence of the Bishop of Saskatchewan, also that of Thomas Bunn. It appears that the life of Major Boulton was spared by the intercession of the Bishop and Mr. Smith. We are not told by what authority he was condemned to die. We are not told that any court sat ; that the court, if it did sit, possessed the power of life and death, or that the sentence was given in accordance with the laws of the land. No minutes of a Council of War is furnished us; no statement is made that Boulton had done anything which, according to the laws of war, justified his death. All we know is that the man having power exercised his will and said he will die—when I say power I mean powder and shot. It appears from the evidence of Bishop McLean and Thomas Bunn that this man Riel made it a condition of sparing Boulton's life and of liberating the prisoners, if the English-speaking people or all persons in opposition to him should choose twelve delegates, and his friends should choose twelve delegates—I mean by his friends his partizans; that is the power he then held was exercised to intimidate the other portions of the population in opposition to him. The first meeting spoken of is the 9th of March. His Grace Archbishop Taché spoke of being at that meeting or in that Assembly on or about the 9th of March. Bunn says it first met on the 9th March, and it continued its sittings, from the papers which have been fyled and from the positive statement of Father Ritchot, until at least the 24th of March; that it does not appear that that body ever framed any Bill of Rights, but from the whole evidence, Father Ritchot would rather lead us to believe that some adviser of Riel and Riel together framed a new Bill of Rights, adding important clauses to the last one. The evidence states that that body elected under the circumstances which you have heard witnesses state, undertook to legislate, and that a Bill was introduced about cutting hay, a Bill about public works, a Bill about constables, and a Bill that the members of the Convention should be paid five dollars per day. Whether they passed into law or not, whether they received the final sanction of the Convention, does not appear. It does not say whether it was necessary for the President to give his sanction, whether he had the power of voting or not. The delegates received commissions as they have been called, or letters of commission, that is credentials as delegates to present the Bill of Rights to the Ottawa Government; they were informed of their appointment long before, and because they were selected by the Convention, which for the sake of perspicuity we will call the Convention of the 25th of January. The paper they received was a document called a commission, and it stated that they were appointed by the Provisional Government to proceed to Ottawa; it was over the signature of Thomas Bunn as Secretary of State. The letter given to Archbishop Taché on his arrival at Ottawa states that he was made a special commissioner to the people of the North-West. In speaking of his commission I say I shall keep within the words of the official papers themselves, and it is but right that I should say to you that the documents from the Government at Ottawa to Bishop Taché and with which he was invested, and also to Mr. Smith and Vicar-General Thibault, and Mr. De Salaberry, were addressed to the people of the North-West, and to no Provisional Government. They did not recognize the existence of any body of men as being in the position in which the Government were treating them at all, still it is all but right to say this remark applies as well to the official documents relative to the delegates as to the official documents I have already mentioned. Still at the same time in the letters, some of which in the official papers are replies from the delegates and from Archbishop Taché, the Archbishop assumed the position that there was a Provisional authority in the North-West, but the Government in replying to them never in the slightest degree admitted that position. The event of the 4th March took place while this state of things was continuing, but you should know that when Bishop Taché left Ottawa he came to the people of the North-West. When Archbishop Taché came here, this deed we are now investigating had not taken place. When the Archbishop left Ottawa according to the letter, he had not the slightest conception that any such deed had been committed. You must also bear in mind that those who held despotic sway were then in possession of the generous intentions of the Canadian Government and the Imperial Government to the people of the North-West, and that the people were more isolated than they are now. Misinformation might then have reasonably existed, but that cannot be said after Mr. Smith's arrival, the arrival of Vicar-General Thibault and Mr. De Salaberry, that cannot be said to be the case, for the very theory of the British North America Act guarantees to the people the same rights as the people of the other Provinces who were banded together in the confederation. Now, gentlemen, it is for you to decide, it is for you to say from the evidence in the witness box whether or not the physical power guarded by certain leaders was under the circumstances a justifiable organization. If so could they plead that they were supported by the majority of the settlers in the settlement? Did the people assemble and delegate power to establish a Government and to create a one-man power? If it is necessary for you to determine that question, how must you answer it? If you determine it in the affirmative, where is the evidence to be found upon which that verdict rests? But, suppose you did, was it not a Government that should be governed by the law? If so, I ask you was it governed by the law of the land? We have heard that not one solitary thing had been done towards repairing roads and bridges. Was that Government elected for the purpose of interrupting carts and travellers on the road, to force and seize and expropriate private and public property from the owners and appropriate it to themselves? Was the Government a shield to the innocent, an avenger of the guilty? If only one of their acts was in accordance with British law and organization, I fail to see it. From the evidence does it not appear that this man said, " We have guns, we have men under command, and our will shall be law of the land and the terror of the community?" Say, gentlemen, if you can call it by courtesy a government? Do you mean that they can put to death one solitary individual without cause or trial? If one, why not two? If two, why not ten? If you can justify one bloody deed, if they had taken out the whole forty-eight would you have justified that slaughter? Instead of keeping poor old Hallet for a month with irons on his hands and feet, with only a buffalo robe, with no fire for a month, torturing him in that way—if you can justify that, you could justify them had they taken out poor old Hallet and shot him. I ask every rational man if the logic is not irresistible, if they had a right to kill the one, would they not have been equally justified in shooting the whole forty-eight prisoners? I shall now dismiss this branch of the charge to you. Hitherto I have been reasoning with you on what has been called the *de facto* existence of the Provisional Government, but I tell you that no organization can be set up as a justification for an act not sanctioned by British laws. Besides being a *de facto* Government, it must be a Government *de jure*, that has a legal basis. This is a very broad distinction. The settlement of Red River or Rupert's Land was under the protection of the laws of Great Britain, and the constitution and the laws cannot tolerate any organization that has not its sanction and its authority, but any revolt or organization of that kind cannot be set up as a justification for the excuse of sovereignty. The Queen by her Council must recognise the independent and absolute existence of that organization; the Governor General with all his Council could not do it; the House of Commons in England could not do it; the House of Lords could not do it; both of them could not do it. It could only be done by the Queen herself acting under her responsible advisers in England, and therefore this organization cannot set up its organization in a British Court of justice as a justification; they must produce the sanction of Her Majesty to that organization. Therefore, gentlemen, in the investigation of this case I charge you that you are simply to look at the fact of the killing, the parties engaged in that killing; if it were done deliberately, then I charge you that the parties engaged in killing are murderers. I say a killing contemplated beforehand—that in law is murder. It is said that to make a homicide murder, it must be done in malice ; that is the technical expression ; the meaning is that any act that is done deliberately and with intention to take away human life in law is done maliciously. It does not require any personal ill will, but it means that if it was done designedly, that human life is to be destroyed, it does not require any manifestations of malice, such as we ordinarily call it. The books give an illustration like this. Suppose a man were to shoot recklessly his gun into a crowd, killing someone; that would be murder because he did it sedately, and death ensuirg, the party would be called a murderer. I repeat then, gentlemen, that after all that has been said, whatever opinion you may form in respect of that organization, whether you say it was a one-man power or whether it was a definite Government or not, whatever you may call it, I repeat in so far as you or I am concerned, it can have no influence or weight in determining this question whatever. It may have hereafter, but it can have none now. . This is why I permitted the learned Counsels every latitude, so that the prisoner might have the benefit of it hereafter, but in so far as you or I am concerned, it must have no influence one way or other in the disposition of this case. I will now proceed to speak of the first part of the proposition, whether or not there was a homicide, and whether or not the prisoner at the bar is guilty of that murder. I did think of reading over the entire evidence, but it is so voluminous that it would take nearly a week; I will, however, refer to the evidence of one or two of the most important witnesses. I will read the whole of the evidence if you think that it is necessary. (The jury here intimated that it would be just as well to read only the evidence of what His Lordship considers the most important witnesses.) I must make an observation with reference to aiders, abetters and accessories. When several are acting together and a felony is committed, it is not necessary that all should be directly acting in that felony. For example, in the robbery of a house one person stands at a distance keeping watch on the road, one at the gate, and one enters the house and commits the robbery; all act together to accomplish the same purpose, all are equally guilty. In the consideration of this case, if the prisoner agreed along with others that Scott should be put to death and killed, whether he agreed to it or not if he assented to it, and agents were employed to execute that determination, if the prisoner were near enough by to assist, he is just as guilty as if he fired the guns himself. Now, I state this to you, and the oath that binds—binds you to make that decision according to law. I tell you what the law is; if that were not the law, what would be the consequence? Men would commit murder or felonies and employ agents to execute their designs, being always within reach if necessary to accomplish it themselves, yet escape the responsibilities of the evidence. We now come to the consideration whether or not the party is dead. All of the witnesses who speak of the occurrence of 4th of March agree substantially as to their statements; there is in fact no contradiction. They all agree that Scott was taken out on the east side of the Fort wall, that guns were fired at him, that some of the balls pierced him, that blood flowed, that at least all agree that two bullet perforations appeared on the body, one on the breast and one a little higher up, some speak of a third that grazed the shoulder. Mr. Young says he observed perforations in the coat at the back, and that it was some distance down from the shoulder, so that apparently the ball passed from out of the back. Most of the witnesses agree on the first firing, that there was a cry or a shout as if a man was hurt; that he was on his knees and fell forward, his hands being tied behind him; that they all agree that at that time there were indications that life was not extinct; that a man named Guilmette got a pistol in some way and shot it at Scott's ear; there was a kind of quivering sensation following that shot, and that the body fell down more prostrate; witnesses both for the prosecution and the defence say that the body was put in a rough box; one man says that the man that was taken up collapsed like a sleeping man. It is agreed by all that the body in this box was carried into the Fort near the bastion. Many witnesses say, some for the prosecution and some for prisoner, that noises were heard from that box. I have no recollection that some of the witnesses saw any blood flowing from the last wound, some saw it on the snow, some speak of it on the face or ground, but one witness for the prisoner who had carried in the box says he did not observe any blood at all. They carried in the box, that was in the afternoon of the 4th of March, on a

Friday. Mr. Young, in this connection, says immediately after the shot he asked Riel for the body; he hesitated and finally declined giving it, but after that he saw at the box Goulet and Guilmette; one of them, Guilmette, said, "If you want this body, go and get a sleigh and take it away." He said he would be glad to do so if he would be permitted, but he did not get it. He went to parties in town to use their influence to get the body for Christian burial, he was informed that if he could get the guarantee of the Bishop of Rupert's Land that no demonstration would be made, he would be permitted to get the body. Bishop Machray went with him the next morning, they saw Riel and informed him of the request that had been made for the body and the conditions. Riel appeared to be embarrassed; he said the Adjutant-General would not permit it; he insisted upon it that as Adjutant-General he had a right to dispose of the body. The witness says he implored Riel that he wanted to give satisfaction to Scott's mother by giving her son the last rites of Christian burial. When he mentioned the name of the mother of Scott, the witness says that Riel seemed to be distressed. He said he was sorry that he could not grant his request, the Adjutant-General had insisted that he had a right to dispose of the body. It would appear from some of the witnesses that the box with the body was carried into the eastern bastion. One witness, Hupe, says that Scott was not dead, that he put his ear close to the box and heard the expression, "I say, I say." One of the witnesses for the prosecution says that while he was standing near the eastern bastion, he heard a sound that appeared to be in the bastion where this body was supposed to be; the expression was something like, "O Lord! O Lord!" In the same connection there was a person said he heard similar sounds proceeding from the bastion. On Saturday night, or near it, they dug a hole near Dr. Cowan's house said to be; a grave. It was said that Scott's body in the box was put in that hole and was buried. In all the cross-examination I do not recollect that any one was present when that box was put in the ground, and one has stated on oath that the body was in the box when it was put in the ground. On Saturday night or Sunday morning at two o'clock, a witness states that he was on guard near the eastern gate. He says it was very dark, and a cutter drove to the gate from the court yard, a large cutter in which were three men; one of them spoke abruptly, "Open the gate;" he gave no countersign, but spoke out hastily, "Open that gate;" he says the man was Goulet from his voice. He did not see anything in the cutter, it was too dark to see anybody in it; they dashed through the gate and drove towards the Assiniboine. There was ice on the river, and sleighs could pass up and down the river. After the troops came here, Mr. Young and some other persons obtained permission to open the grave and get the body of Scott; they opened the supposed grave, and found the box, but there was no body in it. From the 4th of March down to this poor Scott has never been heard of. The body dead was within the power and disposition of the prisoner and those acting with him. They have given no account of it, and a letter is put in signed by the prisoner as an official document. This is dated the 3rd of January, 1873, at St. Vital, signed by Riel and Lepine. In that letter allusion is made to something, and it will be for you to say what that allusion refers to: "Seeing that punishment long deserved could alone restrict this excited man, and in order to secure the full triumph of our intentions, we had recourse to the full authority of government."

It being one o'clock, His Lordship left the chair for one hour.

Before recess I was reading to you as a last item of the evidence of Scott's death, a statement over the hand of the prisoner, in which he alluded to the affair of the 4th of March. He couples Scott with something that was done on the 4th of March. What was it? Now the prosecution laid before you these several facts and circumstances to convince you that Scott died from what was done to him on that occasion, and that he is now dead. The circumstances as given to you in evidence as to the cutter have afforded the means by which the body was disposed of. The prisoner and his confederates had the body in their charge after it was shot, and made away with that body so that it cannot be found. They cannot escape this responsibility : if the body is now living, did not cease to exist at that time, who should know it, who in all the world were better informed than the prisoner ? Was the body thrown into the ocean and weighted with chains, or disposed of by cremation, or in any other way so dissipating it that it cannot be found, it never will release the prisoner from the responsibility of murder. I will leave that question of fact to be taken in connection with the statement made by the prisoner under his own hand. Assuming Scott to be dead, is the prisoner so connected with his death as to render him responsible for it ? I have to tell you that the killing of a human being done at leisure or designedly is murder, that any other person aiding and abetting in that killing sedately and designedly is guilty of murder. Now, gentlemen, when was this killing, and when was it intended ? John Bruce says that about fifteen days before he saw Scott shot, he was at the Fort, and saw the Adjutant-General, the prisoner. He asked him when he was going to liberate the prisoners. The prisoner replied, " Before long ; we will shoot a couple of them before we do it." He says that when the Schultz prisoners were taken, he asked the same question about the liberation and received the same reply ; he thought he was answering jocosely, not seriously, as he (Bruce) thought it was so shocking for any one seriously to say in earnest. The next thing we hear is what Michel Dumas says ; I had better read his own words : " I was a soldier in the Fort ; saw Scott two or three times, knew him by sight ; I heard Scott was to be shot about a week previous to the shooting ; I heard it from the poor such as I am ; some quiet people like myself heard it from those moving about the Fort, and they told me that it was said Scott was to be shot ; I did not hear of any charges against Scott." Then it appears, if we can believe the witnesses, that they had been talking of this in the Fort, having in their hands the power of killing Scott, and that he was to be shot at least a week before the event took place. The other person who states this is Joseph Nolin. He says, in speaking of the court martial, or whatever you call it, " I was first to hear of it. I heard of it about 3 o'clock of that day from Riel himself." He was not asked the question whether he had heard whether anything was to take place, but he heard about 3 o'clock that this convocation of the prisoner and others was to decide the fate of Scott. The prosecution would have you informed from this statement that the killing of Scott, if he were killed, was not only a deliberate but a long-premeditated matter. I will take you now to the night before Scott was shot. Murray swears that at night, between 8 and 9 o'clock, it was after dark at any rate, on the very night of the afternoon that Joseph Nolin swears that Scott was to be tried, Riel, O'Donohue and the prisoner came into the guard-room, in the building where the prisoners were confined, and in the room where Murray was warming himself at the stove ; he says Riel spoke to him abruptly, and said, " Who are you ? Are you a Canadian ?" He said he replied, "I am one of that party ; Scott's room was in the north-west angle of the building ; ours was in the south-west angle. After that I went into our room and shut the door and looked through the keyhole. I heard an uproar at Scott's door, as I thought the door was in charge of a guard. I heard Scott say, ' I want to get out for a call of nature ;' the guard refused to let him go out, and shut the door ; after a little I heard another uproar, the door was again opened, Riel then went to the door. Scott then said, ' I want to go out ; ' some discussion took place ; Scott said then he wanted to be treated civil, Riel replied that he did not deserve to be treated civilly, and called him a dog. Still Scott persisted in going down-stairs, a scuffle then took place, in which Riel joined. The door was shut ; Scott did not go down." It is important to bear in mind that Murray says that it was in the evening about 8 or 9 o'clock, and the prisoner and O'Donohue were seen with Riel. Now, I ask you what were the object of those three men there that night at that time ? When Nolin says that it had been determined to try Scott, was it for the purpose of getting into a difficulty with one or two of the prisoners, to get an excuse to justify the act? Have you heard from the whole of this trial, or did you ever hear one solitary excuse for doing what was done? The next thing we hear is the evidence of Joseph Nolin, which must have commenced immediately after the scuffle at Scott's door. His evidence in this: "I reside at Point de Chene since the summer of 1869. During the winter of '69 - '70 I resided at St. Boniface; I have known the prisoner for a long time; I was one of the party at that time at Fort Garry; I went there in January, and left in May; at the time I went, it was the Provisional Government who had possession, and when I left, it was so called; Riel was President, the prisoner was Adjutant-General, George Goulet was Lieut.-General; there were captains by the name of Baptiste Lepine, Joseph Delorme, André Nault, Ritchot and Lajemoniere. I did not know O'Donohue; I was secretary to the prisoner; there were some prisoners taken in February; I heard there were prisoners in the Fort; I heard there were prisoners there before the Portage prisoners, and I know where the Portage prisoners were kept; they were kept under guard; I knew Thomas Scott; I knew him to be one of the Portage prisoners; he was kept in the same building as the rest; my duties as secretary to the prisoner were to attend to the Council of Captains; I kept an account of the stores; towards the spring they were written, and orders for the Captains were made by the Adjutant-General; I wrote them out and delivered them to the Captains; these orders were written daily by the prisoner; I did nothing except by the orders of the Adjutant-General; the soldiers were paid in goods and provisions. On the evening of the 3rd of March, Scott was tried by a council of war—the same evening that Murray describes what took place in the guard-room. The prisoner presided at the council. There were at the council acting Ritchot, André Nault, Elzear Goulet, Elzear Lajemoniere, Baptiste Lepine, Joseph Delorme. I was secretary of the council. On the evening of the 3rd of March the meeting was for the purpose of trying Scott, to examine what evil he had done. (The Judge here remarked parenthetically that one cannot help being reminded of an event that took place 2000 years ago, "To see what evil he had done.") Scott was not present at the examination. There were some witnesses examined who saw what Scott had done. Riel was one, Ed. Turner was another, Joseph Delorme was another. I think there were others. These witnesses were examined by the Captains who composed the council. While the witnesses were examined, Scott was not present. The witnesses were sworn by me; I do not remember what evidence was given; Scott was accused of having rebelled against the Provisional Government and of having struck a captain of the guard; there was only one who made a speech, viz: Riel; I remember he spoke against Scott; after the evidence, Scott was brought before the council; Riel asked me to read to Scott what had passed before the council; I did not read anything, as I had taken only notes; then Riel explained to Scott himself the evidence which had been given before the council in English; he was then condemned to die; Riel told Scott before he left the room that he must die; after Riel had explained the evidence to Scott, he asked him if he had anything to say; Scott said something, I do not know what; Riel did not ask him if he had any witnesses; no written accusation or charge was given to Scott; the taking and giving of evidence, the bringing in of Scott, the speech of Riel, his explanations to Scott, the decision of the council and condemnation were all done within two or three hours; the council commenced its sittings between 7 and 8 o'clock and concluded their labors at one sitting." Now, gentlemen, you take the evidence along with that of Murray who says with Mr. Young that it was very short work. If the witnesses are to be believed, no formal resolution was recorded of the condemnation. Nothing formal was written down that evening. "I took some notes in pencil of the proceedings. The notes in pencil I refer to were notes of the evidence. The next day I transcribed these notes. I gave them to the Adjutant-General (the prisoner.) The first motion for death was moved by G. Ritchot, seconded by André

Nault. Goulet and Delorme voted yea along with the mover and seconder. Lajemoniere voted that it would be better to exile him. Baptiste Lepine voted nay. Ambroise (the prisoner) said the majority want his death and he shall be put to death. Riel explained to Scott his sentence. Riel asked Scott if he had no request to make, if he wanted to send for a minister; I do not know what answer Scott made to Riel; Riel said if he wanted a minister, if he was at the Stone Fort he would send for him; Riel said he would take his shackles off, and would send him to his room; he would have pen, ink and paper to write; he told him the next day he would be shot; Scott was then taken to his room; Scott was handcuffed when taken before the council; I saw the prisoner the next morning about 8 o'clock; the prisoner came to my room and asked me to write a *procès-verbal*, that is a minute of what passed before the council; I did what was required; Riel examined the minute and said it was not formal." (To the Jury)—Does it suggest itself to your minds that Riel and the prisoner were in communication, because Nolin in his evidence says that Riel called once that morning about the process? "The prisoner called and I gave it to him that morning about 8 or 9 o'clock; he called for the minutes twice; it was shown to Riel who remodeled it in form; I rewrote and then the prisoner called for it; I gave it to him; I saw Scott that morning going out of the gate." (The remainder of what Nolin saw was read by His Lordship.) I have read the evidence of Joseph Nolin, who lays the most complete foundation for this prosecution. If you believe that evidence, if you believe what he says is substantially true of what did occur on the night of the 3rd and the morning and noon of the 4th of March, I tell you as a matter of law that the prisoner is guilty of the murder of Scott. Upon you rests the responsibility of determining the truth, and there is no escaping from the conclusion if the evidence be true, that the prisoner at the bar is guilty of that murder. That evidence is everything that the law requires to constitute evidence. He presided at the council of the men who deliberated and decided that the man Scott should be shot. He was a consenting party who interested himself in the act or in respect of it in the morning. He was either inside the Fort or outside the Fort. He was not one of the firing party that shot their guns at Scott, but he certainly was within such distance either within or without the Fort to lend his own hand to the commission of the deed. I tell you that a person in that position is guilty of the accusation charged against him.

This is not all of Nolin's evidence. He was cross-examined very fully. "After I saw Scott I went up within three paces of Scott's body; the only thing I observed was a kind of a scratch on the upper part of the left shoulder; I think it was the left; at the time I went up to the body the box was inside the Fort; I had seen it previously to my going out; the box was brought out to the little gate; where the box was I saw some persons, two or three, carrying that box; when the box was brought to the corpse I believe it was put in the box and taken inside the Fort; I am not sure that I saw the body put in the box; I did not see the box after it was carried into the gate; Modeste Lajemoniere was often seen by me in the Fort; I don't know where the body or box went afterwards." The cross-examination substantially confirms Nolin's examination in chief. Gentlemen, I tell you that the conclusion and the whole proceeds were commenced and finished within an hour or two. They gave no patient hearing or investigation on a charge of rebellion against that despotic government of guns, powder and lead, and the fact is proved by Nolin that no proof was given of that rebellion. Nolin says in his evidence that it was not proved that Scott had taken the oath not to fight against Riel, that no evidence of that was given at all, and it is said that it could not be denied that he broke out of prison and went to the Portage. It is not proved that he had taken up arms for the purpose of opposing the movement at all. The evidence is that after being in prison for a while, he broke out and went to the Portage and joined his party for the release of the prisoners. That liberation having been already done, he was returning peacefully to his home. As to bringing a charge of striking a captain, I have stated to you what Murray says. Whatever may have been his offence, they had no right to put him to death, and if the evidence is to be believed, he was one of the most innocent men in the world. Take the evidence of Modeste Lajemoniere, who says that he saw Scott from the attic window of Dr. Cowan's house. He looked and saw Scott pass out of the gate. He says a man by the name of Guay was with him (Lajemoniere); at that moment while he was at the window he turned around and saw Riel and the prisoner. One of them made use of the expression, "Then in God's truth they are bringing him down," or words like these. He does not say which of the two men uttered them. He says, "I left the prisoner and Riel in the attic and came down and went to the southern gate until all was over. I then went to the little gate." His Lordship here explained what might be considered an apparent inconsistency between the statements of the Rev. Mr. Young and others and Modeste Lajemoniere to the effect that after Lajemoniere had come down-stairs and gone to the south gate, Riel and Lepine could have descended and gone out by the eastern gate, as it would take them only a moment. That Riel was there, every witness of the matter swears to be a fact. Several witnesses saw the prisoner there also. But, gentlemen of the jury, it makes no difference whether he was outside or inside, if he deliberately consented to the death of that man, and was assenting to the execution being carried out, he is just as guilty as if he fired the whole six guns himself, certainly much more than the six men who had been made drunk before they could sum up courage to commit that slaughter, because you see that every witness speaks of the men being more or less tipsy, and one of the witnesses states that Guilmette was so drunk that he sank down. Can it be possible that the prisoner and those acting with him could not get six executors without first blunting their intellectual and their moral senses by giving them whiskey and strong drink? As I told you I am going over to repeat the evidence. You must always mind this that several persons looking at the same occurrence, one will see one thing and one will remark another thing, and when they come to describe what took place, one will say he saw one thing, and one will say that he saw another thing that actually did take place, while one did not see what the other saw. It is a very common circumstance, and it does not apply only to the sense of sight, but also to that of hearing. A person may talk and hear words quite within the power of your hearing, but if your attention is directed to something else, you will not hear a word. In that way, of course, an apparent conflict of evidence, both for the prisoner and against him, is entirely swept away. You would suppose that unless a person came here to perjure himself, that the man who says that he actually spoke to the prisoner near Scott, François Charette, and saw the prisoner and the pistol, and that the prisoner told him to go into the Fort, that he had no business there, and he was even pressed by a kick, you would think that unless the man wanted to perjure himself grossly, you would feel disposed to believe what he states. I repeat to you there is no conflict of evidence. The main question is, did the prisoner sit on that judgment, sit when that *coterie* of persons were there that night? Did he say, "The majority want his death and he shall be put to death?" Was he around with those men the next morning? Was he within reach of that execution that took place? I do not care what he was doing. If he never came down from the attic, he is just as guilty as if he had fired the shots himself. There is no misunderstanding the way in which I lay down the law. If I am wrong I can be set right, but if you go astray the mishap is irreparable. Now, gentlemen, divest yourselves of any other aim or object but the truth. Is Scott dead, and did he come to his death by reason of what happened on the 4th of March, during the day or during the night, and is he now dead? And here I must call your attention to the admissions of the prisoner in his own letter. They have a bearing upon the question. Then, if he is dead, did the prisoner act along with those individuals who said he should die or he shall die? Is that the truth or is it not? Did he look on and see that sentence carried out? If he did; if you believe that—and you are bound by your oaths—then, I tell you, the prisoner at the bar is guilty. If you believe that Scott is living, or if you believe that the prisoner was not at that council, did not look on and say that Scott was to be executed, then of course you will say the prisoner is not guilty. Both in the interests of the prisoner and in the interests of public justice, you should come to a conclusion one way or other. There should be no disagreement of a jury in a case of this kind. One does not well see how there can be a disagreement. All human opinion must come to one or other of these conclusions. Now, gentlemen, in conclusion, let no unjust consideration influence you. I charge you in the most solemn manner to allow no considerations of the opinions of the world, or any persons whatever, to have any influence on your minds or on your judgments, but balance all that has been said to you, both in the witness box, by the counsels, and by the Court, and then recall the solemn oath you have taken. See that you are not only deciding for yourselves, but for the future of your children and of your country, and that for if you are accountable to the Great Being to whom we all owe our existence. Balance in your minds all these circumstances, facts, and statements, and hold the scales as if you were on the brink of eternity.

The jury retired at half-past four o'clock. At seven o'clock they returned with the verdict—" Guilty, with a recommendation to mercy."

The Court then adjourned, His Lordship having occupied five hours and a half in delivering his charge.

After the verdict, the following motions against sentence being pronounced, were presented by the prisoner's counsel, Mr. Chapleau, and fyled :—

I.

Motion on behalf of prisoner that sentence be not pronounced against said prisoner, according to verdict of murder found against him by the Jury in the case; but that such verdict be declared null and void, and set aside, and judgment in the case arrested for following reasons, to wit :

1. Because the Jury was directed by the Court that no evidence had been produced on behalf of the prisoner, that the prisoner, at the time he presided at the Court Martial that tried and sentenced the man Scott, was acting in the regular exercise of his functions as the Adjutant-General in the Provisional Government of Assiniboia— the said Government having been recognized by Her Majesty's representatives in this country—whereas such evidence was offered and produced.

2. Because the said Jury were instructed by the Court that no evidence could be received on behalf of the prisoner of the actual and regular recognition, by the Dominion of Canada and Her Majesty's representative, Sir Clinton Murdock, and His Excellency the Governor-General of Canada, of the said Provisional Government of Assiniboia, of which the prisoner was an officer on the 4th of March, 1870, by the negociations and verbal pledges given by those high officials to the Delegates of the said Provisional Government.

3. Because the Court directed the Jury that the existence and authority of the said Provisional Government of Assiniboia was never recognized by the people of the Red River settlements at the time when the prisoner was acting as an officer of that Government.

4. Because the Court directed the Jury that the documents signed on the 5th April, 1870, by William McTavish, the then Governor of the Hudson's Bay

Company and President of the Council, being a written agreement between the said William McTavish and Louis Riel, the President of the said Provisional Government, was no legal evidence of the existence and authority of the said Provisional Government.

II.

Motion on behalf of prisoner that sentence be not pronounced against said prisoner according to verdict of murder found against him by the Jury of the case—that the said verdict be declared null and void, and set aside, and judgment in the case arrested for following reasons, to wit:

1. They could have no legal jurisdiction to try, hear and determine upon the alleged crime of prisoner.

2. That it appears that the offence of which prisoner is accused was not committed within the jurisdiction of this Court.

3. That in empannelling the Jury to try issue on this case, the names of the Jurors were not called alternately from each of the English and French list in the order in which the names of the Jurors stand on said list, inasmuch as the name of Peter Harkness, *alias* Peter Harkut, he being one of the Jurors whose names were in the French list, was immediately called after the name of Joseph Berthelet, whose name stands on the said French list.

4. Because often the list of Jurors purporting to be the French list, having been gone through and exhausted by the challenges of the defence and the orders to stand aside by the Crown, the Court, instead of calling again the name of the first Juror remaining unchallenged on said list, as required by law and practice, directed the name of Duncan McDougall, which stood the thirteenth in the said French list, to be called, and allowed there and then the Crown to challenge peremptorily the said Duncan McDougall as one of the Jurors of this trial, and the Court after the name of the said Duncan McDougall had been so called and challenged, proceeded and directed to call the name of Moise Goulet, which stood the second on the said French list, the counsel for the defence having at the same time objected to this mode of calling the Jurors.

CHAPLEAU & ROYAL.

WINNIPEG, October 28th, 1874.

WEDNESDAY, November 4th.

After routine His Lordship Chief Justice Wood in passing sentence made the following remarks. (Owing to the discourtesy and officiousness of Mr. Sheriff Armstrong of Winnipeg, who refused to permit a shorthand reporter to occupy a position within hearing, the remarks of His Lordship were not taken down at the time, but were afterwards kindly furnished by a gentleman who happened to take some notes.)

THE SENTENCE.

After the prisoner had been asked if he had anything to say why the sentence of the Court should not be passed on him, and his counsel, Mr. Chapleau, had read a memorandum containing certain legal objections which His Lordship overruled, His Lordship, amidst the most profound silence and with emotions which he with difficulty suppressed, proceeded in a measured and solemn tone:—

Prisoner, you stand convicted of having, on the 4th of March, 1870, at Fort

Garry, in that portion of Rupert's Land which has since become the Province of Manitoba, murdered Thomas Scott. An unlawful, ordinary homicide is a startling and shocking occurrence in a civilized and Christian community at any time, but the killing of Scott is taken out of the category of common homicides. So dreadful and so horrible was it that even those who at first felt disposed to sympathize with the cause of the insurrectionary movement would not believe it possible until the dark deed was perpetrated. The knowledge of it sent a thrill of horror throughout the Dominion of Canada and the civilized world, and struck the hearts of the settlers of Red River with shuddering terror; and although now over four years have passed away, that crime is still regarded by the people of Red River and the Dominion of Canada with unabated abhorrence; and not a solitary individual has ever dared to speak or write a single sentence, I will not say in justification, but even in extenuation, palliation, excuse or apology of its enormity; and the evidence given on your trial, instead of relieving, has added to and increased the dark shadows surrounding that awful tragedy. A jury, the majority of whom are natives of Red River, for two weeks have patiently listened to all that could be said in your defence. Your counsel, most sympathetic, learned, able and eloquent gentlemen, have done all that could be done in your behalf. In your defence they were allowed the widest latitude; but to the credit of human nature and to the honor of the profession be it said, during their entire defence they had not one syllable in justification or apology to offer for the awful crime of which you have been convicted. They did for you all that great ability and great eloquence with the greatest liberty of defence could accomplish. The question of your guilt or innocence was fairly left to that jury by the Court — your counsel having taken no exception to the charge. That jury have pronounced you guilty; and I must say I do not well see how they could have done otherwise. Indeed I do not believe twenty respectable French *Métis* can be found in the whole Red River Settlement who would not have come to the same conclusion—and who do not now approve of the verdict of that jury—whatever native Canadians may say in respect of it. You can claim no consideration on the ground of ignorance or misapprehension. Père Ritchot swears he advised you and others of the risk and the danger you incurred in the movement in which you and your *confrères* were engaged. Long prior to the commission of this offence, you had before you the Proclamation of the Governor General, issued by the order of the Queen, forgiving you and your associates in treason all you and they had done up to that time; *provided you returned to an observance of the laws and obedience to the lawful authority of this land*. You were assured by official documents under the hand of the Governor General and proceeding from the Privy Council of Canada, that all possible grievances, if any existed, should be redressed; that the most generous and liberal policy towards the inhabitants of Red River should be pursued in dealing with the North West Territories, and in thus carrying out the policy of the Empire — that all their possessory and other rights should be respected; — in short you were informed that the Imperial measure of uniting Rupert's Land and the Indian Territories to Canada had been conceived as much in the interests of the population of Red River as in that of Canada and the Empire at large. To enforce those views and to render conviction of their truth irresistible, gentlemen of unquestionable integrity and such as must have commanded your confidence and that of the misguided men over whom you assumed to exercise control, or with whom you were associated in your unreasonable and unlawful rebellion to the constituted authority of the country, were sent to you as special commissioners. For what was done by you and your associates from that time onward, whatever may be said as to what was done prior thereto, you and your associates stand before the world without a shadow of excuse or justification. You would not heed the warning—you would not listen to what you knew was the truth. You imprisoned, and I may say from what has been disclosed on this trial, tortued those innocent of even actively opposing your mad proceedings. You robbed Her Majesty's loyal subjects of their property and plundered wherever you could do so with impunity. And, lastly you crowned the long catalogue of your crimes with the slaughter of Thomas Scott for no other offence than loyalty to his Queen. But it is not my province to say anything by which one additional sting should be added to that remorse which in all charity it is to be hoped you now experience for the past. I have made these remarks to prepare you for what I now say to you, that I dare not hold out any hope that mercy will be extended to you for the crime of which you have been convicted. In my heart of hearts I pity your wife and children, your relations and friends. They must keenly feel your situation. Had you taken the advice of your brother Baptiste on that fatal evening of the 3rd of March, you would not now be where you are. It is one of the inevitable consequences of crime to involve all relations and connections in its punishment, and knowing this, it alone should have arrested you in your mad career. *You did not spare poor Scott.* You did not think of, or if you did, you did not regard his poor old mother or his relations. Where his ashes repose you may know, but we do not. Whether his body was made away with so as not to be found, to be set up as a defence as has been done on this trial, or because it was so mangled and mutilated that even you were ashamed it should ever be seen, is unknown. What was done with Scott's body you must know. Taking all the facts in the evidence together, well might the ever-to-be-lamented Sir George E. Cartier, in a private and confidential communication to Lord Lisgar, say, " *The killing of Scott was an excessive abuse of power and cruel brutality.*" The jury have recommended you to mercy. All the exceptions taken by your counsel, together with the entire evidence and proceedings and the recommendation to mercy, will be transmitted to the Secretary of State for Canada and by him laid before His Excellency the Governor-General in Council. In addition to that your counsel will have an opportunity of presenting to the Executive any considerations they may think advisable outside the record. I have but one course left open for me, and that is to pronounce on you the final sentence of the law. I have made the day of your execution more distant than I otherwise might have done in consequence of the distance and the length of time necessary in communicating between Manitoba and Ottawa ; and to give you ample opportunity for self-examination, for reflecting over your past life, and for preparation for the awful change which awaits you. You, unlike Scott, will not be forced to prepare to leave this and enter the invisible world in a few short hours. When the Rev. Mr. Young came to you like an angel of mercy and with streaming eyes begged you to spare Scott's life only for a few short hours, to enable him to meet his God, you inhumanly denied and refused his request with a brevity and emphasis in keeping with every act surrounding this human butchery. After Scott's death this same messenger of Heaven, bathed in tears, went to Riel along with the Bishop of Rupert's Land, and humbly implored Riel to give him the body that he might give it the last sad rites of the Church, intimating that he was about to write to his poor old mother the untimely death of her son, and that it would be consolation to her to know that her son had received Christian burial. Even his heart softened under this appeal. But you, he declared, claimed that you had the disposition of the body and utterly refused to surrender it for burial. To all entreaties to spare life for a brief period before death, and to give up the body for burial after death, you were alike inflexible. Search the annals of the barbarous tribes which for centuries have roamed over the vast prairies of the North-West, and in them you will fail to find a parallel in savage atrocity. There is no spirit of vengeance in these proceedings. It is the triumph of law over the unbridled audacity of crime. As this, in all probability, is the last opportunity I shall ever have on earth of addressing you, I thought it my duty, however painful it might be, to address these plain and candid observations to you that you might realise your true position and prepare to meet your God. The sentence of the law upon you is that you be taken from the place where you now are to the common gaol of this Province, and there be kept in solitary confinement until the twenty-ninth day of January, 1875, and on that day, between the hours of eight and ten o'clock in the forenoon, you be taken thence to the place of execution, and there be hanged by the neck until you are dead, and may the God of pity have mercy upon your soul.

ERRATA.

Page 7, 5th line—instead of *amendable*, read *amenable*.

Page 10, 17th line—instead of *goal*, read *gaol*.

Page 39, 13th line—instead of 10, read 2.

Page 56, 30th line—instead of *Girard*, read *Senator Girard*.

Page 84, line before last, and 11th line of page 85—instead of *summonse*, read *summarise*.

Page 99, 9th and 17th lines—strike off the word *not*.

Page 102, 24th line—instead of *as*, read *that*.

Page 104, 18th and 22nd lines—instead of *Panquin*, read *Poche*.

Page 110, 23rd line—instead of *hear*, read *have*.

Printed by The Burland Desbarats Lithographic Company,
319 St. Antoine Street, Montreal.

Selkirk House,

WINNIPEG, MANITOBA,

H. HOUDE, Proprietor.

A FIRST-CLASS HOUSE WITH A WELL FURNISHED BAR.

GOOD ATTENDANCE,

And all the Delicacies of the Season.—MEALS AT ALL HOURS.

HEAD-QUARTERS' HOTEL,

E. W. WEED, Proprietor,

BRAINERD, MINNESOTA.

ONLY FIRST-CLASS HOUSE IN THE CITY.

All trains arrive at and depart from the door. Travelers to and from all points in Manitoba and the North-West will find the HEAD-QUARTERS suitable in all respects.

MERCHANTS' HOTEL,

ST. PAUL, MINNESOTA,

A. ALLEN, PROPRIETOR.

Canadians and others on their way to Manitoba will find the "MERCHANTS" a first-class house in all essentials.

SIGN OF THE BEAVER.

A. DAOUST,

BUYER AND DEALER IN ALL KINDS OF

DRY GOODS, GROCERIES & GENERAL MERCHANDIZE,

Devlin's Building, nearly opposite Bentley's, WINNIPEG, MA.

Constantly on hand a choice assortment of Buffalo Robes and Furs. Traders requiring Outfits and Supplies will find my assortments equal, in all respects, to their requirements, and at reasonable prices.

The Burland-Desbarats Lithographic Co.,

115 ST. FRANCOIS-XAVIER ST., & 311 to 319 ST. ANTOINE ST.,

MONTREAL,

Possesses unequalled facilities in the ARTISTIC, TYPOGRAPHICAL and PRINTING Departments of their Works, and is prepared to execute every class of Printing required by

BANKS, COMPANIES, MERCHANTS, BREWERS, DRUGGISTS, LAWYERS, NOTARIES, ARCHITECTS, SURVEYORS, &C.

Fac-similes of old Books, Manuscript, Engravings, Maps, Plans, &c., produced at the shortest notice. We invite orders from all parts of the Dominion, and are even prepared to send our products to the United States. All who favor us will acknowledge that we surpass all competitors in

ELEGANCE OF WORKMANSHIP, MODERATION IN PRICE, PROMPTNESS IN EXECUTION.

STUART MACDONALD,

Barrister, Attorney and Solicitor in Chancery,

CONVEYANCER, NOTARY PUBLIC AND COMMISSIONER

For taking Affidavits in and for the Province of Manitoba.

LAW OFFICE: DOMINION PUBLIC WORKS BUILDING,

WINNIPEG CITY, MAN.

N. B.—Attends the County Courts in the Province of Manitoba. All description of legal information furnished; Land Claims located and Patents secured.

J. R. Benson's Livery Stable,

RORIC STREET,

Near the Post Office,   **WINNIPEG, MAN.**

The largest and best stock of Livery Rigs and Horses in the City or Province. Requirements met at all hours, night and day.

FIRST-CLASS TURN-OUT A SPECIALTY.

Orders may be left at the STABLES, or at the Office of the EXCHANGE HOTEL.

ROBERT STALKER,

MAIN ST., POINT DOUGLAS,

Harness-Maker,

DEALER IN TRUNKS, BLANKETS AND HARNESS.

☞ ALL WORK WARRANTED. ☜

BANKING HOUSE OF A. McMICKEN,

WINNIPEG, MANITOBA.

Issues Drafts on Ontario, Quebec and Saint Paul,

AND DEALS IN FOREIGN EXCHANGE.

Collections made. — Deposits received on Interest or Open Account.

Correspondents: Bank of Montreal; First National Bank, St. Paul; Dawson & Co., Bankers, St. Paul; First National Bank, Duluth; Bank of Duluth, Duluth; Cook Co. National Bank, Chicago; Sparks, McPherson & Co., Minneapolis.

LIVERY STABLE,

IN REAR OF THE ROYAL HOTEL,

NOTRE DAME STREET EAST, WINNIPEG, MAN.

The subscriber begs leave to inform the public that he can supply all who may require it with the BEST RIGS to be found in the City or Province. Patronage respectfully solicited.

W. N. BAILEY.

FLAT BOAT AND COMMISSION STORE,
NOTRE DAME STREET, WINNIPEG, MANITOBA.

H. HODGES,
DEALER IN

Flour, Feed, Groceries, Provisions, Boots and Shoes,
GENTS' FURNISHING GOODS, &c.

ROCAN & MORNEAU,
BUTCHERS,
Proprietors of the Winnipeg Meat Market,
OPPOSITE MERCHANTS BANK,
MAIN STREET, WINNIPEG, MANITOBA.

Always on hand the best stock that the season and the country afford. A liberal reduction made to regular customers. We make it a specialty to keep a choice assortment.

Mathew Davis,
GENERAL BLACKSMITH AND JOBBER,

NOTRE DAME STREET, WINNIPEG,
(Opposite Macaulay's Mill.)
MILL WORK & IMPLEMENTS OF ALL KINDS NEATLY REPAIRED.
Horseshoeing a Specialty.
ALL WORK WARRANTED.

THE GERALD HOUSE,
Messrs. GERALD and WHITFIELD, Proprietors,
ASSINIBOINE STREET, WINNIPEG, MANITOBA.

The GERALD HOUSE is now conducted by us on the most modern and approved style. In connection with our establishment are EXTENSIVE STABLING FACILITIES for those needing them. The GERALD HOUSE will be found a Farmer's Home in all essential particulars. Patronage is respectfully solicited.

BOWLER & CATHCART,
Bakers and Confectioners,
GENERAL GROCERIES,
MAIN STREET, POINT DOUGLAS.

SMITH, MUNRO & CO.,
WHOLESALE AND RETAIL DEALERS IN
Heavy & Shelf Hardware, Stoves, Tinware, Paints,
OILS, GLASS, &c., &c.,
MAIN STREET, WINNIPEG, MANITOBA.

J. B. HAINES,
MANUFACTURER OF
HARNESS, SADDLES & TRUNKS.
Harness, Saddles, Bridles, Whips, &c., always on hand.

MAIN STREET,

(Next to Bentley's,)   WINNIPEG, MAN.

A. & F. GINGRAS,
MAIN STREET, WINNIPEG,
(Opposite the Site of the Old Parliament Buildings,)

Importers and Dealers in Dry Goods, Groceries and General Merchandize.

MARCHANDISES SECHES, EPICERIES, HARDES FAITES, PELLETERIES,

PEAUX DE VACHES, ROBES DE BUFFLES, PEMMICAN EN SACS, VIANDES SECHES.

GIVE US A CALL.

Winnipeg Marble Works.
DAVID EDE,
Dealer in Italian and American Marble Monuments,

HEAD STONES, TABLETS, MANTLETS, &c.,

WINNIPEG, MANITOBA.

Livery Stable,
W. H. HARVEY, Proprietor,

LOCATION IN THE REAR OF W. H. LYON'S,

Just a little West of Central Main Street,

WINNIPEG.

Stock unequalled; splendid Rigs. Orders attended to night and day. First-class Turn-out a specialty.

A. G. B. BANNATYNE,

IMPORTER AND DEALER IN

Groceries, Wines, Liquors, Cigars,

PORK, BACON, HAMS, FLOUR & FEED,

IN THE NEW BRICK BUILDING, NORTH OF THE "OLD STAND,"

MAIN STREET, WINNIPEG.

Undoubtedly the best assortment ever offered for sale in the country before, and the largest, choicest and most varied stock in Winnipeg.

THRESHING MACHINES, REAPERS AND MOWERS.

W. H. LYON,

WHOLESALE AND RETAIL DEALER IN

DRY GOODS, CLOTHING, GROCERIES,

Wines, Liquors, &c.,

WINNIPEG, MANITOBA.

JAMES HENDERSON & CO.,

DEALERS IN

Gents' Furnishing Goods,

READY-MADE CLOTHING, HATS AND FURS,

MAIN STREET,

WINNIPEG, MAN.

SHAVING AND HAIR DRESSING SALOON,

McGUIRE & DUMAS, Proprietors,

(NEXT DOOR TO CITY HALL,)   MAIN STREET, WINNIPEG, Ma.

THE BEST ESTABLISHMENT NORTH-WEST OF ST. PAUL.

A good and efficient staff constantly employed. Particular attention being paid to the latest styles. Shaving, Hair Dressing and Shampooing done in the most approved and artistic styles.

HOURS, FROM 8 TO 8.—SATURDAY EVENINGS UNTIL 11.—CLOSED ON SUNDAYS.

Always on hand Cigars, Fancy Articles of all kinds, Finest Oils in the Province, all kinds of Perfumery, Toilet Articles of all descriptions, Hair Brushes and Italian Cosmetics.

CLARK & WEEDON,

𝕽𝖊𝖆𝖑 𝕰𝖘𝖙𝖆𝖙𝖊 𝕴𝖓𝖛𝖊𝖘𝖙𝖒𝖊𝖓𝖙,

HOUSE AGENTS & AUCTIONEERS,

HAVE FOR SALE

A large number of Good Farms

IN EVERY PART OF THE PROVINCE,

AND TOWN LOTS,

AT PRICES WITHIN THE MEANS OF ALL.

Houses to Rent.

LAND WARRANTS FOR SALE.

☞ MONTHLY CIRCULAR ISSUED FREE.

MAIN STREET, near the Court House,

WINNIPEG.